Tales from My Father's Home
Kupishok, Lithuania
(Kupiškis, Lithuania)

Dr. Shlomo Kodesh

Published by JewishGen

**An Affiliate of the Museum of Jewish Heritage—A Living Memorial to the Holocaust
New York**

Tales from my Father's Home
Kupishok, Lithuania
(Kupiškis, Lithuania)

Translation of: *Sipurim Me'Beit Abba*

First Printing: July 2021, Tamuz 5781

Project Coordinator: Ann Rabinowitz
Layout and Name Indexing: Jonathan Wind
Cover Design: Rachel Kolokoff Hopper

Published by JewishGen, Inc.
An Affiliate of the Museum of Jewish Heritage
A Living Memorial to the Holocaust
36 Battery Place, New York, NY 10280

Printed in the United States of America by Lightning Source, Inc.

Library of Congress Control Number (LCCN): 2021941989
ISBN: 978-1-954176-17-1 (hard cover: 368 pages, alk. paper)

Introduction to the English Translation

One of the challenges for researchers of family roots and the Holocaust is the issue of the material being created in languages that modern or younger researchers do not speak or are not familiar with. It was much easier when the majority of Jews spoke the mame loshen, the colloquial term for Yiddish, or loshen koydesh , which refers to Hebrew as the "holy tongue," rather than German, Hungarian, French, Ladino and other languages of the Jewish world.

As a coordinator of the Kupiskis SIG, a special interest group of those born in Kupiskis, Lithuania, and their descendants, which came into being in the early 1990s, I heard of a Kupishoker named Shlomo Kodesh quite early in my research and I was eager to convert his Hebrew works about Kupiskis into English. He was a Zionist Kupishoker who left Lithuania in 1933 for British Mandate Palestine, and he was quite familiar with the Interwar Years and post World War II years in Lithuania. His works resonate in an imaginative and creative way about his father's world that was no more.

Early members of our Kupiskis SIG, such as Linda Cantor, Shirley Epstein, Harvey Krueger, Prof. Dov Levin, Howard Margol, Stanley Mayersohn, and Harold Padow, all spoke of the works of Shlomo Kodesh and how wonderful it would be to have them translated into English from the Hebrew. To that end, I got in touch with Shlomo and encouraged him to finish his translation, which he strongly wanted to complete before the end of his life.

Unfortunately, it was not to be. He passed away in his early nineties leaving an unfinished, but translated English draft. Since then, I had tried many times to find a publisher for the translated book, but the prohibitive cost prevented its completion. It was only with the help of the JewishGen Yizkor Book Project that we were able to produce the book which you are able to read today in clear English, accompanied by photographs from Shlomo's own personal collection.

It is now 2021 and my own seventy-fifth year and my promise to Shlomo to have his memories of his ancestral shtetl of Kupiskis and his life in other portions of Lithuania has come to pass at long last. In addition, my correspondence with him and his writings dealing with this work have been donated to the Judaica Library of the University of Miami, Coral Gables, Florida.

I know that Shlomo and his family would have been tremendously pleased to have the translation of the book of his youth available in the wider Jewish world.

Ann Rabinowitz
Coordinator, Kupiskis SIG
Former Litvak SIG Board Member

Cover Credits

Front and Back Cover Background Photographs: Wildflowers by Rachel Kolokoff Hopper.

Front and Back Cover Background Color and Texture: Rachel Kolokoff Hopper.

Front Cover Background Photograph: Kupiskis Jewish Cemetery in 1910 (https://kehilalinks.jewishgen.org/kupiskis/kupcem.htm).

Back Cover Text (edited): From the original book, pages 4-8.

Back Cover Photograph Upper Left: Dr. Shlomo Kodesh from the back cover of the original book.

Back Cover Middle Photograph from the Original Book: Shlomo Kodesh, as a high school student, 1920 – Kaunas (Kovno), page 210.

Back Cover Lower Photographs from the Original Book: My parents, Chanah Kodesh and Meir Kodesh, page 71.

JewishGen and the Yizkor Books in Print Project

This book has been published by the **Yizkor Books in Print Project**, as part of the **Yizkor Book Project** of JewishGen, Inc.

JewishGen, Inc. is a non-profit organization founded in 1987 as a resource for Jewish genealogy. Its website [www.jewishgen.org] serves as an international clearinghouse and resource center to assist individuals who are researching the history of their Jewish families and the places where they lived. JewishGen provides databases, facilitates discussion groups, and coordinates projects relating to Jewish genealogy and the history of the Jewish people. In 2003, JewishGen became an affiliate of the **Museum of Jewish Heritage—A Living Memorial to the Holocaust** in New York.

The **JewishGen Yizkor Book Project** was organized to make more widely known the existence of Yizkor (Memorial) Books written by survivors and former residents of various Jewish communities throughout the world. Later, volunteers connected to the different destroyed communities began cooperating to have these books translated from the original language—usually Hebrew or Yiddish—into English, thus enabling a wider audience to have access to the valuable information contained within them. As each chapter of these books was translated, it was posted on the JewishGen website and made available to the general public.

The **Yizkor Books in Print Project** began in 2011 as an initiative to print and publish Yizkor Books that had been fully translated, so that hard copies would be available for purchase by the descendants of these communities and also by scholars, universities, synagogues, libraries, and museums.

These Yizkor books have been produced almost entirely through the volunteer effort of researchers from around the world, assisted by donations from private individuals. The books are printed and sold at near cost, so as to make them as affordable as possible. Our goal is to make this important genre of Jewish literature and history available in English in book form, so that people can have the personal histories of their ancestral towns on their bookshelves for themselves and for their children and grandchildren.

A list of all published translated Yizkor Books in the project with prices and ordering information can be found at:
http://www.jewishgen.org/Yizkor/ybip.html

Lance Ackerfeld, Yizkor Book Project Manager
Joel Alpert, Yizkor-Book-in-Print Project Coordinator
Susan Rosin, Yizkor-Book-in-Print Project Associate Coordinator

JewishGen
Yizkor Book Project

This book is presented by the
Yizkor-Books-In-Print Project
Project Coordinator: Joel Alpert
Associate Project Coordinator: Susan Rosin

Part of the Yizkor Books Project of JewishGen. Inc.
Project Manager: Lance Ackerfeld

These books have been produced solely through efforts of volunteers
from around the world. The books are printed using the Print-on-Demand technology and sold at
near cost, to make them as affordable as possible.

Our goal is to make this intimate history of the destroyed Jewish shtetls
of Eastern Europe available in book form in English, so that people can
experience the near-personal histories of their ancestral town on their
bookshelves and those of their children and grandchildren.

All donations to the Yizkor Books Project, which translated the books,
are sincerely appreciated.

Please send donations to:

Yizkor Book Project
JewishGen, Inc.
36 Battery Place
New York, NY, 10280

JewishGen, Inc. is an affiliate of the
Museum of Jewish Heritage
A Living Memorial to the Holocaust

Notes to the Reader:

We apologize ahead of time for the poor quality of images in the book. Often these images had been scanned from the original Yizkor books which were of poor quality to begin with, being copies of old photographs. Each transfer results in loss of quality. We have done the best we could, given the original material and the resources and technology at hand. Even though images often appear of higher quality on computer screens, that does not transfer to high quality images in print. A reader can view the original scans on the web sites listed below.

Within the text the reader will note "{34}" standing ahead of a paragraph. This indicates that the material translated below was on page 34 of the original book. However, when a paragraph was split between two pages in the original book, the marker is placed in this book after the end of the paragraph for ease of reading.

In order to obtain a list of all Shoah victims from Kupishuk, Poland, the reader should access the Yad Vashem web site listed below; one can also search for specific family names using family name option. These lists are continually updated by Yad Vashem, so it is worthwhile to periodically search these lists.

There is much valuable information available on this web site, including the Pages of Testimony, etc.
http://yvng.yadvashem.org

A list of this book and all books available in the Yizkor-Book-In-Print Project along with prices is available at:
http://www.jewishgen.org/Yizkor/ybip.html

Geopolitical Information:

Kupiškis, Lithuania is located 55°50' N 24°58' E and 81 miles N of Vilnius

	Town	District	Province	Country
Before WWI (c. 1900):	Kupishki	Vilkomir	Kovno	Russian Empire
Between the wars (c. 1930):	Kupiškis	Panevėžys		Lithuania
After WWII (c. 1950):	Kupiškis			Soviet Union
Today (c. 2000):	Kupiškis			Lithuania

Alternate names for the town:

Kupiškis [Lith], Kupishok [Yid], Kupishki [Rus], Kupiszki [Pol], Kupischken [Ger], Kupišķi [Latv], Kupiškio

Nearby Jewish Communities:

Viešintos 9 miles S
Subačius 10 miles WSW
Skapiškis 10 miles ENE
Šimonys 10 miles SE
Geležiai 10 miles W
Vabalninkas 12 miles NW
Pandėlys 16 miles NE
Troškūnai 17 miles SSW
Svėdasai 19 miles ESE
Papilys 20 miles N
Kamajai 21 miles E
Panemunėlis 21 miles ENE
Anykščiai 21 miles SSE
Debeikiai 22 miles SE
Raguva 23 miles SW
Traupis 23 miles SSW
Krinčinas 24 miles NW

Kvetkai 24 miles NNE
Neciuniskiai 25 miles ESE
Pumpenai 25 miles WNW
Panevėžys 25 miles WSW
Rokiškis 26 miles ENE
Suvainiškis 26 miles NNE
Vyžuonos 26 miles SE
Nereta, Latvia 26 miles NNE
Biržai 27 miles NNW
Užpaliai 27 miles ESE
Pasvalys 27 miles NW
Kavarskas 28 miles S
Jūžintai 28 miles E
Pušalotas 28 miles W
Mikališkis 29 miles W
Kurkliai 29 miles SSE
Kirkilai 29 miles NNW
Onuškis 30 miles NE

Jewish Population: 2,661 (in 1897), 1,444 (in 1923)

Siauliai

Klaipeda

Rokiskis

Kupiskis *

Lithuania

Taurage

Sventzian

● Jonava

Kaunas

Vilnius

Marijampole

Map of Lithuania with **Kupiskis**

Tales from My Father's Home
Kupishok, Lithuania
(Kupiškis, Lithuania)

Dr. Shlomo Kodesh

TABLE OF CONTENTS

Introduction

Written by Dr. Shlomo Kodesh

Translation into English by Guy Chuck, Udi Danon and Ellis Pearlman

Every man has a story – his own life story. It starts in his father's home, in the fields and meadows of a man's childhood. This, undoubtedly, is the nucleus. This nucleus is well preserved, and it blossoms on rare occasions in the conditions which stimulate growth. The development of the story is not continuous. It has its breaks and winter slumber, but it awakens and presses on with some changes. Occasionally, it repeats itself but in other cases sails on to unexpected destinations.

This is the way my story moves too. It opens in the small township of Kupishok, which, for me, includes the whole of my Lithuania, the Jewish Lithuania, the Lithuania that is gone forever.

I have invariably been a man of opinion, in short – a prattler. As a child, I was the head of all the talkers, regardless of place: Synagogue, family table, even more so with friends. I have always been fortunate to have had a proper circle of listeners. My imagination and eloquence aided me to depict events and situations so that they interested the listeners.

The constant reading of tales and stories nurtured this skill of mine still further and it later became a way of life. Anything that came out of my pen or mouth was often embodied in a story. Sometimes, it appeared as a story inside a story, which is not necessarily recommended by the creators of strict literary and linguistic rules. However, the rule makers do not always go along with human nature.

As I said, I embarked on the Lithuanian stories in Lithuania. I remember that whenever I went through a special experience, I instantly had the urge to tell people about it, either orally or in writing. Years later I understood that my stories actually met the needs and tastes of many people. Human beings are story lovers by definition. This lust embraces all ages, status and communities. People obviously have diverse tastes and levels of intelligence. If you are lucky enough, you succeed in reaching your listeners. They will always be with you and occasionally – behind you.

The best Biblical prophecies have been written in the form of tales. Let me remind you of the fables of 'The Vineyard' and 'The Vision of the Dry Bones.' The Jewish heritage possesses these values in abundance and so do other nations. Hassidism too has made its way with the help of story-telling.

Consequently, I surmised that the teacher would be more successful in his class if he explains his material through a story. This idea is well-suited for a special education discussion but let's return to our business at hand.

The Lithuanian stories started in my hometown. When I left the country, the stories continued to accompany me. Nevertheless, the story inclination has become even stronger after the great ruin. Moreover, the experiences that I used to consider meaningless and unimportant appear today as significant and worth describing. Sentiment, you may ask? Nostalgia?

Possibly yes and there is no point in being ashamed of it. Nonetheless, there is something which is above all that: It is the light of the leading star, the code of life we are searching for and bound to find in middle-age. As is said in 'Sayings of the Fathers (chapter 5)': 'Fifty is the age of wisdom.' Occasionally it is the age of complete loss, confusion and weakness. This is the philosophy of eat and drink since tomorrow we may die. This can be adopted by an individual as well as by a community. Jerusalem, too - the capital of the independent State of Israel - has not yet produced prominent moral values but has been swept in the direction of imitiating others. Instead, it should have shaped new ideas following the belief from our glorious past – 'For out of Zion shall go forth the law – (Isaiah 2:3).'

Here are my stories. I was hesitant to call them memoirs in the sense of eternal memory, as memoirs oblige precision. They have to follow a chronological order, exact names and other accuracies.

I write this as I approach the age of ninety. It is a peculiar age since memory frequently goes back several generations, allowing you to recall events in detail. It is not the same when one tries to remember what happened yesterday or an hour ago. In the latter case, the ability of storing things in one's memory is very limited - now you see it, now you don't. I have tried my utmost to be as much to-the-point as possible without exaggerating and rambling. There is a lot to tell and there is no bigger joy than that. All the more, my impaired vision limits my writing by hand. Instead, the tape-recorder, this precious instrument, confronts me with the heroes of my life who are mostly dead. They come up from their graves exactly as they used to be. I argue with them, crack jokes with them and at times get angry. It is not boring at all!

The characters of my stories are the descendants of generations to come. Thank God, up until now, I have not bothered my household with my inner world. Someone like me, always worried and thoughtful since my youth up to this hoary age, does not usually have enough time for relatives.

Every generation has its manners. My generation rebelled against the fathers' heritage. This spiritual gap between the older and younger generations is not a good example for the sons. There are enough reasons for close relationships between various generations since it encourages the younger ones to return to their roots, at least the family ones. I present this story to you, my descendants on all sides, in order to let you enjoy it and broaden your horizons.

My students are plentiful, and I still meet them on various occasions in different frameworks. It happened that during a conversation I suddenly recalled that this year I celebrate the 75th anniversary of teaching. When I was fifteen, I was officially appointed the Hebrew and religion teacher at the school which I myself attended at the time. The appointment was made by the school inspector during the German occupation. It happened right after the death of my father, Meir Kodesh, may his memory be blessed, who had held this teaching post until he passed away suddenly. The brave inspector even surprised me by offering to pay me the full salary my father received: twenty marks per month in cash.

Since then, I have been breathing the classroom air for seventy-five years and my students are spread out all over the planet. Destiny has been kind to me, having brought me to the lovely city of Ashdod whose leaders gave me the opportunity to teach for another fifteen years in the realm of Adult Education. In this Zionist city, I have acquired many more friends and students, all of whom I love. The stories of old Lithuania are usually not part of their own life experience but with a bit of curiosity and patience, I hope, they will spend some hours on broadening their outlook through reading this book.

The last ones to mention are the Litvaks, the Jews of my country of origin wherever they are. Not many of us have remained alive after the horrible Nazi burning. The people of my generation are slowly disappearing the natural way. Precisely for this reason, I sincerely hope that the Lithuanian Jews and their descendants will find something of the old aura of their devastated homes in this book.

As for the style - I knew a different Hebrew too. All the same, it seems to me that my readers would prefer the stories of Shlomo Kodesh in his original style. These are my stories and language.

Ashdod, 1993.

Father's Forgiveness

"And Jacob loved Joseph, his youngest son, more than all his sons, and made him a coat of many colors." The coat of many colors was undoubtedly luxurious, and very beautiful. For if it were not, why would the Pentateuch mention it as a sign of Jacob's great love for his son Joseph?

I envied not Joseph, not for the coat of many colors he had been given, nor for his father's love for him, who loved him more than all his brothers. I did not envy him; in fact, I even pitied him. In my heart I felt pity for him, as one pities his fellow man, doomed to share the same fate.

I was my father's youngest child, and he loved me more than all the others. I experienced this first-hand and I know what Joseph went through. I could certainly relate to Joseph with respect to my own identity. I, who am merely the son of Rabbi Meir Kodesh from a small village in Lithuania, was neither content nor pleased with my life. How much more so was Joseph, the son of Jacob, the grandson of our forefather Abraham. Our forefather Jacob, I imagined, did not allow his beloved son, poor Joseph, an idle moment for playing games and fooling with children's tricks or pranks.

My father watched over me - loving me the way he did - lest I waste, Heaven forbid, an hour of Torah study, prayer, and doing good deeds; lest I heed the call of Satan the destroyer in the form of the evil inclination. The evil inclination, which has existed since the days of Creation, is what tempted our foremother Eve to eat of the fruit of the Tree of Knowledge.

It is that which schemed against our forefather Abraham to try and keep him from fulfilling God's commandments to bind his son; and it certainly did not leave Joseph, the son of Jacob, alone just as it did not leave me and all Jewish children alone.

It is the evil inclination, cursed be it, which cannot but tempt Jewish children, innocent ones, to stray from the path of righteousness. It is the evil inclination, which would entice me to neglect Torah study, scram from the synagogue during the repetition of the Amidah prayer by the cantor, and slip away to the backyard to play with 'buttons' instead of responding 'Amen' along with the congregation?

I was aware of all this and, nonetheless, I am not ashamed to confess: On more than one occasion I was seized by the evil inclination - my soul failed me and I heeded its call to engage in child's play, which my father and rabbi and all great and wise Jews viewed as foolishness and considered invalid - bearing no interest in this world and certainly yielding no principle in the hereafter, a world of good.

The fact is, my father was also familiar with all the deeds of the evil inclination, and stood by my side to help me defend myself and ward off its evil counsel. Surely this resembled the ways of our forefather Jacob with respect to Joseph, his youngest son.

Verily, from the depths of my soul I could hear Jacob speaking with his beloved son, that same morning conversation between a righteous father and his spoiled son, lying back in his warm bed and indulging in a pleasant morning hour's sleep and sweet dreams. While Joseph was still pampering himself in the tent of his mother Rachel, the fairest of all of Jacob's tents, his father's hand, a bony, cold hand, stroked him "Arise, Joseph my beloved son. The time of the morning prayer is nigh. The herds have gone off to graze, and you, my son, are still immersed in slumber. You have slept enough. Remember the first paragraph in the 'Shulhan Aruch', the authoritative code of Jewish laws: 'Spring like a lion to the service of the Lord'. My son, get out of bed, strong as a tiger and swift as a deer, or shall we pray with the second minyan today, and cover another page of Gemara before the service?" Joseph felt lazy; oh, how lazy he felt to leave his warm bed and his beautiful dreams behind!

He tried to ignore his father's just words and to toss and turn to the other side of the bed, but his father Jacob's stroking became more frequent and more vigorous, not quite petting, and not quite patting. Sweet dreams faded and vanished as Joseph got out of bed against his will, covering his head with the skull cap which had slipped off during his sleep, muttering the prayer of thanksgiving, while he was bitter about that 'hidden treasure', that pleasant morning hour's sleep that was no more...

That is how I imagined Joseph, without the evil eye, and I pitied him. Joseph, the youngest child, was also extremely fair to look upon, as it is written: "Girls stepped up to gaze", which Rashi interpreted as meaning that damsels would stop to stare at his beauty. However, he had the ill fate of having to sit, at his father's command, all day and evening in 'the Lord's tent' with a page of Gemara open in front of him.

In my imagination I envisaged Joseph swaying with all his strength to drive off evil thoughts - the devil's work, humming the teachings of the Sages to a sad melody. How delightful would it have been had the wickedness of the evil inclination in his heart succumbed to the swaying of his body and been frightened by his melody, and not pulled him away like a marionette toward the sons of maidservants.

These children would play happily near the tent with 'buttons,' polished stones and shards of porcelain, to their heart's content. His heart went out to them, his body pressed against a big, hard stone which Shem - the son of Noah who was known to be the world's first Torah scholar - had sat on in his day. After Shem, continuing Torah study on the very same stone were Abraham, Isaac, and his father Jacob.

***

I was ten years old, a student of the Gemara for three years already, like the rest of my peers in the village. Valiantly, we all swam in a sea of Talmud; the melody of the Gemara was caught up in our throats and we were well-versed in endless pages of Talmud from the following tractates: Ketuvot, Gitin, Beitzah, Baba Kama and Baba Matzia. These were real assets, invaluable words of Torah seasoned with the commentary of Maimonides and the dialectic annotations to the Talmud. The diligent among the young scholars were quick to thumb through the interpretations of the Sages appearing at the end of the books of the Talmud: the interpretations of our teacher, Rabbi Meir Schiff, the 'Pnei Yehoshua', and the like. 'Towers' of Torah pages which only learned men climbed and ascended were in their possession.

This was the way of Torah in Talmudist Lithuania during my youth. This was the purpose of our lives; we studied Torah from early morning until late in the evening. I also studied in this fashion and was not much different from my peers where Torah and wisdom were concerned. Only in my father's eyes was I so wonderful because he loved me more than all his children, as I was his youngest child, his last hope to raise a son learned in Torah who would perform good deeds.

***

Alas, his grown-up son and daughters did not choose to follow in his footsteps. Their hearts were filled with other ideas, and they left our father's house, taking the wrong path. My father, the sharp-witted scholar who could deeply ponder questions of Torah, presenting the issue in the clearest terms and employing deductive reasoning so keenly, never took the time to examine the ways of my grown-up brother and sisters, to ask them about their beliefs and inquire as to what they regarded as sacred to the point of self-sacrifice. He knew one thing, that it was the wrong way, the ways of the Gentiles.

His righteous forefathers, the Hassidim of the Habad sect who were honest, respectable merchants, did not fathom such ways, and such scholars and God-fearing men earned their honorable place in the annals of the righteous. In the eyes of my father, his daughters' struggle and war against the Russian czar and the world order of the rich and poor was an abomination. Is it not written in the Torah: "Poverty shall not be removed from the land?"

He absolutely abhorred people who cast off all restraint, particularly those who would throw off the yoke of kingship. Czar Nicholas II, who reigned on his throne in St. Petersburg at the time, was a wicked one, the descendant of wicked ones who hated the Jews and issued evil decrees against the children of Israel. But this was nothing new, not to my father nor in the eyes of the other learned Jews in the village.

Such was the custom of the kingdom, to restrict Jews and to oppress them. Thus said our Sages of Blessed Memory: "All those who make trouble for Israel become rulers," and every year we read from the Passover Haggadah: "On more than one occasion, one rose to destroy us; but in every generation, there are those who rise to destroy us and the Lord, Blessed Be He, delivers us from their hands." How was this anything new? This was the Diaspora and was expected. The entire world knew this, even a baby in its crib! It was only his daughters that stubbornly insisted on changing the world of the Six Days of Creation.

My father derived no satisfaction from his daughters. On the outside, they appeared to be good girls – comely, with golden hearts that would have pity on any poor or depressed person, and they were wise. Remorse tore apart my poor father, and he regretted the grave error he had made in their upbringing. What did he think would come of this nonsense - heeding the counsel of a woman - my mother - to send their daughters to attend the village school? This was an evil kingdom, which was not content with the laws and evil decrees it constantly issued against the Jews in order to extort money from them through taxes and rates and bribes. But it did not make do with these and sought to take their souls as well.

***

From the wicked shall emerge forth evil, and the same school in the village which opened and was supposedly suitable for Jewish children became a grave and a net to ensnare the feet of Jewish children, to lead them astray from the path of good: Not 'Jewish children' but rather 'Jewish girls'. For although the same school accepted both boys and girls, no Jew in the village was unwise as to hand over his son to Moloch - to take a child out of the 'heder' (religious elementary school) and out of the yeshiva, and have him waste his time supposedly learning the teachings of the Gentiles.

Things had not gone that far yet. The sermon delivered by 'the rabbi on behalf of the kingdom' (as distinguished from the true rabbis whose honor and purpose lies with the Torah) one Sabbath - praising the Enlightenment and speaking of the 'home-owners' who had the heart to send their children to study the language of the land and the wisdom of arithmetic, the wonders of geography and the genesis of trees and stones, animals and beasts, insects and reptiles - was also ineffective.

'The rabbi on behalf of the kingdom' was skilled in delivering public sermons at the command of the authorities. 'The law of the land is binding,' and the Jews of the city had no choice but to unwillingly accept the torment of this type of sermon, which contained neither the flavor of Torah nor the sweetness of a moral, like typical sermons did. Rather, what was the substance of the lecture? Prattle about 'fairy-like Enlightenment' and about a new age that had descended upon the world, that it was precisely the wisdom of the Gentiles that was appropriate for that day and age.

It followed that by law and common sense, the Jews of the village must take their sons out of the heder and the yeshiva and send them to the same so-called 'house of Torah' which the kingdom had set up for them. In this place, new teachings awaited them, which their fathers and their fathers' fathers had never known, with the same 'uchitel' (teacher) who had come to our parts to teach. Only the Lord of Hosts knew where this fellow had come from, to impart his teachings to so many pupils.

***

The 'home-owners' smiled when they heard the name of the 'appointed head of the yeshiva' (as opposed to a true head of a yeshiva), who was none other than an old-looking young man with spectacles whose 'pince-nez' (glasses) would slip down his nose whenever he sneezed or spoke, and miraculously was left dangling thanks to a silk thread he wore around his ear, saving it from being completely broken.

This young man was the talk of the village and was the laughing-stock and object of jokes. Since this 'uchitel' was a source of total wonder, his very Jewishness was questioned. He spoke Yiddish like one of us, and even spiced his words with a Biblical verse or with a saying of the Sages as any one of us, but had the manner of a Gentile, being absent from the synagogue on weekdays. Even on the Sabbath, he would arrive around the time of the reading of the Torah and would finish praying, wonder of wonders, at the same time as the entire congregation.

Instead of a hat, he covered his head with a sort of cap that had a gleaming visor, with a silver insignia in front. He carried a very thin stick which he would roll around in his hand while he walked, which was not functional as a support for someone who required a walking stick, but rather used as an object of ostentatious display which the sons of the Polish landowners would flamboyantly wave before 'shiksa' on-lookers.

And while on the subject, this very same teacher would talk to the wife of the drugstore proprietor a great deal. You could find him at the drugstore every spare moment, as if his entire body was ailing and required medication every day of the week. To make a long story short, this describes the man and his nature. Was this 'uncivilized' man to be entrusted with the souls of Jewish children? There was no substance to this in reality, since no Jewish child, as noted, actually transferred schools from the heder to the village school, with the exception of Dr. Zebadia's son, who never mingled with the Jewish children, and ended up just as he had started off, an 'apostate for spite', going about bareheaded, and speaking to his father and mother, as well as to his Gentile nanny, in the language of the Gentiles.

All the same, lo and behold, the power of Satan! Although that teacher failed to lead a single Jewish boy astray from the straight path, the number of students attending the school near the 'non-Jewish place of worship' (the church) gradually increased, namely the girl students. Word in the village had it that knowledge of Russian was considered a great virtue for matchmaking.

Rumor spread in the women's section of the synagogue that matchmakers considered the ability of the maiden in question to speak the language of the land to be one of the virtues of a bride instead of a dowry or at least lowered the cost of the dowry by a few hundred rubles. After all, this was a big deal. There was not a home where maidens could not be found, and there was not a Jew in our city with dowry money in his pocket.

If this is how fathers were, how much more so were the mothers. After all, by their nature, mothers would worry about a match for their daughter, almost from the day the baby was born: a few prayers and supplications, a few heartbreaking sighs, a few tears shed which would wet the 'Offering of Meal' siddur in supplication to God Most High - who joins couples and decrees who shall marry whom - to send their daughter a worthy mate.

Whether this selfsame daughter had come of age or was still a baby playing in the sand, engaging in child's play, was all immaterial. It did not matter if parents worried over their daughter marrying early or late, for prayer - and not simply waiting for a miracle to happen - could fulfill at least some of their wishes .

Every penny counted in raising dowry money: A sheet that could be sewn into a gown - a towel, a tablecloth, or a feather-filled cushion. Nonetheless, all these could not cover the entire expense, for there were many daughters, thank Heaven, in a typical Jewish household, whose members often went hungry.

The Lord of Hosts saw the plight of the daughters' parents and generously endowed these maidens with virtues: There were fair ones and there were smart ones; there were those skilled in handicrafts such as sewing and weaving; there was the type that was a natural in trade who excelled in her father's shop; and another, who spent a lot of time in the kitchen and had a refined taste in baking and cooking.

The common denominator of all these virtues was that word got around about them among the public so that mothers of grooms were eager to bring into their homes brides so blessed. They would manage to persuade their husbands to lower the sum of the dowries set for the groom.

Ever since proficiency of the Russian language became regarded as a virtue of damsels, my mother started to coax my father into allowing Mina Haya, my 15-year-old eldest sister, to join the neighbors' daughter who attended the school, leaving her house each morning carrying a pile of books and a notebook.

At first, my father dismissed my mother's argument as weak and considered it an affront. He said, "The good and merciful God, who provides in His goodness, sustaining great and small - would He turn His back on those who performed His will and not provide them sustenance to raise sons and daughters in the way of Torah, to enter matrimony, and to do good deeds?" He had no need for these frivolities, and would not lead his life or run his household according to what his foolish neighbors might say. His daughters would not share company with a boy wearing a pince-nez, frittering their time.

Father and mother each held their own strong opinion. But a living was becoming more difficult to earn, and many were the Jew's needs in those trying times, until my father submitted and gave Mina Haya permission to accompany the neighbors' daughter. It was my father's moment of weakness; he did not forgive himself for the rest of his life. "The fool believes everything," he would utter to himself in his sorrow.

***

Mina Haya proved to be a smart student. In just a few days, she learned the entire Torah, which took her friend months to learn, and she earned a citywide reputation as a bright knowledgeable person. Even mother, being a mother, was not modest about her daughter's success in school, and sang her praises when her daughter was not around. And so Mina Haya, in this manner, was lured to this 'impurity', attended classes, completed her studies and received all sorts of honors, certificates, gifts, books and the like.

As far back as when she was seventeen, my father felt that she had overdone it, and tried to save his daughter from the claws of the wicked, but is was too late. Moreover, two years later, the second daughter, my sister Peska, also took the path of her sister and began to attend the school – with a predictable end, a rather shameful and painful one at that.

***

As the girls grew up, my father's grief intensified. In less than two years, Meir Kodesh's daughters were found to have rebelled against the kingdom of God. Woe to such reproach! The eyes of God watch all those rebels - men and women - who have gatherings in the forests and speak ill of the Russian king and his subjects. Mina was almost arrested committing such an act, when the Cossacks encircled Firgeh Forest, the designated place of secret assemblies, where countless couples would flock under the guise of a field trip, as if to catch a breath of fresh air.

When they arrived at a small lake in the forest, these couples would gather in a great assembly, young men and women, many from respectable households. It was no secret that even Hirschkeh, the son of a Hassidic rabbi, joined the same group, despite the disappointment of his father.

What were they doing there until after Havdalah (the benediction over wine, spices and a flame at the conclusion of Sabbath days and festivals)? Things that were uttered there by the great rebels remained a secret, which were not revealed to any but the most trustworthy people, friends and confidants.

By contrast, those same melodies and tunes they used to sing there in unison became publicly known. They were melancholy, sad melodies -

songs of want which they used to sing about the troubles of poor seamstresses who would sew nice dresses for the daughters of the rich lords, when they themselves wore rags; and songs about the cobbler who would supposedly talk to his hammer and awl, telling about his impoverished condition. Apparently, these were things everyone knew and were no novelty. Nevertheless, they were exciting and stirred people. That is the power of a melody, such that if you were to sing about things everyone knew to the tune of a new melody, the lyrics would become as new, and invoke anguish and longing, or the opposite... great joy. There were also other melodies that the young men and women would hum in company or in solitude - all sorts of oaths and vows against the emperor and his men, songs of rebellion and of insolence against oppression, which they would sing angrily and vehemently, thereby lifting the hearts of these rebels against the kingdom.

All these melodies did not remain a secret. On the contrary, they spread by word of mouth and caught on quite well. Many of the townspeople were music fans. The same melodies were played morning and evening in workshops and stores; older sisters would put their siblings to sleep with these tunes; and yeshiva students, by contrast, would sway over the pages of the Gemara in the heder, diligently pondering a difficult Talmudic subject to the melody of the same holy oath which the 'gang' took to fight the czar to the bitter end.

***

There was the incident involving Meir Motis, who led the Mussaf service during the High Holidays, who stood and introduced a new addition to the version of the Mussaf service's song of prayer and sang "providing sustenance in his mercy" to the tune of a melody the 'gang' would sing.

This was a novelty and came as a surprise. Many 'home-owners' turned up their noses in revulsion but, on the other hand, there were many who actually praised the cantor, since there is a most important principle in the Torah – 'invoking sanctity.' Meir Motis did well, so they say, in elevating a weekday melody to a level of holiness. They supported their argument by citing those who would sing the holiest, most elevated of melodies in the Hassidic rabbis' courts, who sought and discovered melodies of Gentile shepherds, and elevated them to holiness with Hassidism and steadfast devotion to our Father in Heaven. Verily, they earned the mark of distinction reserved for the righteous.

***

Let me now describe the typical household scene of the home-owners of the town, and also in my home. At the same time, each home was different. Behold, the households of Uncle Samuel and Uncle Jacob Gefen were hard hit by the same injury, the latter being a learned Jew who proposed sharp-witted new interpretations of the Law in a work he composed entitled "These are the Generations of Jacob." The home of Yitzhak Moshe, the butcher, was not spared this affliction either, nor were dozens of other 'home- owners', all God fearing, all perfectly faithful.

Their sons and daughters were similarly influenced by these affairs of the kingdom, neglected study of Torah to a greater or lesser degree, and were lax in observing the commandments. Nevertheless, it was not the end of the world for them, neither did their households cave in on them. Indeed, they all remained steadfast to their father's morals, rebuked their sons and daughters and, when they discovered that their words came to naught, they yielded like merciful fathers. Their hearts bled in secret, and they put on a smiling face in public, the way fathers lovingly accept all the childish deeds of their children. Such fathers entertained hopes for their children's future: "When they grow up, they will be wiser."

Not so with my father! He followed a straight path and was stubborn and zealous about his beliefs. He was soft-hearted and was easy to please in financial dealings and lay matters. However, when it came to beliefs and opinions, his heart hardened, and he became uncompromising. He was not comforted by misery in company and fought for what was sacred in his eyes to the point of self-sacrifice.

He was a compassionate father. If one of his children were sick, he was restless, and there wasn't anything that was too difficult for him to do for the sake of his sick child: Ease his pain and give him strength with the help of all types of medication; amuse him and make him smile.

However, that same compassionate and merciful father withheld his love and mercy even from his loved ones when it came to throwing off the yoke of the kingdom of Heaven or taking matters of holiness or age-old traditions lightly. No compromises were to be made as far as he was concerned. He could not and would not understand neither the spirit of his son or daughter nor the spirit of the times. These matters were to be performed unconditionally and he moved not a hair's breadth from his position.

***

There was no room for both worlds under one roof. Like father like son, the good deeds of parents are a good omen for children. Sons and daughters would take after their fathers in their zeal and their faith in the Torah to which they were steadfast and would observe the Torah with all their souls and for which they would sacrifice their lives. Father endured even the most difficult tribulations of his life; his son left the house, going his separate way, and he did not stop him, even though deep down, he loved him profoundly and missed him greatly, leaving him with broken body and spirit.

Parting from my sister Mina Haya went exactly this way: One day, at the end of the Sabbath lunch, my sister made an astonishing announcement: Tomorrow at daybreak, she would take the morning train to the city of Vilna. She would be going to Vilna to study midwifery. She related that she had already written and received an acceptance letter. She even saved money for train fare from the pennies she received from mother for minor errands. Her friends gave her an address of a cheap hotel in Vilna where she would stay.

She made the announcement with such incomparable stubbornness. Silence - stillness following the shock - prevailed in the house. Afterwards, my mother began to cry bitterly, and all the children sitting around the table joined her. I was a baby and was not yet aware of what was happening, but I remember that I started to sob very loudly and my oldest sister embraced me and calmed me down the best she could.

Only my father remained collected, like the calmness of the Sabbath. He quieted all the sobbers, reminded my mother of the sin of being sad on the Sabbath, and my mother stopped crying and also brought my father a small glass containing the 'remaining water for ritual washing' with which to wash his fingertips before the grace after meals.

Following the grace after meals, my father would retire to his room, as customary on the Sabbath and rest, indulging in the enjoyment of the Sabbath. After an hour he would arise. This week, he followed his custom. Since my mother remained in her room and complained of a headache, father drank tea alone, and perused a book of morals.

He then left for the synagogue for the afternoon and evening prayers. He returned home, performed Havdalah, said the blessing over spices, said the verses to the two versions of Elijah the Prophet, one a Lubavitcher Hassidic tune and the other a Copost Hassidic melody. Even though the Lubavitcher Hassidim and the Copost Hassidim were of the same flesh and blood - all Hassidim of the Habad sect, they had separated nonetheless, and Copost Hassidim sang Elijah the Prophet to a different melody on Saturday night. My father did not take part in this dispute, which separated hearts - between my uncles - even in my grandfather's house. My father would chant both versions in order to discharge his obligation.

Only after the entire ceremony did he go to his room and remain locked up there for an hour. A profound sadness and a void which could have filled the world pervaded the house. Everyone whispered as if there was a poor sick person, Heaven forbid, in the house. After an hour, my father came out of his room and entered the dining room. In his hand he held a twenty-ruble note. He called his eldest daughter, who was locked up in her room after making her shocking announcement. My father gave her money and told her, "This is for your initial expenses. You will receive this allowance every month. Be careful with your studies since it is sanctified work in which lives are at stake. Go in peace and be a faithful Jewess; be careful not to violate the Sabbath, which has the weight of all the sins in the world," he said, extending her a hand. My sister fell upon his neck weeping. I believe this was the first time I saw my eldest sister crying with such emotion. My father patted her head and went to his room. The next morning, he did not go out to accompany her and left the gloomy task of parting from his daughter to my mother.

A few others followed in my sisters' footsteps, whether to study midwifery or other skills taught in the big city, where they learned a new lesson in wont and in poverty. They observed the commandments in a different way of life but with the same devotion and love of Torah as their perfectly faithful, God fearing fathers had.

***

My father was unfortunate. When it came time for my older brother to study in the yeshiva, my father tried, for the first time in his life, to deviate from an age-old custom and suffered a double punishment for this sin: mental anguish and deep remorse.

Rumor spread to our city that in the same 'holy community' of the city of Lida, the city's rabbi, Rabbi Jacob Beinish, the founder of the Mizrahi religious Zionist movement, had opened a new type of yeshiva. In this yeshiva, in which Talmud, Gemara and writings of Rabbinic authorities on Halachic matters were properly taught, subjects of secondary importance were taught along with Torah. The Russian language and arithmetic, the same 'Greek wisdom' for which the Sages had (cynically) set an hour which was neither day nor night. In this yeshiva, an hour of study was devoted to this subject every day.

What was the purpose of all this? To withstand the tide of the spirit of the times, and to subdue Satan from within. If it had already been decreed that Jewish young men would devote their time to Zionist wisdom, it was better that this be done under the kosher supervision of an ultra-Orthodox, God fearing head of a yeshiva.

My father heard this story, which left a deep impression on him. Adversity makes a man wise, and what good did his stubbornness toward his daughters do him? Instead of sending his son to the Lubavitcher yeshiva, as was the practice of fathers, he sent him to the city of Lida. For the secret had been discovered, and it became common knowledge that a few of the best young men had left the yeshiva in Libavitsh, preferring an external wisdom, in their manifold iniquities. After all, his son Shmuel, a sharp-witted young man, had a good memory. Who could guarantee my father that even Shmuel would not be led astray, Heaven forbid, by that same spirit of apostasy, and would not leave the yeshiva in his thirst for knowledge the Gentiles possessed? The rabbi of the holy community of Lida was right. Young men would 'taste' of that knowledge, and yet have their fill of the Divine Torah, thereby enjoying the best of both worlds. In this manner they would cheat Satan, who seeks to plot schemes in order to lead wise students astray from the path of the upright. Still my father often felt quilty for having deviated from this age-old custom, that he was not sending Schmuel to Libavitsh, in accordance with Hassidic custom.

He did not derive satisfaction from Shmuel either. My older brother was a very handsome young man, who excelled in the aptitude for writing. Verily, he was a great scribe. Father, who was also eloquent and spoke in rhetorical language, very much enjoyed reading Shmuel's beautiful long letters which he would send from the yeshiva. They were written in the holy language in poetic form, sweet as honey and most notably, in beautiful, ornate handwriting. In those days, the shape of a letter carried the same weight as the content of a verse, and writers would write ornately, producing very small and beautiful letters. People would envy this work of art and they would try and imitate it by writing nicely, adding their own touch. My brother inherited from his father language and writing, and his letters would pass from one person to another at the Hassidic minyan. Educated home-owners enjoyed reading his letters, and the fathers of daughters even sighed "Shmuel is a fine young man. He is very handsome and speaks wisely,"
repeatedly praising Shmuel before his wife and growing daughter.

Indeed, my father was not a lucky man, and the hope he had in his son also met with disappointment. My mother, upon seeing my father saddened and complaining that satisfaction had departed his home, accused the Evil Eye. "People have smitten us with their evil eye," my mother would spill her heart before Tzippa, her sister and neighbor in the house, shedding a tear on her sleeve and adding: "I always told my husband that it is better to never show a smiling face than to arouse the jealousy of others. However, he thought everyone rejoiced in his happiness, but he in fact sparked the envy of many."

What had taken hold of my brother? He did not heed the advice of his sisters nor was he involved in the affairs of the kingdom - to dethrone the czar, create a world of compassion and raise the poor from the dung heaps. My brother chose a different path, which was also crooked in my father's eyes. My brother Shmuel took the path of Zionism, which to me meant immediate redemption. From the yeshiva he brought to my father the message of those seeking Zion. The same rabbi who founded the Lida yeshiva was a member of the Love of Zion movement and his heart yearned for redemption in the land of our forefathers. He permitted his students to dream about the revival of the Jews in the Holy Land and to express the sweet longing for Zion and Jerusalem through a Gemara melody.

Good men who were sharp-witted and learned in Torah abandoned their pages of Gemara and went their way to learn a trade or whatever they might pursue. My brother Shmuel however, was among those who abandoned the Torah and, if that was not enough, rumor had it that he was a sinner - a sinner himself who also caused others to sin. He was eloquent and had a strong influence on his friends.

He hung around, tempting yeshiva students to go to the city of Vilna, and train themselves to work in manual labor with which to make a livelihood upon making Aliyah and which Palestine was in need of. Innocent young men were lured and went with him to Vilna. But these men sinned and relented. Not having a cent in their pockets, they did not eat for days in the big city, slept in hostels for the poor, and ate a little jam until they ran out of strength and their spirit broke. As the saying goes: "Where the repentant sinners stand, the holy righteous may not."

The young men completely repented, studied the Six Orders of the Talmud and writings of Rabbinic authorities on Halachic matters, but did not forsake Zion. They preserved the love of Zion in their hearts and urged praise for Palestine.

Only this stubborn character, my brother, did not return to the yeshiva. Only sixteen, he had become obstinate. Many things happened to him, and he underwent various trials and tribulations. He experienced hunger, along with his sisters who lived in the same city. They shared their morsel of bread with their brother, who abandoned Torah. Finally, luck came his way when he found himself a job setting letters in a printing press. He toiled at hard labor and barely managed to make a living. My father's hopes that my brother would come to his senses and return to his home and his Torah were in vain. He did not return to the yeshiva, and my father's anguish grew.

As at other times, my father tried to do something about it. He would close his shop and go to the city of Vilna to have a word with his son and turn him back from a crooked path of folly but he always returned from that journey angry and despondent.

Finally, he left his son alone and stopped traveling to Vilna. My father became silent and did not say a word about what had gone on between a stubborn, zealous father and a stubborn, zealous son.

Their last such meeting was held in an attic, in a dark room filled with mildew. It was Shmuel abode in a poor Vilna backstreet. My father had returned from evening prayers, and my brother had returned from work. The two dined together and sat near the fire to warm their frozen bodies in that wretched apartment. At this point they became embroiled in a major dispute and did not reach a middle ground. Father argued against Shmuel, citing the persuasive argument of the commandment to honor one's father and mother bearing the same weight as many other commandments, a virtue awarded with a long life and all things good. He even said that he did not intend to make him go back to the yeshiva against his will. On the contrary, if Shmuel's soul did not crave Torah – only to exploit it, that is, to earn a living at the rabbinate's expense – he could come back home with him, put his shoulder to the business and set time aside for Torah like other married yeshiva students who would study Torah and persue an occupation, enjoying both worlds.

Father spoke more and more with a dual tone: one of conciliation and one of rage, but neither were of help. My brother was eloquent, an eminent Zionist preacher. He became embroiled in a major argument with our father,and answered him point by point. He cited the Gaonites (title of the heads of Babylonian Talmud academies) who were lovers of Zion for all generations, who acted to rebuild Zion on its ruins. He described the affliction of the Jews in the Diaspora - evil decrees from without and degeneration from within. Men were guided by greed, and the earth beneath would tremble. Greatly excited, he concluded with a verse by Bialik: "Will the dead come to life even when a shofar is blown and the standard be raised?"

Getting to the point, the walls of this attic never heard such vulgar, explosive statements, sharpness of tongue and effusion of spirit which eventually exhausted my father. It was a wee hour of the morning when Shmuel saw his father fall asleep in a sitting position at the edge of his bed, his head resting against the wall, his sleep troubled by his heavy breathing. It grieved Shmuel to see our father's anguish and took pity on him. He covered him with a warm blanket, and he himself sat on the other end of the bed, trying to keep warm with his old coat. This was how he slept until it was time for morning prayer.

At daybreak, father woke up startled, and realized that he had slept a troubled sleep. He saw his son sound asleep, pale and thin, that same tattered coat covering him. His soul grieved. He then conjured up scenes of the debate and the rebuttals made by Shmuelkeh, employing both valid and invalid arguments. Very gently, he removed the warm blanket from his body to cover Shmuel in order to keep him warm. He dipped his hands in a bowl of water in the corner of the room, whispered the Recitation Verses (Psalms 145-150, recited during the morning prayers), boiled a cup of hot water on a soot-covered kerosene cooking stove and wrapped himself up in a tallis and tefillin.

My father prayed with a broken heart and broken spirit. In the meantime, Shmuel awoke. He gave father a conciliatory smile, and also hurried to wash his hands. Shmuel pleased his strict father as he also stood for a short prayer, putting on his own tefillin. Afterwards, each went his own way; my father went home to his afflictions and his aching soul, and my brother to the Ha'Olam Bureau, the Zionist publication where he was employed as a proofreader and enjoyed his work. Zionists would read Ha'Olam to drew comfort from the teachings of Herzl. For his part, my brother aided their cause, while making a living under difficult circumstances.

After my father returned home, he grieved, but seldom revealed his suffering and anger, preferring to remain silent, containing his grief. Moreover, from that point on, he started turning a blind eye to the compassionate deeds of my mother who would send the children who had left home an allowance now and then to get by. My brother and sisters divided the present of their good mother, and their souls were enlivened from afar. My father knew of the matter but did not rebuke her. His heart was not hardened, but the heart of a compassionate Jewish father who would not hold back an additional allowance to his children who had left home. Only He Who can read man's thoughts knew why his soul grieved so.

***

Mother bore seven children and but five had survived. Two had died too young for my father to be proud of them. Shlomo Zalmankeh, the youngest child, had not yet been plagued by Evil. No wonder all his love and hopes, anxiety and bitter experiences with his son Shmuel and his daughters were at stake, and all depended on his educating me. My father decided not to repeat the same mistakes.

He carefully pondered the matter and reached the general conclusion that all the evil that had befallen his household was due to friends who had been a bad influence. He decided that I would not be drawn into the trap of no-good friends. One must not split hairs where a soul is at stake, and one must not be lax when it comes to Torah study. In that regard, my father could be counted on. In the words of the Jewish psalmist: "They (the Lord's judgments) are more desirable than gold, than fine gold."

My father allowed himself to drastically break away from the age-old custom of the town, observed in Lithuania for generations: dividing the period of Torah study among a few teachers in the city, by the age of the child and level of study. It is said, "Five-year-olds will study Bible", and you couldn't find a more decent, honest teacher for beginners than Moshe Wellweiss.

Everyone knew that Moshe Wellweiss was a musician, a joker, who would make brides and grooms happy with Hassidic melodies and humor. But his wife and their eight children could not be supported with jest and Hassidic melodies. He became a nursery school teacher, and earned a living as a teacher in addition to earning a living as a clown.

Opinions were divided: There were those who said Rabbi Moshe Wellweiss, with all due respect, was not a great Talmudist, which is why he taught only toddlers, whereas others said this was not so. He was learned enough in Torah to teach older students Bible, Rashi commentary and even Gemara.

So what was the matter? Small children were very fond of Moshe Wellweiss, since he himself had the soul of a child and would laugh wholeheartedly at any bit of humor, like a baby all excited by something he sees for the first time. Anyhow, there were two primary times, the time every child in town needed to be able to properly read Hebrew and the other, to begin translating a verse from the Book of Genesis. Once a five-year-old could understand a verse from the Pentateuch, what was the purpose of his being in Moshe Wellweiss's 'heder', the teacher for beginners?

For the 'heder' where Bible and the beginning of the Gemara were taught was in a small house on the verge of collapse, the house of Moshe Zondil. He was also known as the intermediate level teacher, a hint that Moshe Zondil was an excellent teacher for beginners but was not yet a Talmudist.

His students did not have it easy, and they received both the carrot and the stick for their sins and sinful intentions. He was strict and would scold his pupils over important and trivial matters alike. Nonetheless, he had such an influence that many a student - in fact all the married yeshiva students of the city, themselves fathers - would go to Moshe Zondil's place after the Sabbath morning service to properly greet him with a "Good Sabbath Rabbi," as if they were still his 'heder' students, still influenced by his teachings.

Sharp-witted and very diligent children studied Bible with Melamed's 'heder' only one year. From the second year, they would advance to the most purposeful course of study with Rabbi Moshe Mordechai, where they would study until their bar mitzvah. Mediocre students studied Bible for two years, and those requiring remedial instruction studied three years or more.

When a student versed in Judaism came of bar mitzvah age or older, he had two options: study Torah or choose an occupation. If he opted for Torah, there were small, crowded yeshivas which were always ready to accept yeshiva students who were diligent at Torah study. Communal workers of every respectable town established small yeshivas for yeshiva students, or large yeshivas for older, married students who craved to study Torah and preferred to be immersed in Torah study to mundane matters and concern for their livelihood.

***

Whenever a town in Lithuania built a yeshiva under its jurisdiction, the pious women would rally around the flag to sustain these students to provide them their daily bread. There was not a household in the town which did not offer a 'hosting day' for a yeshiva student one day of each week. It was no disgrace (God forbid), to partake of a stranger's meal. On the contrary, these lads earned their hosts the merit of having fulfilled the commandments to promote Torah study and sustain wise students, the most important commandment and the greatest merit. As the Sages once said: "The study of Torah is more important than anything else."

This was the way of Torah in my town. This is how Jews were brought up in Lithuania, in the ways of Torah and in worldly affairs, where Torah superseded the latter. There was not a male in the town who tended to the business of his father or his father-in-law before having had his fill of Torah and before his soul was instilled with the fear of God. How was I, Shlomo Zalmankeh, the son of Rabbi Meir, different from all the other lads? I attended class in Moshe Wellweiss's 'heder' together with my peers, I participated along with my classmates, and we murmured in unison: "kamatz, aleph, patach, beit, tzereh, gimmel, shuruk, daled (names of Hebrew diphthongs)." We all studied the melodious sounds of the letters of the alphabet, which would sweeten the yolk of Torah.

Along with the rest of my class, I got to the siddur and to the Torah portion of Lech Lecha, after which I advanced to be taught by the strict Moshe Zondil. There, we studied the Pentateuch and Rashi, in the course of which I was properly and fittingly slapped on the cheek. On the Sabbath, we would read 'Ethics of Our Fathers' to the melody of the Day of Rest. We clung to the Torah, but did not desist from playing children's games. We played hide-and-seek and, slowly but surely, we advanced to the heart of the matter, to the first pages of the very easy part of the Gemara, the Beitzah tractate - revolving around an egg that was born on a festival, with the subsequent dispute between the strict school of Shamai and the lenient school of Hillel. Up to this point, everything was in order, nothing new under the sun as far as I was concerned.

I finished my second year in Moshe Zondil's 'heder' (my father was a Bible fan and did not disturb me during Bible class until I had learned all twenty four books from start to finish), and already Rabbi Moshe Mordechai, the Gemara teacher, was pinching my cheek in the synagogue - a harbinger of things to come. God willing, I would be one of his students next year, hopefully a good year. And then, as when God overturned Sodom and Gomorra, something happened in the town which had never before occurred - a miracle. Rabbi Meir, a fervent Hassid of the Habad sect, took a separate path from the ways of his fathers. Instead of sending his son to the Gemara 'heder' taught by Rabbi Moshe Mordechai, he retained a rabbi to teach him privately. He was no ordinary rabbi, but precisely the young 'mitnagged' (opponent of the Hassidim) rabbi, who had spent many years in the Slobodeka Yeshiva, the famous yeshiva of 'The Moralist' . The condition was that the young rabbi would teach me a page of Gemara three hours a day, and my father was prepared to pay the rabbi a fortune in tuition, twenty-five rubles for a half hour. What was the purpose of all this? To keep his youngest son at arm's length from friends who were a bad influence, God forbid.

My father did not rely solely on others, the young rabbi included. Not only did he put all his money into my education, he devoted every spare moment of his life to me and to my Torah study. Heaven forbid that he should err this time, as he had in educating his older son. He assumed the duty of being at his youngest son's side in the fierce battle against the evil inclination, which incites and is seductive. I was always with my father. I would pray the first minyan with him, even on weekdays. Have you ever seen a child my age getting up for the first minyan at sunrise? Others would be fast asleep, while I would accompany my father to the synagogue. Wisdom belongs to the morning, with double the gain. In the meantime, only an hour was left to thumb through a book of morals or the Lubavitcher Rabbi's 'Tani' book together with father. My father had a hidden intent, that the 'mitnagged' rabbi would not have an evil influence on me. Talmudic erudition is one thing and Hassidism is another. One should beware of a married yeshiva student prodigy, that is, respect him but suspect him.

All this applied to weekdays, the days of Creation, when father would divide his time between many business matters, family matters, Hassidic devotion and community matters. On the Sabbath, the day of rest, things were different. This was a completely holy day for me, the beloved youngest child, to peruse the book after lunch and visit the rabbi's home to hear him share a reliable testimony on the ways of Torah as well as sip a cup of 'Kosher for Sabbath' tea served by the young wife of the rabbi.

You would think poor Shlomo Zalmankeh, bound to his father's love with his life passing him by, neither children's games nor friends, no childhood mischief or pranks. Yes, but no! The truth was that I had two spirits dominating me as a child, and the one contradicted the other.

I was a mischievous child who invented games and played pranks. Playing with friends provided me with excitement and Haim Bar, the attendant, had several additional occupations. He was also a watchmaker and an expert umbrella repairman. But all three livelihoods were not enough to sustain his large family. This Haim Bar was my archenemy, who pursued me to the bitter end and did not let me run around the pulpit in the synagogue like my friends did. This Haim Bar called me by the derogatory name of 'Purim grogger', and one of his claims was that the minyan was quiet and peaceful until Rabbi Meir's 'jewel' stepped in. Woe for the calamity as soon as this 'jewel' - that is myself - entered the synagogue! Noise and commotion and screams and children running around all over the synagogue. I could not but admit that Haim Bar had gotten carried away by his anger. It was no fault of mine that my peers were drawn to me and would 'anoint me king', and that I would frequently play war as kings do? This is the way of the world, with the war cry sounded in preparation for battle, for wars have not been waged quietly from time immemorial.

However, I also enjoyed solitude. I always had a fervent imagination, and I could lose myself in daydreams and conjure up pictures of anything I wanted. Moreover, a product of my imagination that got into my head, which I fancied, could not be put out of my mind, like other children who would get caught up in a momentary imagination. I was different. A fantasy which I was fixed on I would pursue for days and would immediately put all my energy into it.

I had a long daydream in which I was in an ideal world, my own private world, where I was my own master. Of course, in my world of make-believe, I indulged in all the honors and delights in the world. I was a prince and a world-renown genius of Torah, like the Gaon from Vilna in his time, righteous as Righteous Joseph and handsome as he, wise as King Solomon and rich as Korach. I did whatever I pleased with my treasures and with the Divine wisdom that inspired me, all drawn from my own strength; how much more so from the day I found books belonging to other imaginative people, who added stories embellished with animals and birds, trees of the field and creeping things.

Over time, I accepted my fate, through solitude and private lessons. A small room was designated for me at home, a room which signified pure holiness to me and my Torah. My father even decided my daily routine, which was unlike that of any of the other children my age. In the morning hours, when everyone would agree the mind is clear, my father would wake me and humorously say: "Arise, Arise Rabbi Shlomo Zalmankeh. Arise, Arise thou lion cub of Judah!" This was an allusion to the first paragraph in the Shulhan Aruch: "You shall serve the Lord with lion-like resolve."

By the time the 'cub' rubbed his eyes, trying to get another moment's sweet slumber, his ears would awake to the sound of a tablespoon striking a glass: a clear sign of that sweet beverage my father would bother to prepare for my pleasure out of his love for me and his desire to refresh me, to give me added strength and intensify my desire for Torah. This drink was known as 'eggnog',and was made of two egg yolks beaten and mixed with very fine sugar, like those spices from the Pitum Haktoret (ingredients of frankincense) prayer.

Father would hum that prayer, a customary prelude to the morning prayer, while he mixed and prepared the eggnog. After the yolks were beaten and mixed with the sugar, forming a thick solution - the color of amber and having 'the taste of Paradise', father would pour milk into this glass, which filled with a yellowish liquid, creating a thick sweet foam which tempted the palate to taste this sweet liquid.

No one else could prepare eggnog with such confidence and ease of mind. My father earned a reputation and was considered an expert in preparing this masterpiece, something he could take pride in. (I still wonder about the origin of the term 'eggnog' and the association between the great Gog and Magog who are nothing but murderous blood spillers, who would be revealed to the world in the punishment to precede the End of Days, yet that morning drink reinvigorates and gladdens the soul.) Getting to the point, somehow, with the help of "He Who removeth slumber from my eyes", I was rescued from the throes of sweet morning sleep, and my lips whispered the thanksgiving prayer which does not mention the name of God (and therefore may be said without washing the hands). In the meantime, I would get dressed and prepare myself for the ritual washing of the hands, perform all the morning mitzvahs pertaining to the body, and would be prepared to sip of that ever so sweet 'eggnog', which tasted like ambrosia. Father would sit comfortably beside me, slowly sipping a glass of hot water and taking a slice of that splendid butter-flavored roll my mother baked. Lest you should ask "Partaking of food before the morning prayer, how could you?", rest assured. My father performed the mitzvah ordained by the Lubavitcher Rabbi, that is, the decree to 'carefully watch yourself' which commanded that one not let his body grow weak, lest this result in weakness of the heart, which my father had started to feel in recent years. We finished drinking our eggnog and sipping a cup of tea. The hour of morning prayer was nigh. But father was in no hurry to part company, for we still had that page of

Gemara Kala ahead of us, which we would study together as a prelude to the morning prayer.

***

It is natural for babies to observe grown-ups and try to be like them, imitating their manners and lifestyle. Haven't you seen baby boys playing around, wearing their father's long pants and their grandfather's spectacles on their nose? And what about all those girls who would supposedly display motherly love to a lifeless doll? This is how young boys and girls behave, assuming the manners of their fathers and mothers. Children play grown-ups, and adults do not hold them accountable.

Things in my childhood were different. After all, our Hassidic forefathers intended to spare us the punishment of a childhood devoid of the fear of God and suppression of desire. In their love and out of their concern for our souls, lest they be blemished, they imposed upon us, from early childhood, the yoke of the Divine kingdom and of Torah. Mature and discerning sons were quick to outgrow signs of childhood, and the sooner the better. We were aware of this and wanted to be like adults in every way. Many boys would wear long pants, and a small fringed tallis was visible in all its holy splendor, hanging out of our clothes as if to declare the mitzvah to wear a tzitzit. We prayed with intent, swaying our bodies and closing our eyes so as not to let Satan interfere with our concentration of thought. Like real adults, we beat our chests with little fists as hard as we could during the confessional and, one by one, with broken hearts and tears in our eyes, declared all our many sins, including those we could comprehend and those we could not fathom - sins we had committed as small children, sins we did not commit, and sins whose meaning we did not know.

We did not fall short of our forefathers in the study of Torah or in our excitement over a Gemara melody, be it gay or sad. Like them, we performed the meal related customs and dipped a slice of bread - over which we had recited the blessing - in salt, making noise as we cooled off our soup, grabbing a quick bite on weekdays but nothing over and above what we required for minimal nourishment to avoid neglecting study of the Torah. However, we ate at ease on the Sabbath and festivals in order to experience the delight of these special days.

***

During breaks from Torah study, we would work in our fathers' businesses and were permitted to learn the ins and outs of business and trade. These hours when we were engaged in business were a break away from the monotonous life of Torah and mitzvahs. On busy market days and fair days, there were also many Gentiles in the shop. Every buyer would haggle craftily, come and go, and then return. In the meantime, his evil inclination would tempt him to steal. On such days, we would not go to school and would run errands for our parents, who were poor, miserable salespersons. We stood with them during such time of stress and served as full-fledged helpers. We arranged and weighed the merchandise and, most importantly, we were very watchful and never took our eyes off the buyers who would handle the goods, supposedly examining their quality, slipping it into their canvas bag at a moment when our attention was distracted. The quick among them would escape from the shop during busy hours, with the spoil in their hands, depriving our parents of their livelihood. At such times, we were adults in most respects. "How good it was that everything had its time." Our time would come when we would grow up, God willing, marry and perform good deeds and pleasurable acts allowed only grown-ups.

Nevertheless, there was an underlying matter in dispute between fathers and sons over one sign of adulthood: We had a strong craving for this mark of maturity - possibly a lust - which we believed we were entitled to for our merits in swimming the sea of Talmud like adults with great perseverance and refined dialectic. Why were our parents and teachers so adamant precisely on this matter, to forbid us this pleasure with the excuse that it is improper for minors, heder pupils, particularly Moshe Mordechai's students? We did not understand, even when we were offered very convincing explanations: Physical punishment - being slapped or flogged. There were parents and teachers who would resort to this form of punishment in front of classmates to serve as a deterrent.

It shall be presumed that the discerning readers among you have already gotten to the bottom of this desire which we craved as children, which was none other than the desire to smoke. Today we are all wise and know that smoking is merely a bad habit, the temptation of the evil inclination to encourage squandering the money of men and ruining their health. In those days, doctors were not yet aware of the dangers of this epidemic. Far from it, smoking a 'papyrus '(cigarette) was considered a custom radiating importance, and we kids were stricken with this desire and were not wise enough to abhor it and abstain. On the contrary, the best and most faithful among us - sin-fearing, steadfast to the Torah and praying with intent - would succumb to the sin of taking a small bit of tobacco from our fathers' table and, with no one watching, learn how to roll the thinnest piece of paper with our fingers into the shape of a pipe, a receptacle for tobacco, glue the end of that pipe with saliva, and lo: They held a 'papyrus' in their hands, which needed only to be lit. One sin leads to another; since that 'papyrus' had to be lit so that no one would see it, we had to snatch a matchbox from our mother's stovetop or from anywhere else while no one was watching, get away with this forbidden spoil to a place out of sight. This was the time and place to learn the secret of inhaling the smoke through the throat and blowing it out through the nostrils, requiring a high level of mastery, and we little ragamuffins would compete to see who was better at inhaling smoke, exhaling, and blowing the smoke out.

In my manifold iniquities, I was no better than my friends. At first, this improper act was not the most pleasant experience. I felt the bitter taste of the smoke that entered my nose; I coughed; my eyes swelled with tears; and I would spit out the moist tobacco which touched my palate with an acid taste. Despite it all, I endured it and did not desist from that same wasteful act, but persisted. Who knows where these deceitful acts of mine could have led me had my lusts driven me from one sin to another - to excess. 'Usually the thief is caught in the end.' But thanks to a miracle, I did not incur the punishment I deserved on account of this sin. And in this regard, I must tell about my Aunt Rachel - the widow Rachel, my father's sister.

I had many aunts, on both my parents' sides, whether fair and good-hearted or quarrelsome and embittered. What they all had in common was that they were all spoiled, hostile to each other all year round, who would make up during family get-togethers on holidays and festivals. Aunt Rachel was one of a kind.

My grandfather had been blessed with many sons and daughters, all but one of whom he had married off in his lifetime and for whom he had built homes. He did not live to marry off his youngest child. It was my father's duty, as the eldest child in the family, to marry off his youngest sister to a learned man, comme il faut. Father went to Libavitsh and returned with a fine young man, a choice groom, learned and of good upbringing, visibly intelligent and sensitive to Hassidic teachings and melodies. However, he was delicate, all wrapped up in spirituality, tall and pale, who would eat little and be immersed in meditation, business and vain pleasures of this world being the last thing on his mind.

My father went to great lengths to have lenders loan him money and opened a business for Rachel and her husband, a sort of department store. It was a small store, four by four, with no window and very hot. Miraculously, however, buyers who chanced upon this small store entered empty-handed and left with bags full of various merchandise such as salt-herring, a tin pail for the home and yard, kegs of tar for carriage wheels, varieties of embroidered work and lace for wedding veils or coffin decorations (for Gentiles). Perhaps it can be deduced that the business did not lack various types of tobacco for filling pipes and for rolling cigarettes.

Part 2

It is common knowledge that proprietors make little profit from selling tobacco and papyruses (cigarettes), since the hand of the kingdom would reach into this business, taking the lion's share of the profits and leaving the storekeepers with the most meager profit. Moreover, that covetous authority would impose an excise tax on tobacco venders, who had to obtain a special license which cost a great deal of money. Nevertheless, the crowded shelves of my Aunt Rachel's store was not short of this merchandise.

Why was it Rachel's store? After all, it was my Uncle Mendel, her husband, who was obligated to provide for her by law and by custom. Halacha and custom were one thing, and human nature was another. My Uncle Mendel did not like doing business with Gentiles. He had hardly learned their language and had never learned to do business. He was very conscientious in business and was extra careful about swindling and tricking anybody. It was his policy not to charge more than five pennies for merchandise which cost five pennies. Apparently, his deeds were worthy of recognition. Praise is one thing and bad luck is another. Uncle Mendel hurt his own livelihood, as Gentiles were skilled in haggling and lowering the price. This was the nature of a buyer, to suspect a Jewish merchant of jacking up the price of the merchandise, and anyone who watched his money would bargain with him.

Buyers were wont to bargain with Uncle Mendel, but they did not succeed, for they could search for bargains elsewhere. They might find what they were seeking, and they might not. In the meantime, there were fewer and fewer customers in his store. Aunt Rachel was sharp-tongued and knew a thing or two about shopkeeping and tried her best to persuade her young husband to stop his charity work at the shop. Doing deeds for God was one thing; doing deeds for men was another. It was difficult for a Jew to make a living, and still Gentiles would envy the Jew's livelihood. If a seller did not act wisely to lure buyers to purchase the merchandise in his store at a fair profit, how would he earn his livelihood?

And the Jewish shopkeeper's needs are many. Mendel listened to his young wife's moralizing, trying to straighten things out in his head. She was certainly right! A livelihood was no light matter, as proven by the following: The Lubavitcher Rabbi, may he live long and happily, would spend hours upon hours alone with his followers, hear their wishes and their bitterness regarding matters of livelihood, and would give them his blessings. To quote the saying of Our Sages of Blessed Memory: "He who does good deeds at all times is one who supports his wife and children."

For did Mendel not assume this duty when the Ketubah (Jewish marriage certificate) was read under the wedding canopy? A Jewish man's obligations are to earn a livelihood and provide for his family's needs. In other words, his wife Rachel was right, and he appeased her and made promises regarding the future - that he would eventually learn to do business, even though business was a mystery to him at the time. My Aunt Rachel accepted the promises her husband made and even tried to reassure him. Being shrewd in business was a skill in its own right and was something that needed to be learned. In the meantime, he would go home, drink a hot beverage and browse through a book, and she would take his place in the store.

My aunt loved her husband with all her heart and, when he was not around, would praise his integrity and overlook his weak judgment in matters of business. They got along well; Mendel would occupy himself with Torah and fear of heaven, and she would make up for his deficiency in the vain pleasures of this world. My aunt was content with her lot and was expecting a baby.

However, my aunt would not reap satisfaction. A disaster suddenly befell her: In the synagogue, wrapped in a tallis and tefillin, Mendel kneeled over and died. Mendel was eulogized and declared a saint and a Tzadik (righteous man) who had ascended to heaven in the prime of his life in a holy blazing fire. Residents of the city paid him respects and held a funeral the likes of which had not been seen in the town for many years. His grave was dug next to the old rabbi's 'tent'. Unfortunately, all the honor bestowed and praises heaped upon him did not alleviate my Aunt Rachel's cup of sorrow in the least.

After her initial shock, she fell silent and said not a word. She hardly shed a tear and would stare in wonder at the masses of consolers who came to her house during the first days of mourning and afterwards too.

Even during the prayer for the dead in which the name of the deceased is mentioned - a sign for women in mourning to break out with heart-rending wailing - even then, my aunt remained silent and quiet, as if her husband's death had not yet sunk in. Only after the thirty days of mourning, she began to weep over her beloved husband, and her sorrow only grew daily: Rachel was not to be comforted.

There was a Divine decree to the effect that the future of the deceased would be forgotten. My aunt would not accept this decree. On the contrary, she began to unload her distressed soul in many ways, lamenting and eulogizing her husband's faultless soul and remained in a continuous state of mourning. In her heartfelt distress she even uttered severe criticism of and made claims against members of the family in general and my father, her eldest brother, in particular. A person should not be held accountable for the harsh words he utters in his grief. Rachel made such accusations against my father, saying he ignored his brother-in-law by not insisting on consulting with doctors about strengthening Mendel's heart. Over time, she hurled more and more accusations bearing the weight of the original sin: Why had he not performed a sufficiently thorough check of Mendel's past and lineage? Perhaps he had not heard that his whole family was frail? That even Mendel's mother died in her youth, and that he inherited her weak heart. These were mere words uttered in rage, which my aunt herself regretted and for which she requested her brother's forgiveness, not having intended to reproach him, God forbid, but that her troubles had come from a broken heart. My father granted her complete forgiveness and made sure to support her.

Rachel unwillingly returned to the store, but with a heavy heart. She no longer lured shoppers to buy; no longer stood next to them when they sorted through the merchandise; no longer spoke highly of the merchandise and stopped being an aggressive salesperson. Consequently, on account of her deep mourning, she neglected the business and her livelihood was drastically affected. Few buyers would now frequent her store and, financially speaking, she was in dire straits.

My aunt cut back on expenses and did not pay the three-ruble fee for the license to sell tobacco, which the kingdom would exact for its coffers. She relied on miracles to keep the royal emissaries from catching her red-handed, those same 'angels of terror' who were the various inspectors that would suddenly peer into stores, inspect the license to sell tobacco, checking countertops and drawers, in case the Jewish shopkeepers concealed 'forbidden merchandise'.

My aunt would shake like a leaf for fear of the 'aktziznik', the royal inspector, who might suspect the innocent. She viewed any Gentile with an imposing figure who entered her store carrying a briefcase under his arms with suspicion, and this disturbed her.

Each evening, she collected the forbidden merchandise into a wicker basket, which she would take home and return to the store the next day, keeping it hidden in a special drawer. Licensed shopkeepers, by contrast, would arrange their merchandise on shelves to capture the attention of buyers.

Over time, Rachel let her fear get the best of her and dared not keep any forbidden merchandise in her small apartment in our neighborhood. Instead, she hid it in our house, since father was more loyal to her than anyone in the world. The officials did not suspect father of trading in tobacco. Still, being extra cautious by nature, father did not store that forbidden tobacco in a place that was visible, not even in his own house. Instead, he kept it in a black bookcase safely closed with a big heavy lock. What safer place was there than the top shelf of the bookcase which was located in the large parlor, where no wicked 'aktziznik' would ever think of searching? This was a very large bookcase which had always been designated as my 'tent of Torah', being the beloved youngest child. I spent many hours of the day in this room, in solitude, engaged in Torah study. My father would tend to his affairs and my mother would go to the fabrics store while I, little Shlomo Zalmankeh, was left all alone in the parlor, the Gemara properly open in front of me in line with my father's wishes.

Perhaps father had never intended to conceal his hiding this treasure in the bookcase. Why would he conceal anything from me? Would I inform the 'aktziznik'? At the same time, there was no point being forthright with me regarding this ordinary affair which was none of my business.

One way or the other, it was not father that revealed to me the secret of the tobacco treasure. I accidentally discovered it on my own. I loved to rummage through that top shelf; perhaps I would find another book in the holy language (Hebrew), one of those small books containing stories as sweet as honey, offering diversion from the difficult subjects of the sea of Talmud. Everyone knows that the last section of the order Nezikin (the fourth division of the Mishnah) was a difficult part of the Gemara to study; those far wiser than me had wrinkled their brows trying to understand these words of Torah which were more profound than the sea is deep. Even though I was already over ten years of age and had completed three years of Gemara study, studying those same profound pages was no easy task.

When I opened up the Gemara, the text of a paragraph of the Mishnah lay before me, what appeared to be only a few lines. That same paragraph was supplemented by extensive annotations to the Talmud, evidence of the heated debate, profound views, and difficult problems surrounding the subject. Do not pity me and do not feel sorry for me! I loved the last section; I explored its depth and, with the sharp-wittedness of a child, brought up new problems and answers to difficult questions - Torah dialectic. It was just that at times I was overcome with a desire to take a study break and to peruse those secular books in the Hebrew language which I once inadvertently found in the bookcase, and I strongly yearned to read them and be entertained by their stories.

I did not imagine moving the long ladder and reaching the opening of the attic. It was not within the ability of a ten-year-old boy to move it, with its huge rungs, from place to place, what with the fear that my father might catch me red-handed. Nevertheless, on account of my inclination, I overcame this fear and found an opportune time when my father was not at home. When my mother had gone out to weed the vegetable garden in our yard, I thought it to be the right time to make the great ascent to the top shelves of the bookcase. How? I moved the table on which the Torah rested and placed it up against the bookcase. I placed my chair of honor on the table and, with a measure of skill, added on top of all that my father's foot stool. It was like a three-story construction built with turrets. I climbed the odd-looking turret, encouraging myself to make the great ascent, holding on to the bookcase and all its contents. That is how I reached the last rung and started feeling around in the dim space between the ledges, hoping to pick up books and Rashi commentary on Talmud, which I yearned for so much.

My pawing fingers stumbled upon a peculiar package, soft and odorous, containing no books. Overcome by my curiosity, I opened up the package, with no ill intentions, God forbid. That is how I discovered the tobacco treasure hidden away from the wicked bribe-seeking overseer. I suddenly felt an urge to roll myself a cigarette from that same worthy find.

The evil inclination disguised itself in a robe of piety, and reminded me of the talk of Rabbi Moshe Mordechai, the famous Gemara teacher. He would say: "How delightful is a cigarette puff which settles a very difficult subject in Gemara and opens a man to new interpretations of the Law..." The evil inclination provoked me, saying: "Do not miss this chance for a cigarette puff. Go and take a full pinch of tobacco, and God willing, you will yet develop the wit for Torah the likes of the country's greatest scholars!"

I have no desire to praise the evil inclination. On the contrary, I loathe it and am very angry with it on account of its wicked nature and its disturbing people's peace of mind with its deceit. The truth reigns supreme, however, and we owe it even to our enemies. We are thankful that this wicked being, the evil inclination, does its work faithfully. Woe to him that, God forbid, is taken prey by that same evil being. He is strongly tempted by his inclinations, is tempted repeatedly, until the evil inclination does what it purposed to do; this I learned first-hand. What if I had immediately agreed and stolen my widow aunt's possession? God forbid, since when I started to feel this find to discover what it was, I was stricken with remorse, those same pangs of conscience which are precisely the glorious work of the good inclination. This righteous being started to persuade me, as it was accustomed to doing, by employing reason and infinite wisdom: "Arise, confounded fellow, and leave this ill device and base design. What you are doing is wrong! Quickly return the tobacco and the paper to its hiding place and go back to studying the tractate of the last section and, thereby, gain the best of both worlds. Standing a test is a great merit which elevates you to the ranks of our forefather, Abraham, and Joseph, the righteous, and their likes..."

Happy is the man whose ears hear the advice of the good inclination and who has the strength to heed it and do what is good and right in the eyes of God and man. Thank God that I most definitely heeded it! After all, was I not born into a good family? Would I rob a widow's possession - not any old widow but my Aunt Rachel, my own flesh and blood? Generally speaking, that craving for smoking is unbecoming to a youth such as myself, for I was still too young. Thank goodness I managed to climb down that ladder; I literally jumped, like one trying to save himself from a big fire, almost toppling the entire bookcase under me and practically breaking my elbow in the act. I dissembled the construction I had made and returned every object to its place and restored every item to its original purpose - the Torah table and the chair of honor before it, where a smart student such as myself would sit. I also returned my father's foot stool to its place by the armchair.

That is how the household objects were restored to their place and original purpose, and how I went back to being myself and to my Torah. However, in my manifold iniquities, this disgraceful episode did not end with that. It can be safely assumed that this self-same wicked being, the evil inclination, does not stand idly by. Like a spotted cat, its claws grab its prey, cruelly tantalizing it, supposedly giving it a chance to escape. Then, it immediately grabs hold of it again and follows through with its designs. That is how this villain dealt with me as well and did not leave me in peace. From that day onward, I became disspirited and my reasoning became impaired.

Everywhere, I bumped into bright students fervently engaged in Torah study, while I conjured up in my mind the treasure. As soon as I would return from the rabbi's house, I entered the room where the great secret was hidden. One day I had barely touched the chair with good intentions of sitting on it and uttering words of Torah, when suddenly the table and chair began to move, the Devil's work. Even the foot stool, the smallest piece of furniture concerned, seemingly moved, like an act of witchcraft, and began climbing over the larger pieces and positioned itself on top of them. All of this began moving toward the bookcase, taking position in front of it and winking at me as if to say: "Will Rabbi Zalmankeh rise for the big Aliyah?" You might consider this a figment of a foolish imagination. It was certainly the case, but this vanity of vanities had let me not alone days upon nights, and denied me peace of mind.

While my mouth and lips were engaged in Torah, my heart was far away elsewhere. You might ask whether I had forgotten those same holy verses (which are a remedy against the evil inclination, which every good boy is well-versed in against those times when, God forbid, his evil inclination assails him). No such thing! I muttered verse after verse: "Though you plan a conspiracy it will be annulled; though you utter words they shall not stand, for God is with us." I also intentionally whispered these same precious words: "The Lord gave me a pure heart, and instilled in me a new, true spirit..." . I carefully uttered these and similar verses with concentration of thought to tear Satan asunder and to ward off sinful thoughts. What can I say?

This time I did not chant the verses. The force of these precious verses had weakened and they had no more impact. I uttered them out loud with difficulty, but my spirit was completely vanquished, trapped in the net of Satan the Destroyer. I was tempted and gullible. Woe is me! I took out a full box of tobacco on that ominous day, and a pack of paper for rolling cigarettes attached to the side of the box. One sin leads to another.

I rummaged through the drawer of the kitchen table and found a package of matchboxes; I took one, doubling the theft. I stuffed all these stolen possessions in my pocket and got away with these 'prohibited objects' to the silo of the cowshed in our yard. It served as a repository for fodder, though it also had a distinct advantage in that it was not all that high and a ladder was close by at all times - so that there was nothing unusual about my ascending and descending it. After all, I had been granted permission from my mother - who was always worried - to climb that ladder and bring down a pile of fragrant hay or set aside a portion for a milking cow's meal. (This cow expected to be visited by one of the household from time to time, for it was lonely there in the dim cowshed.) This is proof that I was very familiar with that climb.

I knew every nook and cranny in the silo, which contained many hiding places. This is where I hid my reading books, which my father deemed a waste of time, between the roof's beams. This is where I chose to hide this unkosher find I had stumbled upon in the bookcase; I climbed into the silo as at other times.

"Do you take me for a complete fool?" God forbid, the only thing I did in the silo was to roll a cigarette and make my get away to another hiding place where there was no risk of a fire starting.

There, I inhaled smoke at my pleasure, coughing like adults would - coughing and clearing their throats while smoking, due to the acrid flavor of the tobacco. I even learned tricks, to have my nostrils serve as a funnel for my mouth, a sort of chimney, and I would simultaneously exhale the fragrant smoke through my mouth. That is one feat in the art of smoking that not every urchin could easily attain.

Looking back today, I honestly doubt if this whole business was enjoyable at all. On the contrary, smoking was an act of bodily torture, for I smoked the plainest variety known as a 'machorka'. This tobacco was pungent and dirt cheap, a blend smoked by the most common people. It had no taste nor smell, but its vapors would enter my nose and leave me choking. Needless to say, I derived no pleasure from this basest of acts. My good inclination did not abandon me when I ascended and descended that hiding place, and would repeatedly remind me of various commandments which would suggest rebellion against the Divine yoke on the part of someone violating them: "Thou shall not steal", "Plunder not a widow" and other such verses which proved me wrong. Furthermore, there was nothing the least bit honorable in the whole act, since it is well-known that there is no pride in solitude. There was not another soul before whom I could boast about this great adventure. On top of it all, during the act I would be attacked by fear and panic that I would be caught in my mischief, that my shame would be exposed in public, and that I would be brought to an even greater punishment.

Nonetheless, I was lured to this no good business like a drunkard who is aware of his sin but lacks the strength to abstain from the wanton drunkenness which took hold of him. His situation becomes worse, he rots in his own suffering, and sinks in the abyss of destruction. Good riddance! I finally reached the bottom of that stolen box. I breathed a sigh of relief. This reprehensible deed of going up and down in the cow's quarters, of trickery, and subsequent sins I had committed after the first, were behind me. In the low ground in our yard, which covered the hill, a stream gently flowed. I threw the empty box into the stream, as if performing a 'tashlich' (on the first day of Rosh Hashanah Jews go to a body of water, empty out their pockets and say: "Cast all of my sins into the depths of the sea" as a sign of repentance). In this 'tashlich' I also threw the matches, reproved myself for the sin I had committed, and completely repented. I prayed with greater concentration in order to atone for my sins.

"Distance us from an evil person and an evil companion; instill in us the good inclination and lead us to do good deeds. .." It seemed to me that this entire prayer had been instituted in the prayer book for me, to clean my evil conscience and to have me return to the path of righteousness. From the Zakkah (combined confession and prayer often recited before the evening service on the eve of Yom Kippur) to Torah study, I diligently persevered. "You will be judged by your own deeds" was a great principle. Since I devoted myself to Torah, the Torah responded to me in kind. I came up with additional annotations, raising logical subjects for debate during my lessons with the Rabbi. Even the good inclination did not prevent others from praising me - whether in my presence or before my father. I made my parents proud and fulfilled the commandment of honoring one's mother and father.

My parents pampered me in all sorts of ways, and showed me their affection by giving me snacks - fruits and sweets - between meals. Around the holiday of Passover, they ordered special clothes for me. These were happy days for me, and I drove out of my mind the remorse and pain caused me on account of the tobacco episode, as if the whole incident had never happened.

Although I had a certain childhood innocence, things do not exist in a void, and neither did my widowed aunt's property. Anything of value has someone who will claim possession over it. How can one explain that many days had passed and no one came to count the merchandise and discover there was a box missing, as if Divine intervention were at play.

It was a year of poverty worldwide. It became increasingly colder that winter and not a Gentile soul came. The Jews would complain, "When will this terrible winter end?" But there are set seasons and times in the calendar. No sooner would winter end and spring would be right around the corner, with the holiday of Passover drawing near. The snow started to thaw and the town gained relief. Peasants gladly left the boundaries of their village and once again came to the city pushing their wares: poultry, potatoes, eggs, and balls of wool. Merchants were waiting to sell, and the townspeople stormed the shops to provide for their households.

It was precisely during that winter with the heavy snows that something unusual happened at home. A relative from a nearby village offered my father a partnership in a firewood business, which he had purchased in a good deal. The business was not running up losses, but the buyer was hard-pressed for money, since the seller firmly insisted on a cash sale of the storehouse without further ado. Father said this was an auspicious partnership, and so the business was formed. Father tripled the amount of money they made and even received a commission.

It was not the custom of our town for a respectable person to be away from home a few days a week, wandering off to distant places in search of a livelihood. It is best to be in one place, whereas being on the road is difficult. But necessity knows no bounds. My father heeded my mother's advice, as he was wont to do, and undertook to withstand the difficulty of being away Monday through Thursday, Thursday being the town market day. My father no doubt very much regretted being on the road away from home. However, most of his sorrow and anxiety were owing to the fact that he would not be seeing me for so long and would be unable to watch over me and my ways in Torah. Every Monday he would leave after moralizing that I not neglect my Torah study, God forbid, when he was not around to watch me.

***

During that same winter when my father was on the move, he could not join me in Torah study, namely the Gemara page discussing the plague of the first-born. My father had a great idea for making the best of the situation: I would perform a mitzvah that my father could not perform, so that the first-born would not have to fast on the eve of the Passover holiday, and to glorify the Torah and give my father a little satisfaction at the same time. In addition to the last section of the Mishnaic order of Nezikim, known to expound on annotations to the

Talmud, my father also let me study the Hagiga tractate by myself, a page of Gemara with Rashi commentary, but without dialectical depth. The Hagiga tractate is one of the smallest in the Talmud, and there was no doubt in my father's mind that that page was simple for me. He knew that I would complete studying it in time for the eve of Passover and properly read the Torah portion instead of him.

This in fact marked a milestone in the Hassidic minyan in my city; not a distinguished member of the community, but a young boy would be reading the end of the tractate, which exempts the first-born from fasting. We kept this a secret to avoid others from wondering about this and whispering. Each Sabbath father would sit down with me after we studied the last section of Nezikin. I clearly witnessed his pleasure at seeing me near completion of the task. There was no doubt that I would complete the tractate on time and that, God willing, I would bring him previously unparalleled joy in the fulfillment of a mitzvah.

I do not recall another eve of Passover so beautiful and filled with splendor as the one we had that year. The spring sun did its utmost to thaw the last piles of snow which still remained at the bottom of gutters and which capped rooftops. It was as if the Holy One, Blessed Be He, had intended to please us for the harsh winter we had undergone, to make it pass without delay. Jets of water slowly streamed from every gutter and emptied out in every direction. The streets filled with harmless, shallow puddles, but it is through these puddles that the world's glory abounds, for they would gleam in the sunlight and radiate myriad rays of light, adding beauty to the warmth of people's hearts and instilling in them the holiday spirit.

**

Young boys do not discuss business. Although I was knowledgeable of the wheeling and dealing of merchants, of the liability claims between the party injured and the injuring party, and learned things during market days when I helped, father had never spoken to me about home economics or matters of livelihood. I did not know, therefore, what reform my father had instituted upon embarking on that partnership, and what profit he had made. Nevertheless, I recognized his cheerful countenance by the jolly Hassidic tunes (such as 'Bim Bam') which he hummed while preparing for the holiday. We welcomed the holiday in a jovial spirit and with a sense of contentment.

***

The morning before the eve of Passover is one for rising bright and early, especially since a number of chores as removing leaven and cleaning dishes and utensils for use during Passover had been put off that year, waiting my father's return. Even the holy task of dusting books was not done by other members of the household, and one can be sure that this mitzvah was left for my father to perform.

He removed, one by one, the books that comprise the great orders of the Mishnah, which were bound in brown leather. These books were printed by the Re'em widow and the Re'em brothers of Vilna. Father very gently removed them from the bookcase, placing them on a special table. Great importance was attached to these holy books, which were objects of deep affection because they contained both the obvious and the obscure: Torah dialectic, sharp-witted questions, problems and interpretations, the light and the glory of Torah which are the Jews' inheritance in this world and the next.

My father handled these books with love and devotion. With a cloth, he carefully wiped their brown leather, careful not to bend any page, God forbid. He dusted each page, extremely careful in going about this task; he lovingly caressed the binding of these books, which had not been used at all this year, as if to redress their purported neglect, a sign that these books would be studied, God willing, in the days ahead.

These books were followed by writings of Rabbinic authorities: Hoshen Mishpat (the fourth part of the Shulhan Aruch), Yoreh De'a (one of the books of the Shulhan Aruch), Shulhan Aruch, Maimonides' Mishnah Torah, and so forth. These are the smaller books of the orders of the Mishnah, which pertain mainly to rules that are to be put into practice. These are the landmarks of the Jewish way of life. They are full of authoritatively established rules and laws, early customs, and questions and answers. Those who ponder Halachic questions can find an answer therein. And all the children of Israel, wherever they might be, can find a straight path to follow and good deeds to perform, in matters that are between God and man, between fellow men, and between man and himself; both in bodily and spiritual needs.

And so, going from one shelf to another, my father cleaned the books which were arranged, for the reader's convenience, from top to bottom in descending order of importance. Above the Halachic books and writings of the Rabbinic authorities was the place of honor of the Hassidic books, the Bible with thirty-two commentaries, compositions written by Torah scholars, and Torah annotations written by famous rabbis and less known scholars.

They were great writers in biblical and Mishnaic language and were instinctively guided by the spirit of the Torah and proposed Torah annotations of their own which they put on thin paper. Verily, when these pages had piled up into mounds of Torah, they were seized by a great measure of good will to perform an act of kindness for the scholars, and to make their annotations known to many. Even though almost all them were poor and had no source of livelihood, and even though printing these compositions cost a great deal of money, the insistent scholar-writers did not give up. They would deny themselves and their households food and clothing and pinch pennies in order to save a few dozen shekels, advance payment for the printers, who would publish the Torah writings. They worked hard until their entire composition was published. Many of them did not live to see that day and died having fulfilled their desires only half-way. However, those who did live to see their desire fulfilled had their spirits wound up in these piles of books, and would turn to the Jewish communities to distribute these Torah texts, and would receive some monetary exchange for the book. As there was no fixed price, the rich and generous paid a high price, and poor scholars made do with pocket money, and did not deny themselves the pleasure of Torah and the mitzvah of encouraging a scholar for the sake of glorifying the Torah.

The compilations piled up in our bookcase by the dozens. My father perused only the most well-known ones, the rest having been disorderly placed in the corner of the bookcase although, on the eve of Passover, they were all removed, and father looked inside them, as he shook off their dust.

My father felt tired that night and did not complete the chore. He left the two uppermost ledges of books for early morning. With dawn, my father arose to finish the job left over from the night before. Would he wake up his youngest son for this holy task? My father did not want to deprive me of an extra hour's sleep, so that I would be alert on this big day. For at last, I faced a big challenge: to stand up and deliver a public sermon on the last page of the Hagiga tractate, and I had to be well rested.

My father, in his pity and love, let me be, to delight in an extra hour's sleep, for my pleasure and for the sake of Torah....

When I eagerly awoke from my sleep to face the great hour that awaited me in the Hassidic minyan, I overheard my father and mother arguing, and my name kept coming up. But why? Alas, what I had forgotten came back to me that morning: The box of tobacco episode!

My father, who had an excellent memory, was set on removing that package from the holy place, and to find it another place, to avoid mixing it with the secular. He rummaged through the attic and discovered, with his sharp eye that the package had been wrapped unprofessionally; this is what aroused his curiosity and suspicion the most. He checked the contents and discovered the missing box. He had no doubt that the box had disappeared, thanks to his good memory and the long contents list printed on the package, which I failed to notice. There was no doubt; an invisible hand had rummaged through that package and had taken the box. It did not take long for father to suspect his youngest child.

Fathers were not oblivious to youngsters' craving to smoke. Perhaps my father had at that moment recalled a similar act of his during his own childhood. To make a long story short, my father had shuddered and had urgently called mother, as he was accustomed to doing whenever there was trouble. He angrily recounted to her the biblical account of Achan the son of Carmi , drawing an analogy that supposedly mother had taken the box or had collaborated with me in that reprehensible deed.

My father spoke in the harshest of words, suggesting that I had committed a grave sin and transgression which could not be atoned for. Theft and embezzlement! Robbing a widow! Neglecting Torah study! A rebellious son! My father was articulate and spoke with eloquence. My compassionate mother was dismayed at what she heard. Had things gotten so bad?

But mothers will be mothers. She did not justify that same shameful act, but was lenient and suggested that I could be forgiven and could atone for that reprehensible deed.

She began to present my defense (which I would not have particularly enjoyed hearing had I not been convinced of her good intentions). She said I had simply misbehaved, like any mischievous boy. Little children, my mother said, were inclined to imitate behavior, and this was Nature's way. Being hard-pressed for time ahead of the eve of Passover, she said she had not kept an eye on me, and began conjuring up her own childhood memories when she herself was still very young, eager to appear grown-up in her own eyes, wearing a wig belonging to her mother of Blessed Memory, in order to show off. She was caught in the act by her ow mother, and was forgiven.

My mother's defense only fueled my father's anger, hurling at her one claim after another, alluding to me as her 'jewel', meaning that I was only my mother's, and that my father had no share in this disgraceful son. Embroiled in his own anger, he had forgotten the hour when he would pamper me every morning by preparing that most delicious eggnog for me to enjoy.

As she did at such times, my father blew things out of proportion and then suddenly, everything came to a halt as he asked himself: "Is this child a fool? Is a ten-year-old, may he live long, still a child in your eyes? A young man who, thank heaven, is being taught by an eminent scholar, is he a child to you? This son of yours who had perhaps forgotten the explicit Biblical recept "Thou shall not steal!" Or perhaps he did not know that it was forbidden to rob a widow, a beloved aunt?"

Even I, who was party to the matter, knew, oh, how I knew, that this time my strict father and not my compassionate mother, was right. I was certainly willing to lose face or turn to the other side of the bed and become, by some miracle, a newborn baby who was too young to get flogged. I trembled at the memory of being flogged, not because of the physical pain involved during the act - far from it.

I was a courageous lad who was physically healthy. I had suffered bodily pain in the past without complaining. The disgrace at being forced to assume a flogging position is not what bothered me either. We all had this experience at home and in the heder. For there is not a child who has never been flogged at one time or another, for this is only natural. However, I hated being flogged by my own father. I simply could not watch my father; I could not bear looking at the glowing, fearful expression on my father's face before and after. He was scared and frightened, took short breaths, and uttered fragmented, jumbled words. During this act, my father became stripped of his honor and title: The wisest of scholars - and his rank, one of distinguished birth. I was proud of him for these reasons. All this was gone during the flogging; his stature had diminished, and his radiance had vanished on account of my evil inclination.

May you never experience the same, in the early morning or at any time, for that matter. I felt remorse for the sin I had committed, and I pitied myself and my father and compassionate mother, to whom I had caused all this trouble. Fraught with anguish in my warm bed, I suddenly heard words of a different color, words of hope and consolation. My father suddenly recalled something which had vanished from his mind when he had been embroiled in his anger. He laid his eyes on the ancient grandfather clock with the weight and pendulum swinging back and forth. Blessed art Thou Who alters periods and changes seasons!! A miracle happened: The cuckoo remembered to announce the morning hour of the eve of Passover. It started to groan as usual, chiming indistinctly, ringing and then pausing: One and two, and three -

counting to six, announcing to the entire world that, thank goodness, the hour had arrived, and Jews could not waste their precious time this morning on activities unrelated to Passover.

One thing recalled leads to another! It suddenly dawned upon my father that this morning was more honorable than any other, since it was the day before Passover, the fast of the first-born. For heaven's sake, all Jewish first-born in the Hassidic minyan would have their eyes set on me, that is, on that same 'jewel', the rebellious son. Thanks to this 'jewel' and his lesson, this hour of fasting would become an hour of rejoicing in the Torah and bring joy to many! My father came to his senses, realizing that this was not a day for flogging. How are two opposites reconciled? He would lay down a stubborn and rebellious son on a bench on account of a grave sin; he would then get him up off this bench of trouble and seat him in a dignified place on the bench of Torah. My father suddenly lost his train of thought, and at once ceased his tirade and claims against mother.

Father reached my door and my good mother followed. She was uncertain as to his intentions and, in her mercy, wanted me to be judged leniently. I heard my parents' footsteps drawing nearer to my bed and I was afraid of what would happen next. The sun rose right above my head and I feigned a deep early morning sleep. Miraculously, the first thing my father saw was the big Gemara, the Hagiga tractate sitting on the table which I had perused last night, opened to the page pertaining to the public sermon. Even though I was very familiar with the text, I was not counting on my memory. Moreover, I knew all the scholars in the Hassidic minyan. They were very argumentative in matters of Halacha and were sharp-witted in debate. Rabbi Getzil Hoffman, Rabbi Ya'akov Yafeh and their likes would probably give me a hard time by vexing me with very difficult questions I had not yet thought about. Therefore, I thought it best to be prepared and so I had spent the night before the big test going over the page of Gemara and its commentary in order to fully understand the meaning of the Torah and to be able to come up with an answer to any question I might be asked.

My eyes were closed, supposedly, but I kept my left eye slightly open, and covered it with a blanket. Through a small hole in the blanket, I spied on my father and kept track of his movements. He thumbed through the Gemara and threw a glance at me, again perused the Gemara, and paused a while to study certain sections, as he was accustomed to doing. With the upcoming holiday in the back of his head, he put down the book and approached my bed hesitantly. It was then that I saw how the expression on a person's face can change completely. Slowly but surely, his rage abated and grace, compassion and abounding love prevailed.

My father turned to my mother, who had followed him weak-kneed, and hinted that she leaves the room. My mother became frightened. At first she was suspicious, and probably with good reason, fearing that he would do something to me. But she never opposed her husband, and left. Her fear was unfounded. For when mother left the room, my father approached me with quiet steps, slightly lifted the edge of the blanket that covered my face, and said in a quite voice as he petted me: "Zalman, my son, it is Passover eve today; the day is short and there is much work to be done. Arise, my son, it will soon be the hour for morning prayer. Today, everyone arises early for prayer. Get up, Zalmankeh; spring like a lion to the service of the Lord..." (How is that for a 'prelude to a flogging'?) Have no doubt: This time I did not refuse my father with respect to the morning rituals. I 'opened' my eyes fully and began to rub them a bit, pretending to yawn, like one who had just been awakened from a deep slumber. In my heart I uttered a prayer of thanksgiving to the Creator,

Who scrutinizes hearts for redemption and recompense. I said the morning prayers, and sprang out of bed to fulfill the other morning customs.

***

I was unusually quick to do my routine that morning, to perform every obligation and ritual perfectly. Even though I felt with all my heart that a great miracle had happened to me in that I had been spared, by all accounts, a severe punishment which I had expected to receive, I had the feeling that this story was not yet finished. I could have been preached to and rebuked as soon as I entered the dining room, after the ritual washing of the hands. Even when I heard that same familiar shaking sound of the egg yolk and sugar being mixed in a cup, the preparation of eggnog, I feared that my clever father had perhaps chosen precisely this hour for moralizing about iniquity and sin. I summoned my strength, set my gaze on my father, wore an innocent expression, and asked him a banal question:

"What do you think, father, are there enough Gemara texts for all the first-born sons? Perhaps we should take one or two extra Gemara books so that any first-born who wants to follow along as it is being read to completion will be able to so?"

My good mother, who was then in the kitchen, was anxious and had become thoroughly confused in light of developments: Happy for the miracle, not believing her eyes nor what she heard. My compassionate mother was all the more astonished when she heard my father calmly answer my question: "You are right, my son, even though our attendant, Rabbi Shabtai, probably set aside plenty of books, we will act in accordance with the saying: 'It is always best to be on the safe side.' Therefore, we shall take with us both the Gemara from the six orders of the Mishnah as well as the small Gemara, in order to glorify the Torah.

But be careful, Zalmankeh, not to forget this precious book, and put it back in the bookcase after the celebrations which will follow the end of the reading, God willing."

 Thank heavens, for this was when I realized the affair was over and done with. After an upbeat everyday discussion such as this, being scolded by flogging was unimaginable. I did not ponder why I had merited this wonder. Man should not deliberate over the good things that happen to him, but should accept them as things which need not be probed, and this wisdom guided my behavior.

***

The lives of men are crooked and evasive, with ups and downs. They experience endless hours of grief and days of toil against a few good hours. Man was given the gift of forgetfulness to take his mind off bad times. In their stead, what is inscribed in his memory are all those good times and moments of pleasure from his past, with which man nurtures himself at will. Even I have a hidden treasure of pleasant memories, those hours of pleasure and precious moments I was lucky enough to have at one time. They sustain me, making me forget the difficult times I had experienced in the past, uplifting my spirit. They descend upon me like a dew of consolation, putting a smile of satisfaction on my tired, weary face.

One of my best memories from those golden days and those moments of happiness was that same Passover and the celebration of Torah - like a precious stone - we were lucky to witness. It was clear to me that even without that foolish deed of mine and its surprising conclusion, I would have been joyful that same eve of Passover.

I had always been a sermonizer and loved to expound and see God's creatures listening to my words, whether I was talking about mundane affairs - and how much more when I was delivering words of Torah. Such things did not happen every day. It may sound easy - sitting at the head of a community of Jewish elders, each of whom is a father and a grandfather, with their eyes set on me.

The fact that this was the eve of Passover made me feel especially terrific! My heart was full of abounding love for my father, and I was forever grateful to him for he spared me the punishment of flogging and the torment associated with it. I wanted only one thing with all my being, to make him happy and add to his fatherly pride. I knew he loved me, that I was the apple of his eye and his ray of hope for the future, but this time I wanted to repay his love and grant him satisfaction that not all fathers receive.

All my good intentions, all the life's desires of a Jewish boy who had repented, and all my heartfelt joy in doing mitzvahs manifested themselves during my reading of that last page. My voice was as clear and firm as an experienced old-timer's, like that of Rabbi Getzil himself. Silence prevailed in the synagogue during the sermon. I was lucky, for the crowd grew by the minute unlike previous years when, due to the tasks required for the holiday and its extensive preparations, only first-born members of the congregation would engage in Torah at this pressing hour and not forego the joy of this mitzvah and the additional mitzvah of partaking in the meal to follow. Previously, the others would quickly finish their prayers, fold up their tallis and tefillin, and anxiously head home. For this morning, as soon as I opened my mouth and my voice rang out in Torah, the 'home- owners', exempt from the fast, began to take notice. Why was this lad up on the pulpit on this eve of Passover? Was it Simhat Torah today, when children were called to the Torah along with all the other young people? Because of the novelty, people tarried an extra hour, half listening to my words as they finished whispering the Daily Verse from the Book of Psalms which ends the morning prayer.

When they heard the substance of my words and the synopsis of the subject coming from the mouth of a child spoken so clearly and joyfully, they were stricken with a curiosity mixed with the love of Torah, abounding in the heart of every Jewish man in a Lithuanian town. Smiling, they approached the table, wondering what in the world this child had come to teach them. My mind did not go blank when I saw the growing crowd listening to what I was saying. On the contrary, something came over me and elevated my spirit. I forget everything else. I felt like it was only my father and I alone in a 'heavenly sitting', being elevated and ascending to the heights of the holy Torah and Divine radiance.

Over and done with! The congregation joyfully joined me in proclaiming, "May we go from strength to strength!" Only then did I look around for my father, who, out of humility or fear of the Evil Eye, sat at the end of the table. I saw him take a peek at me with a sort of amicable expression I had never before seen. Even though my mother was busy setting the table for the meal celebrating the mitzvah, I saw her shed a tear of a happy Jewish woman who had just been rewarded a bit of satisfaction, for her son had delivered a public sermon, a moment of pride worth all the trouble of child-raising a Jewish woman may experience.

People began proposing toasts. My father was bestowed the honor of saying the first blessing, whereupon he was showered with abundant blessings and congratulations. There was so much joyous commotion about me, including cheek-pinching, accompanied with congratulations. Melodies and levity ensued, and the crowed became more and more excited, filled with endless joy. Rabbi Shabtai saw that no end was in sight and feared that those around the table would regret it once their excitement passed and they realized that the hour was late and that much work was yet to be done. He approached father and whispered in his ear that it was time to say good-bye, that this was not the time for a lengthy celebration. Father began with blessings to the revelers, and ended with holiday greetings to those seated around the table. The 'home-owners' got up reluctantly, and parted ways by wishing one another a happy holiday and praising me for having merited them a mitzvah.

***

It was not the custom of fathers, when I was a child, to show any visible signs of love for their children. However, I was quite aware of my father's warm hand which stroked mine as we walked home. His good mood lingered for the remainder of the day, while he was immersed in preparation for the holiday, setting the table for the Passover Seder, grounding the mixture of fruits, nut, wine and spices for the festive meal, and grating the bitter herbs. All the while he incessantly hummed gay Hassidic tunes, a clear sign of his good mood.

Mother filled my pockets with walnuts, and then quickly sent me off on a pre-holiday errand so that I would earn the merit of performing the mitzvah of honoring one's father and mother and take some of the load off her back in the process.

The holiday set in. We returned home with two poor guests whom father would invite to the Seder every year. The table shone from the carafe of red wine to the polished, sparkling glasses in the radiance of the lit holiday candles. Father wore his shiny white 'kittel', and provided white attire for the guests. I joyfully asked, "Why is this night different from all other nights"? (one of the Four Questions recited in the Haggadah).

Father paused every now and then from the reading, offering some commentary, quoting a Hassidic saying, or telling a joke. My father had many Jewish jokes up his sleeve - seasoned with words of Torah - which he would tell at the table at this joyous occasion. We laughed hard when he told them, after which we resumed reading the Haggadah. We duly drank four cups of wine (drinking even more than the required number of cups by sipping sweet wine between the courses of the meal) and wished our guests, the 'home- owners', and everyone else well.

We finally came to the blessing over the matzah, and all eyes were upon the youngest child, as everyone smiled, waiting for the amusing wheeling and dealing session to commence over the Afikoman (the piece of matzah eaten at the end of the Passover meal; it is first hidden for the youngsters to search for it, and whoever finds it receives a prize.) It was I who found the matzah, and father was willing to agree to a fair bargain in exchange for the Afikoman. I stared at father like a merchant who knows the quality of his merchandise and its value, holding the Afikoman in my clenched fist, to be redeemed with a gift. My father smiled.

"And so you have succeeded, you naughty boy, to snatch the Afikoman from under my nose. What a fool I am for forgetting your evil ways in the past. Here I was, trying to figure out the complicated math of the number of plagues the Egyptians were smitten with in Egypt and at the sea, and you, you ungodly son, seize the opportunity to rob me. Oh well, henceforth I will be sure to watch you in the years to come, God willing. This year, I fell for it. State your price, Zalmankeh; what is your price for the Afikoman?"

I had pondered and deliberated over the matter endlessly beforehand, all in order to receive a fair price for the Afikoman and not miss this one-time opportunity. Last year, in exchange for the Afikoman I received an elegant box, a piggy bank in the form of a fine wooden utensil with a slot. The box itself came with a small lock. I kept the small key to the lock hidden in my sole possession. From now on, coins would only be inserted in the box, but none would be taken out.

In the future, when it would hold no more coins, the same lock would be opened with a small key, revealing the contents. This hidden treasure would hopefully yield a blessing, particularly since I did not rely on miracles and deposited all my Hanukkah gelt, and money I earned from running errands.

***

In the box, I inserted the Oral Law fee for which my Uncle Mendel, the rich uncle in the family, paid me a fixed rate of three kopecks a page. Even though he was considered to be a penny pincher, around me he was a scrupulously honest individual. He did not rely on his memory, but took out the Gemara from the bookcase and browsed through it, while I stood and expounded a sentence or two, page after page. My uncle followed along with me. (So far so good.)

Without a word, he turned page after page, until I made a mistake on the fifth page. As soon as this happened, I stopped. My uncle smiled and generously paid my Gemara fee for page five too, even though I did not complete it; fifteen kopecks of good money and a loving pinch of my cheeks. This large sum of money went into my piggy bank, which bloated by the month.

Two years ago, I received as an exchange for the Afikoman a handsome six-bladed awl, which sparked the envy of every child who saw it. Last night, I made the firm decision that this year I would ask my father for a handsome walking stick. Why a walking stick? I wanted to imitate the doctor's son who was my age, and had a small, handsome stick with a white, tooth-like marble at the top. I very much coveted that stick. It seemed to me unmatched in appearance, and there would be no greater pleasure in the world than waving my stick about as I window-shopped.

***

It seems like only yesterday that the 'book seller' came to the religious academy, and placed his holy wares on the long table in the synagogue. He did not chide us for browsing through his new books. What especially attracted my attention was a small book, a wonderful book written by Rabbi Joseph Dila Rina. I had already heard the story from a friend. While on the subject, I will briefly tell you that story.

Rabbi Rina, a righteous man and a miracle worker, who yearned for redemption, fasted several times and before whom were revealed supreme secrets regarding the coming of the Messiah. Satan stood, fettered in chains, bearing the Divine inscription, and the Rabbi's world had been practically saved from the Devil's reign, clearing the way to total salvation. However, the Rabbi had no such luck. He was faced with Satan's cunning in the form of the Serpent from the Garden of Eden, who pretended to appear weak and faint. He asked permission of Rabbi Joseph to allow him to smell the fragrant incense in order to revitalize its soul.

Rabbi Joseph, a most compassionate person, forgot that the Oppressors derive most of their strength from the smell of incense, and he gave him one sniff. Immediately, Satan broke free of his chains, spread his black wings, and flew upward.

This was a terrible story and I very much wanted to read it in the book I would buy with my own money. There were many great things that can be bought which I desired and which I wanted to purchase with the money I would receive in exchange for the Afikoman in my hand.

***

Father was waiting to hear my demand. Until I made up my mind about what I wanted and stated my preference, something happened in our home which none of us could have imagined.

"I have a secret," I said, "and would like to present my father with my request in private." All those around the table were astonished. It was not customary to approach a father with secrets, and what did the Afikoman have anything to do with big secrets? However, my father, holding his own and intrigued by the wonder of it all, went with me to the adjacent room.

"Mother too," I said firmly, and my mother followed, smiling, but wearing a puzzled expression. My heart began to race and tears filled my eyes. I could barely utter the words I had hastily planned on saying.

"I ask, in exchange for the Afikoman, that...that... father and mother forgive me for the sin that I have sinned in stealing the box of tobacco... and I promise... promise on my word that never in my life - never will I do such a thing, and I will open up my piggy bank and pay Aunt Rachel the price of the theft with my own money..." I finished speaking, and then began to sob, the sound of which penetrated the walls and could be heard by those gathered around the table, causing them quite a fright.

I would have the ill fortune of losing my father in the years ahead, for he passed away in my youth, during difficult times plagued by hunger and terror. In our few years together, although he pampered me a great deal out of his love for me, he never kissed me, for it was not the custom of respectable Jews to kiss their children unless they were about to set off on a long journey, and even then, this was done quickly, so as not leave others astonished at the despair of a respected notable. I had barely eve known what a fatherly kiss felt like.

I therefore remember, to this day, the kiss of forgiveness which I received from father that eve of Passover. It was short and abrupt, but I detected something glistening - which I suspected were tears - in the eyes of father too. My father stroked my head and said: "Zalmankeh, other than the merit of the holy Torah which atones for everything, there is no greater merit than forgiving you. Be a good Jew, Zalmankeh, and let us return to the table. The guests are waiting for us and we must continue and conclude the Seder."

My mother wiped the tears from her eyes while wiping my own, fixing the skullcap on my head as a loving, tender mother would, and we returned to the table to say the blessing of the Hillel sandwich.

Were Elijah the Prophet to enter our home as is his sacred custom, he would certainly have testified that in no home were such praises to the Lord extolled and pleasant melodies sung as in our home that Passover night. I was happy and my soul was pure, and I was content with my lot.

My parents, Chanah Kodesh and Meir Kodesh

Father, I Forgive You

"He who shames his fellow man in public, has no share in the next world." This was extent to which the sages were concerned with the respect of human dignity. And what about the person who shames his own son in public? And what if that son is only nine years old? Why did my father treat me that way? Why did he always ruin my Shabbat? Why did he make a laughing stock of me in front of my friends? Why?

Hirsch Leibke, (Zvi Aryeh), my classmate in 'heder' and my rival in both Torah study and childish pranks, never missed an opportunity to snitch on me to the Rabbi and shame me in public. Indeed, on one occasion this rascal had the good fortune of being provided an opportunity to make fun of me, by none other than my father. That afternoon, in the synagogue yard which was being momentarily used by us as our own private play center, he stood up among his cronies and with great cleverness, he mimicked the voice of the sexton Rabbi Shabtai: "In honor of him donating the sum of Chai (18) agorot (kopeks) to the synagogue coffers." Chai agorot, Chai, Chai, Chai!

And I, sitting near the fence at the side of the yard, was totally engrossed in a game of "chips" with my cousin David, oblivious to the outburst from this Balaam, the son of Peor. There I was, crouched over the pot-hole where our game was in full swing, in which buttons and pebbles were used on most days of the year, substituted on Tu B'Shevat (the 15th of Shevat) with carob stones and walnuts during the week of Passover. I concentrated my gaze at my cousin's determined aim in the direction of the pot-hole but my ears had now picked up the snide remarks coming from Hirsch, who was now announcing for all to hear: "It won't take Zalmenkeh too long to win the whole lot off his cousin. I bet he'll make a generous gift of all his buttons to the Sofit just like his old man would."

The other children, reveling in his sharp sense of humor, burst out laughing and cast looks of contempt in my direction. I kept on playing as if nothing had happened, while inside my stomach was turning from the and humiliation of it all, humiliation that my father had exposed me to in public, for the entire world to see!. "In honor of him donating Chai agorot" - Chai agorot, the mere pittance that was all the poorer community members could afford to give, whereas the distinguished Baale Batim would always show their benevolence on Shabbat when pledges were made, hence their contributions were always generous.

Hirsch Leibke's father, Ben Zion, who was disabled, had donated Chai times five, and he was not exactly one of the wealthiest members of the congregation. Benevolent Yankel Terpido, a delicate and good-hearted boy, remained inconspicuous that Shabbat, preferring not to brag about his father's generosity. And I had my spirit shattered and my heart broken at the sight of my father, an erudite and privileged individual, a respected member of the community, publicly making the smallest contribution possible, Chai agorot and not a penny more.

Many years ago, the members of the Minyan Hassidim prayer group awakened to the realization that a thorough review of the physical state of this place of worship was needed. They decided this time to spend a considerable sum on the proposed venture, a venture for which the synagogue's regular income would not suffice. Consequently, they had no choice but to deviate from their usual custom and embark on a campaign aimed at galvanizing the impoverished congregation into an extraordinary display of philanthropy.

I can no longer recall the primary reason behind the decision to undertake a complete renovation of this holy place. Was it perhaps due to the pretentiousness of the new warden, keen to make his mark while in office? Or perhaps what brought it about was that unfortunate incident when the elderly sexton, Rabbi Shabtai, having gotten up early in the morning to light the fireplace in readiness for morning prayers, fell asleep while stoking the furnace and a smoldering ember slipped out of the fireplace and almost set the entire wooden building alight? Either way, the whole place was in danger of being burnt to the ground and the billowy smoke had left the walls and ceiling charred beyond recognition.

There was, therefore, no alternative but to completely redecorate the building's interior and it was over this issue that there was disagreement as a result of the demand by several of the congregation's senior Baale Batim that the ceiling be embellished with paling boards coated in white lacquer. These boards would be arranged in a convex circle at the center of which a huge candelabra would hang, dispersing light to all corners of the building. The proposed design subsequently became known by the Latin term "Sofit." All were in agreement that the Sofit would be appropriate for the 'Minyan' (prayer group) and the minyan was more than deserving of the proposed venture.

So what exactly was the argument about? Like the rest of their colleagues in the congregation, the Hassidic Jews of my town were poor and destitute and there was no place for splendor and pomposity in a place where poverty was prevalent. Not to mention the fact that such renovations would leave the synagogue interior resembling that of Christian churches or synagogues used by reform Jews. These were the reservations voiced by several members of the minyan - with my father heading the group - who objected to such frivolous expenditures on something that was unnecessary. But most of the congregation members had their minds set on the idea that the 'Sofit' would hang resplendent from the ceiling, providing them with a sense of gratification every time they raised their eyes towards the heavens above. So my father had no choice but to express his protest by way of a show of miserliness, through a miniscule donation of Chai agorot, thereby causing scorn and contempt to be heaped on his youngest son.

This humiliation was to fester in my troubled soul like an indelible scar for many days to come. I felt a slight pain at the sight of the 'Sofit', glowing and ostentatious in all its splendor. I felt like it was constantly tormenting me, saying: "Your miserly father contributed only Chai agorot for me, so I don't belong to you at all."

* * *

My father endured great suffering. Mental distress is harder to bear than, heaven forbid, physical pain. My father's suffering originated in his soul, the sorrow at having raised sons who would not follow in his path, the path of faith, piety and the keeping of Mitzvot. (Commandments), the kind of suffering that leaves a person angry and embittered.

* * *

The Lord God acted charitably with the people of Israel when he fixed Shabbat and holidays during the course of the year and determined that they should be days of rest and pleasure, not sorrow or grief, heaven forbid. With regard to Shabbat and holidays, the commandments of pleasure and rest are mentioned in passing. Such is not the case with those special days whose primary Mitzvah requires us to be joyful and celebrate, days like Purim, Simchat Torah, the 18th of Kislev, the day on which the Rabbi of Liadi was released from prison, and other special days such as the completion of the study of a book, namely a tractate of Gemara, generally taken to refer to a volume from the Babylonian Talmud.

The Babylonian Talmud has numerous features. Invariably, father would study the same volume of Gemara together with me after we returned home from synagogue after morning prayers, the one he taught his pupils in the Gemara class. He would enjoy exploring the deeper meaning of the section of Torah he was studying, aided by the intricate commentaries by the Rashi, the "Rashba", to which he frequently referred. What made it all worthwhile was the fact there is nothing in this world that does not reach its end and a volume of Gemara is no exception.

A learned Torah disciple will on the completion of such a volume of Gemara, feel joyful and in order that the public may be privileged, he will make his own private celebration of Torah study achievement common knowledge. How is this brought about? Following afternoon prayers and, on occasion, morning prayers as well, the sexton, Rabbi Shabtai, would catch the attention of our minyan and standing on the rostrum in the middle of the synagogue, he would announce that a certain individual wished to invite the public to a celebration upon the completion of a volume of Gemara after evening prayers. Between the afternoon and evening service, the wives of the celebrating hosts could be seen hurrying about, setting tables in preparation for the festive event.

As soon as the evening service was over, all would take their seats at the table and the Gemara books would be opened on the very last page. The host or hosts would ensure that the actual completion of the volume of Gemara in question would take place immediately prior to the celebration itself and so, the last few lines - or page for those who were more studious - were kept for joint study, including the accompanying Rashi commentary. As Divine Providence would have it, these lines were never particularly taxing intellectually and did not require any in depth explanation. On the contrary, they usually contained some enchanting homilies to which the assembled company would enjoy listening. The finale would come when the host read the last few lines with the excitement usually displayed when being called up to the reading of the Torah and then the assembled congregation would recite the blessing out loud: "Chazak, chazak venitchazek! Be strong, be strong, and let us gather strength!"

The verses of the following 'Hadran' (encore) would joyously reverberate in the mouths of the assembled company: "We thank and bless thee O Lord that thou hast placed us among the students of Torah and not among the dwelling places of idle folk." As soon as the recital of the Hadran was over, glasses of wine would be filled, everyone would toast a 'Lechayim', and then partake of the selection of sweets that had been baked in honor of the celebration.

My father would always sit at the head of the table by virtue of the fact that it was usually either him or some of his students who would be celebrating the completion of study. The tunes would start as an outpouring of a yearning soul pervaded by sweet sadness and would end as songs of thanksgiving and joy. Father was held to be an authority on Lubavitch melodies. He had heard them in his father's house as a boy. Grandfather, himself a rabbi of a Hassidic community in his hometown, ran a home that was steeped in the traditions of Hassidic customs and melodies that originated in Lubavitch, the spiritual center. Father was never satisfied with traditional melodies and sought to improvise tunes by combining them with other tunes from both far and near. He had a good ear for music and could master the notes from a new melody with ease. Since he was never completely satisfied with other peoples' tunes, he sought to incorporate a few modifications of his own; he would raise or drop the key as he saw fit and the Hassidim would always be more than happy with his revised version of the melody. These tunes eventually become widely known and were always enjoyed by neighbors and visitors alike.

***

I enjoyed relatively few happy days during my childhood; most of them were full of disquiet and discontent. This does not mean that there were constant quarrels in our house, not at all! Mother admired father for his diligence in Torah study and his prestigious ancestry, while father would treat mother with great respect, in accordance with the commandments of the sages. He knew only too well that we all depended on her for the family's livelihood since it was she who brought in an adequate income through her work in the general store that she ran from dawn till dusk.

Father would spend his time assessing the capabilities of potential students, selecting only those talented enough to become Torah scholars in their own right. These were not always to be found among those families with means that could afford to pay proper tuition fees. Mother never compromised her husband's self-dignity, so that he would never feel inferior to her because of her role as the family breadwinner. She would always go through the motions of consulting him on business matters and he was the one who opened the packages of merchandise that mother had brought back from the nearby city of Panevezys, which was the commercial center of the province. He would open the packages in a show of importance and lay all the items out on the table in the shop which was known as 'Tombank' while she would be arranging all the goods on shelves, each item with its own particular place. I used to see myself as the additional partner in the business, wedging myself in between my parents, observing the unpacking of each item with great excitement and interest and being constantly told by both of them to stop interfering and to get out of the way.

This was how my astute mother was able to keep her husband somehow involved in the running of the family business, by arranging goods on the shelves, as if she could never manage it alone without his assistance. In addition, mother would hand over all the petty cash every Shabbat eve to father for safekeeping for as long as was required. He would take the bag from her and placing a bench in front of the large book cabinet, he would climb up and hide the money bag on the top shelf behind a row of books, which consisted of books in Hebrew and Yiddish, books on Hebrew grammar, a few medical books written in classical Hebrew and a few academic works dealing with Gentile ideology. It was behind this array of mundane publications that father would always stash the hard-earned income that mother handed him for safekeeping. His intentions in hiding the money on the top shelf were twofold: firstly, that no one coming into the house should, heaven forbid, be able to lay his hands on the family treasure trove. Furthermore, he could not countenance the act of mixing that which was sacred with the secular. Volumes of Gemara, Mishnah, Midrash and other sacred books would not be placed adjacent to bank notes and silver, copper or even gold coins that had monetary value but no sanctity whatsoever. Better that it rest alongside books that were considered 'defiled and soiled'.

***

Father was indeed a real bookworm! He had inherited his father's library, in keeping with the tradition of handing down such a precious heirloom to the eldest son, and over time had added more books. The books were arranged on the shelves in order of importance. There were those that were classed as 'Dorei Mata' (the lower shelf) which contained the Talmud and works compiled by the Rambam and other renowned authorities on religious law as well as books on Hassidic philosophy, all of which were steeped in sanctity and whose study constituted the upholding of the Mitzvah to engage in Torah study. These books were beautifully made, bound with fine brown leather binding to insure they never got worn out with use. Every Passover eve, we would remove these precious literary works from their places in the cabinet and wipe their leather covers clean of dust with a cloth and shake them in the radiance of the spring sun that would be shining, the dust floating up in tiny radiant clouds as if the letters themselves had leapt off the pages for a brief twirl in the sun's rays. I loved this work and considered it an honor to be chosen to perform it.

Father would busy himself with the airing of those books classed as 'Dorei Maala' (the higher shelf). These were the small books piled up on the top shelves without any distinction or reference, but I still had a keen interest in them and longed to run my cloth over them too. To this very day, I have no idea as to how father came to own such literary publications by the dozen, works on secular enlightenment that were nothing less than sacrilege such as, 'The Love of Zion', 'The Guilt of Samaria' by Abraham Mapu, 'The Donkey's Graveside' by Peretz Smolenskin, the provocative poetry of Yehuda Leib Gordon and other such works, all casting off the yoke of divine sanctity and Hassidic tradition. I have never quite fathomed out exactly what such books were doing in a God-fearing Mitzvah observing home like my father's. This remains a secret that father, may his memory be blessed, took with him to his grave.

***

In later years when I had grown into adulthood and begun to reflect on the anomalies of this universe, I had a sneaking suspicion - may God forgive me for such ruminative thoughts - that father himself might have had something of a penchant for such books in his youth, including such titles as 'He Who Goes Astray' by Peretz Smolenskin, the 'Visions of

Shada'l, Steinberg's 'Hebrew - Russian Dictionary' and even the works of Kalman Shulman that had been written in traditional Hebrew, works that father had publicly condemned on more than one occasion.

It seems that father, a quick-thinking individual who usually thought one step ahead, deluded himself into believing that these improper literary works would never find their way into the hands of his inquisitive youngest son. In view of his lack of height, he deemed it appropriate to hide them on the top shelf of the book cabinet. Oh, father, were you so blind you could not see? I too reached that top shelf one day when nobody was at home. I quickly fetched the step-ladder and placing it next to the book shelf, I climbed up until I was alongside that shelf. Then I took out and handled each book, glanced through it and then made my way back down with two books still clutched firmly in my hand. I hid them in a safe place so I could read them whenever I got the chance.

***

The shame of it all! While studying Torah, with the volume of Gemara open in front of me on a page of the tractate of 'Ketubot' (marital contracts), I recited in the melody reserved for talmudic study a couple of lines of the text. It dealt with the marriage and marital contract of a maiden whose ceremony was set according to religious law, for Tuesday, a day on which good fortune is twofold and not on Wednesday like the marriage of a poor widow. There I sat singing and mumbling the sacred verses of the Gemara so as not to attract the attention of father who was sitting in a nearby room with his pupils. He would eavesdrop on me as best he could so as to hear the words of Torah coming from my lips, reassuring himself that I was not neglecting my studies.

An ass knows his buyer and likewise, a youngest son will know the actions of his suspicious father. I sang a couple of lines in the Gemara melody and then, following the custom of well-versed practitioners, I fell silent while supposedly scrutinizing the commentary by Rashi and other commentators. It was at this juncture that I took time out from my preoccupation with the marriage of the maiden discussed in the Gemara, and with one leap of my mind I found myself in the palace of noble Tziyon, the Tanachite, who was in fact Yedidya and from there I arrived at the rose bed of kind-hearted, beautiful Tamar. I shared my love for Tamar with the valiant hero, Amnon.

The thief will always end up on the gallows! The first in a series of ringing slaps on my face brought me back down to the real world of the tractate 'Ketubot'. It was an unexpected visit by father who had interrupted his class to observe the extent of my diligent study. The silent break for in depth study of the commentaries had apparently lasted a bit too long for his liking. He had taken a break from his class and gently pushed the door of my room ajar. At that very moment I was extremely tense. In a few lines, Amnon would go down on his knees and wax lyrically in the expression of his divine love for Tamar, the most beautiful girl of them all. This was, of course, not the ideal time for father to be making his entrance.

After subjecting me to the full force of his hand with several slaps on my cheek, he turned his attention to the large ornate Gemara book, courtesy of the Reem brothers of Vilna and the Almana printing press that was open in front of me. With one stroke of his hand, he swept aside the repugnant book concealed within its pages and was about to hurl it to the floor in a fit of rage, but he composed himself again and stopped midway. This was after all, a literary work that had been written in traditional Hebrew in spite of the fact that it contained nothing but sheer insipid twaddle with no Torah related content whatsoever.

In years to come when reflecting on that sorry event, it seemed that it was hardly a coincidence that father felt no need to examine the content of the book hidden between the pages of the Gemara, as if he was already familiar with its content from a previous encounter of his own. He finally released my ears which were now burning from his prolonged pinching, a punishment which normally followed a slapped face and shoving the book in one of the pockets of his long coat, he gently propelled me out the door with me weeping at the indignation of the double punishment that had just been meted out to me: The physical and mental distress, the slaps and ear pinching, and the cutting short of the pleasure I had taken in joining Amnon and Tamar during the most touching moments of their romantic interlude.

***

I headed in the direction of the synagogue yard. Although it was not yet time for afternoon prayers, the yard was already filling with heder children who had arrived in time for the hour of worship. The burning sensation on my ears where they had been pinched had still not worn off and my flushed cheeks clearly bore the marks of the handiwork of my heavy-handed father. I was, however, able to recover from the trauma of the physical and mental distress to which I had been recently exposed. I was also able to clear my mind of the maiden who was to be married on Tuesday and all those accompanying commentaries and convoluted footnotes in the Gemara tractate 'Ketubot', aimed at sharpening the mind of the wise disciple, just as I was now able to put the visions created by Abraham Mapu right out of my mind. My instincts were to prove right later that evening when, on returning home after evening prayers, we sat at the dinner table without any reference made to the transgression I had committed earlier on in the day. A truly wise man is he who has acquired experience. You don't get slapped twice for the same indiscretion.

* * *

The passage of time cancels out punishment. That's the way it has been and that's the way it always will be. My instincts never proved me wrong. My mother and sister, who had been working together in the shop, came home tired and shattered. This event had taken place on Sunday, the day on which the Gentiles would attend their churches and on their return from their worship, they would descend on the Jewish shops in droves whereupon they would stock up with the essential goods they required. All the shop owners eagerly waited for this particular time of the week, although this was also an ideal opportunity for shoplifting. What was the only method of guarding against such thieves? Extreme vigilance, so it would appear. The shopkeepers would fix their sights on the customer and his entourage, watching every movement of their hands to ensure no merchandise would inadvertently disappear, while simultaneously waxing as persuasively as possible and weighing and packing the merchandise and counting the money received in payment for its sale. No wonder then, that the weary shop owners would make their way home after nightfall, thoroughly exhausted.

With her remaining breath, mother would blow hard on the smoldering embers on the stove, and then rekindle the fire with the aid of a few dry wooden chips and small tree branches that had been cut down to size. By the good grace of the creator of light, a flame would erupt under the iron tripod on which there rested a pot full of sweet potatoes, a barley or oatmeal broth flavored with a pinch of salt and coated with a layer of milk diluted with water. Blessed be He who giveth strength to the weary. Mother would sit down at the table after washing her hands and tear off a chunk of bread which would then be dipped in salt in order to recite the blessing 'Hamotzi' before starting the meal. Who would dare stoop to the spineless act of dampening her spirits by gossiping to her about the rebellious son who had belittled his Torah study with nonsense? Father did not deviate from his usual custom on the eve of this day of recklessness and, as usual, he did not involve mother in the morality of parenthood and the tribulations of raising a son. The dinner proceeded as usual with light conversation being made on everyday matters. Mother and father did not talk much at the table, she by reason of sheer fatigue and he by way of adhering to the advice of the sages: Do not involve yourself in conversation with a woman. We sipped our barley and potato soup; we ate bread and butter with grains of dried cheese sprinkled on top, courtesy of our lone cud-chewing heifer out in the yard. Father did not skip dessert, half an apple finely peeled. With the evening meal completed, the day's events were now over and we all retired.

The following morning, my father made no further mention of yesterday's incident, although there were clear signs that changes had been made in my study arrangements as a result of the indiscretion of the previous day. The ornate Gemara book, a gift from my grandparents to my father on his wedding, that had been taken down from the row of 'Shas' volumes in my honor was now back in its place on the shelf in the cupboard and in its place on the table lay the smaller soft covered Gemara book commonly used by all the boys, with its darkly colored pages. Likewise, the door that had separated the new room - specially built to allow me to busy myself with Torah study - from the room where the more mediocre pupils of father were seated had mysteriously disappeared. I was able to accept the replacing of the ornate Gemara book with a more mundane equivalent. The doorway was a different matter altogether.

I viewed this change as a bitter blow that I would find hard to deal with, and toyed with the idea of complaining to my mother. Common-sense eventually prevailed within me and made me realize that nothing good would come out of this sordid affair. So I resolved to swallow this bitter pill as best I could and pretend I didn't care, while searching for an idea as to how to evade father's constant supervision.

***

And so it came to pass that on Tishah B'av, the day that is set aside for mourning, fasting and lamentation, I found an opportunity to seclude myself together with a forbidden book written in Yiddish. I settled myself in a pile of hay in the cow shed loft and in an instant I found myself enthralled by the never ending escapades of the "Count Of Monte Cristo", while my family was visiting at the cemetery as is the custom on Tishah B'av.

Upon being caught for my last misdemeanor my father decided to throw in a small tirade on moral virtue for good measure before he left. "Perhaps you have by chance heard, the Hassidic melody about a man bemoaning the loss of his fortune, namely the loss of money instead of bemoaning his wasted youth? To waste precious time on stuff and nonsense on a day of fasting and mourning? One can perhaps understand a person reading a secular book written in traditional Hebrew during the small hours of the morning – if there is no Torah or God-fearing material of any sort present, then at least one has the sanctity of the Hebrew language in its own right. But to waste time reading utter tripe written in common jargon in the middle of a day of mourning?" Words that were like daggers in my heart, for I disobeyed my father.

***

It was, however, not my fault that my sister, Dina, had chosen specifically to collect books in Yiddish, stories of romance and adventure of kings, tycoons, counts and countesses that were bound to capture the imagination of a nine-year-old boy. My sister would keep the books under her pillow with the consent of father, who took pity on her because she was a sickly child and had saved every penny of her hard-earned money to buy them but he expressly forbade her to show them to me. She was not to blame for the fact that I, her kid brother, had developed my own detective instincts and had discovered the hideaway of these pages, pages that swept me away to a world of undying love and adventures of noblemen and aristocrats.

* * *

Later in life, many years after father had departed this world during the course of World War One, I understood that those gloom laden days of occupation, turmoil and confusion of existing world orders left me, a fifteen year old son, scarcely an opportunity to get to know him and talk to him on equal terms. When I finally began to examine and finally comprehend the enigmas and solve all the conundrums and mysteries of my father's home, I realized that father had within him a soul that made him tower over all his contemporaries.

* * *

The 'new room' – as it became known during all its years of existence until its destruction at the hands of the devil's emissaries – was no ordinary room. The entire wing had been built by Tzemach, the one-eyed builder. He was both architect and engineer and with the assistance of his son and son-in-law, he cast the foundation, put up walls made of wooden beams riveted to a steel bracket and hacked out openings where doors and windows would be fitted. It was he who placed a coat of asphalt over the finely chiseled tiles that formed the roof as well as wooden partitions dipped in asphalt in the large pit that had been dug by an experienced Gentile laborer. Thanks to the labors and ingenuity of Tzemach and his assistants, this pit would become a storage cellar imbued with a variety of aromas that changed with the passing of each season, stocked with an ample supply of fruits, vegetables, barrels of sour pickles as well as tens of bottles of mead. (This was a fermented beverage made from water distilled from honey which was Kosher for use during Passover and at Shabbat meals too; the ideal drink for washing down one's cholent).

This new wing was an integral part of the existing building. The dank and dusky cellar abundant with flavors and aromas was indeed a godsend. Such was the attraction it held for me and I would seize the opportunity on the occasional moments of solitude and shifting the cumbersome lid covering the cellar opening, slither down the ladder into my own private world. If your instincts are telling you that those ventures down into the cellar were not without reward on their part, you will have indeed been proven correct. I remember my sins only too well; I had a sweet tooth that was uncontrollable. I never missed an opportunity to satiate my passion for tastes. I was never fussy and would mix any concoction that appealed to me. A sip of Kiddush wine on a weekday, a bite out of an apple or pear coupled with a sampling of the cracklings of goose that mother had stood frying in the kitchen late at night. My sharp teeth gnawed their way through yeast dough set aside for Hanukkah pancakes with the same voracious appetite with which I would set upon the aromatic cucumbers that had been pickled in brine, red peppers and other spices while floating in the barrel set aside for that purpose.

But he who understands the subtleties of the heart and evaluates the debilitating craving of the soul for that which is divine yet out of reach in the sunbathed world up above, also knows how unreservedly my wandering soul was immersed in the wonders of that dusky cellar. I wove the fabric of my own private world with golden thread. I told myself stories with countless episodes in which I was always the hero facing down all challenges both real and surreal and even those that were beyond the imagination of a mischievous sharp tongued and impetuous boy. This is the absolute truth.

* * *

To claim that father and mother had, in effect, built a complete additional wing to the original dwelling which mother had provided as a dowry on her marriage is totally wrong. The new wing with its spacious and brightly lit kitchen situated on top of the aforementioned cellar was nothing more than an embellishment for the primary purpose of building an exclusive room for Torah study. Later on, however, a good-sized bed was placed in the room and a cupboard for clothes made from bright oak wood stood by the bedside. Useful household accessories always prove their worth, but these served no other purpose than the hosting of a fellow Torah student who was to sit at the table that had been placed in the room along with the book cabinet and two plain chairs that had no arm supports.

The hectic activity went on for a whole year; piles of wooden beams and pails of asphalt and whitewash were scattered all over, not to mention the late night discussions, the bills and measurements and the loud arguments with numerous suppliers and tradesmen. All of this was compounded by the noise and mayhem, the banging of hammers and the grating of hacksaws, the slapping of whitewash brushes and the clattering of window panes. Father found himself completely disoriented by the combined cacophony of human voices and grating noise of heavy duty tools but tried his utmost to carry on as usual amidst the total devastation inside our house.

What a relief when the project was finished!

* * *

Father was a man of vision who put his faith in divine providence. He dreamed passionately of succeeding in ensuring that his youngest and dearest son would not follow in the footsteps of his older brothers and sisters and abandon the Torah of his forefathers after leaving home. Could it be possible that he had not been stringent enough in the upbringing of his other children by not insisting they be educated in accordance with his beliefs, an act which might have stopped them from turning their backs on him when they became adults? He would not make that mistake again for sure. This time he would smother his restless renegade son with the best Torah tutor that could be found.

The teacher hat had been entrusted with the task of getting the boy to apply himself to his Gemara studies subsequently proved unsatisfactory. It was not just Moshe Gershon Bruchs, the teacher with the foul breath and soiled hands, who had no luck with the hotheaded seven-year old.

At the time, I spoke with my father and brothers in traditional Hebrew, and was an expert on the Bible. I was enthralled with the fables taken from the book 'Legends of Israel' (written by someone named Lerner), that were as sweet as honey and which I almost knew by heart. Perhaps the teacher realized that the 'creep'- as I became known in light of the nasty tricks I played on him and his wife - had already managed to compile his own commentary on the book of Genesis, written in tiny letters on bits of paper and blank pages torn out of books that I had illicitly appropriated for that purpose? This commentary, true as it was to the Hassidic form of homiletics, had been picked up by me from my father who always quoted from the Lubavitch doctrine and from 'streimel' wearing dignitaries who would visit our town from time to time and who, in deference to our family lineage, would always stay at our home.

I liked neither my Rabbi nor the Gemara tractate 'Gittin' that I was supposed to be studying. To this day, I have maintained a dislike for this particular tractate and the issues discussed therein. Father kept me and my teacher together in this double house of horrors for one period only and it was with a sigh of relief that we parted company from each other at the end of our study period.

***

My next teacher, Rabbi Moshe Mordecai, respected and honored as he was, had precious little success in getting me to apply myself to a page of Gemara with the accompanying commentaries, even though the volume of Gemara in question was the complex tractate of Baba Batra. I did, however, manage to curry favor with my teacher on one isolated occasion when following a heated discussion, I asked a surprisingly original question, thereby receiving words of praise from the rabbi of the town who had come to the class that day to test the pupils. Pinching my cheek, he went as far as to deliver a version of a famous adage of the sages specially revised in my honor by pronouncing: "He who is neither a minor as such, yet not an adult either but a minor who is well versed in Torah is truly an adult."

For that brief period my teacher was overjoyed with me since honor achieved by pupils is also honor for their teachers but it didn't take long for the novelty to wear off. Ultimately it was my antics he would remember, namely my raucous laughter which would spread to my classmates, and my leading role in the 'break time battles' between David's followers (and who else would play David but I?) and Goliath's men who were the cronies of gutless Hirsch Leibke, my sworn enemy and rival for status among the rest of our crowd.

***

When it came to delivering a verdict on my progress in general to father, Rabbi Moshe Mordecai was blunt, forthright and unequivocal. "This boy has talent. He has a good grasp of subject matter and a sharp mind. He is, however, captivated by the evil spirit, may heaven preserve us, and I have no idea as where to he got it from. I have tried both reasoning and flogging him but to no avail. He is a clown by nature and ingenious at causing mischief. Do not be discouraged Rabbi Meir by his lacking in Torah. This boy has the merits of previous generations in his favor and as the sages said, "The Torah always keeps a vigil over those who can accommodate it within their souls", but as far as piety is concerned I can offer no salvation whatsoever. The sages have said, "Everything except piety is entrusted to the hands of God in heaven."

"What do you suggest Rabbi?" father pressed him, his heart sinking all the while. "He won't be much good in Yeshiva at his age since he is only ten. I doubt very much whether his mother could bring herself to part from him in any case."

That evening I heard voices raised in angry debate coming from my parents' bedroom. Father accused mother of pampering her youngest offspring to the extent that he abandoned the path of righteousness, thereby allowing the evil spirit, may heaven preserve us, to gain ever-increasing control over him. This time, however, mother was having none of it. She asked him whether he had been any more successful in the education of piety of their older children. They had been forced to leave home in order to escape his perpetual rebukes and had relocated to a city that was distant enough to ensure he exerted no further control over them.

"What good has your Puritanism brought us? You have stuck to your guns and they have stuck to theirs. The boy is inclined towards Zionism and the girls to socialism. The eldest was arrested on charges of treason and was lucky not to have faced trial and a subsequent jail sentence. If Moshe Mordecai doesn't want the boy, then fair enough. He can master a page of Gemara plus commentaries without his teacher's help. The pace of the boys' Gemara class is far too slow for him. You yourself admitted he is getting bored. So can you honestly expect him not to go astray? He is way ahead of the others. Go to Lubavitch and see the Rabbi there; perhaps he may be able to give us some advice."

The discussion between them went on for another hour with the angry tone eventually giving way to rational dialogue. By this time, I could no longer hear their words from my side of the partition, which separated my bedroom from that of my parents. The next morning, I felt a marked improvement in the atmosphere when I accompanied father to the early minyan for morning prayers, yet something had changed.

***

When I was especially mischievous, father would very often instruct me to lower my trousers and bend over a bench whereupon he would proceed to whip me with a broomstick, an experience no less painful than a slapped face but far more humiliating. Consequently, I became more and more insubordinate and ignored my father's order to lower my trousers and bend over the bench when ordered. I would often continue to resist even to the point of twitching and kicking.

On one occasion father felt he could save time by doing two jobs at once, namely mixing his eggnog and flogging me on the bench. One of the principal rules in life is that one should never bite off more than one can chew. Father clearly got carried away on this occasion; he stood the glass on the end of the bench and at the same time he grasped me firmly with the aim of stretching me over the bench for the usual flogging. He succeeded with great difficulty in pinning me to the bench, with his free hand poised to strike at the usual spot on my posterior but in the course of violently thrashing about; I kicked the glass on the end of the bench. It fell to the floor shattering on impact; its contents splattered everywhere. At that moment I sympathized with father at the apparent loss. The glass had broken and the eggnog was gone. I had barely finished buttoning up my trousers and washing my hands in the sink in case they had touched an immodest part of my anatomy when father was on the job again. Flogging is a task on its own and preparing eggnog is a task on its own and neither should encroach on the other's preserve.

***

On this particular morning, following the late consultation between my parents, I was served a glass of this potent concoction in a clear show of affection. Using a teaspoon, father skimmed the layer of foam off the liquid and fed me himself. Afterwards,he stirred the remaining liquid in the glass and placed it by my side, making light conversation with me all the while, a clear indication that he was in a relaxed state of mind, something that rarely happened in our house.

The advice offered by mother was clearly behind this change in temperament although by advice I do not refer to mother's recommendation that father travel to Lubavitch to seek help from the Rabbi that would reinvigorate his youngest son with the piety he currently lacked. (Father was a devout Hassid who continued the tradition set by his predecessors and ardently followed the teachings of Hassidic faith and the Lubavitcher Rabbi. However, he made one exception where Hassidic practices were concerned. The Lubavitch doctrine was a source of Torah and inspiration and as such it was not to be involved in personal matters. Hence father did not travel all the way to Lubavitch to ask for mercy on his youngest son).

***

Mother's good advice was in fact a casual reference to the possibility of individual study, known as 'Farzeich' in Yiddish, which was considered to be an advanced level of Torah study. Those eminent Yeshiva students, who had totally immersed themselves in Gemara, Tosafoth, and other commentaries to the point of saturation, no longer required the help of a teacher to take them through a volume of Gemara page by page. All they needed was a lesson or two a week and once they got involved in a discourse on a complex issue, they could manage on their own. This process usually called for the reading of several verses of Gemara by the principal of the Yeshiva who would then get things going by making a singularly complex point. Then, rallying all his skill and expertise in the logical interpretation of Torah, he would attempt to answer his own question by drawing on sources used to solve a similar issue in a different context.

Ironically, before the principal had managed to expedite his train of thought to the full, one of the top pupils would pose another query on the same matter, which had the effect of refuting the principal. Often, he would dismiss an answer that he himself had only just suggested, having drawn on a source in another volume of Gemara. This would be the signal for other students to pitch in enthusiastically with their own ideas and interpretations, each disputing the material introduced by his colleagues. The atmosphere would become heated and the razor-sharp wits at play would introduce hair-splitting analyses that grew in precision as the debate progressed.

It was only towards the end of the lesson that the principal would finally be satisfied that there was a straightforward answer. A clear-cut and lucid paragraph from the Mishnah would emerge as the solution to the puzzle they had just been debating. The answers to all the queries and points that had just been raised were crystal clear. Any shadow of doubt had finally been lifted. There were no outbursts or sighs of relief afterwards. The intense atmosphere simply died away. The principal would smile with satisfaction, as if he had just returned victorious from battle and the students would fix their teacher with a look of admiration and appreciation for the exhilarating Torah experience he had just led them through. After the principal had left the room, the students would continue their deliberating in small groups until finally, each person went his separate way.

All this took place once or twice a week. On the other days, when there was no teacher present, each yeshiva student would choose his own tractate and then study it either on his own or together with a couple of friends. Like a true disciple of Torah, he would split his day between group and individual study. Each student would have his own melody when intoning the verses of Torah while his eyes would be simultaneously scanning the plethora of commentaries, both those on the sides of each page and those hidden between the appendices at the back of the book. He would flit back and forth between the two parts of the book bursting into melody each time he cast his eyes over successive verses of the Gemara and Mishnah in front of him.

These were, of course, all students aged 17 and 18 who were soon to be led to the marital canopy following which they would continue their studies at the 'Kollelim', the colleges for married students that were attached to the yeshiva. But we are talking here about a ten year-old kid. Could anyone possibly expect him to learn on his own? At his age, the only things on his mind were games and other activities that were devoid of any Torah or piety. He needed a teacher that would provide him with an intensive program of Torah on a daily basis.

There would be no place for rank-and-file teachers this time round as learned as they may be. Who could be more eminent a Torah scholar than Rabbi Yossef Alperovitch, the leader of the Hassidic community? He was an extremely busy man whose time was fully taken up with the task of adjudicating in matters concerning Kashrut, and civil disputes, as well as involvement in other communal chores such as the giving of lessons in Torah and Hassidic literature, a task that the Rabbi was duty bound to fulfill.

The service requested did not call for professional teaching, as this would have constituted a disregard for the Rabbi's position. All they were asking him to do was to bring one solitary boy back into the fold of Torah, namely the youngest son of Rabbi Meir, a learned scholar in his own right with a prestigious lineage in his favor. The Rabbi would sit with me for two hours each morning following morning prayers and together we would study a certain tractate of Gemara. I would then return home and continue on my own. My father would be on hand if I ran into any difficulties during my studies. All he had to do was open the door and salvation would be at hand. Between afternoon and evening prayers, he would take an hour of free time to sit with me and start on another tractate out of interest, just an extra page of Gemara plus Rashi commentary each day, nothing more.

***

Father told mother about his brilliant idea and sought her guidance. One day after morning prayers, father approached the Rabbi after services and made his proposition. "One does not refuse those destined for greatness", he urged but in the end, it was the proposed fee of twenty-five rubles per 'period' (six months) that did the trick. The Rabbi was supporting his intellectually gifted sons who had gone away to study Torah at a well-known institution, and he was always in need of extra income.

Father took me to see the Rabbi at his home. He gave me a brief test in Torah and stroked my cheek, a clear indication of how satisfied he was. The Rabbi's wife served father tea and a piece of the cake left over from the Shabbat festivities (known as 'Helekich' in Yiddish) and then offered me a piece as well. After I recited the blessing and the Rabbi and father had answered 'Amen' in unison, we took our leave, imbued with hope for the success of this venture.

Had father gone a bit too far in his expectations of me? Can a high-spirited boy control his temperament? The answer to that question was unclear. We all thought the idea would work well. I liked my room and my distinguished teacher too. I would read through the pages of the Gemara that the Rabbi had instructed me to look through and then attempt to come up with an answer of my own to the questions he had given me.

***

Anyone who has had occasion to study Torah will never pass up an opportunity to discover an intricate answer to a complex question and then bring it to the attention of Torah scholars. I, too, would avail myself of this challenging activity, while browsing through the Gemara. I would linger over a page dealing with legends that was usually crammed with text leaving very little room for the commentaries. Those who compiled the Mishnah and legends did imaginative pupils a great service when they allowed differing subjects to overlap. In the heat of a discussion of an issue disputed by the House of Shamai and the House of Hillel, they would halt the discussion midway and as if intending to revitalize the atmosphere, they would launch into a narrative relating the eccentricities of Rabbi Bar Chana or moving accounts of the passing away of righteous men. This trend was reflected even more prominently in those verses of the Talmud that dealt with relations with men and women and whose assignation was unclear, verses that were read with uninhibited delight by many. Scholars of all ages consider it a challenge to be able to sift through books, find such lines and then read them in seclusion thereby provoking the evil spirit which places vile thoughts in the minds of prying Torah students.

***

I enjoyed the time I spent alone in my room as well as the hours I spent together with my teacher, Rabbi Yossef Alperovitch. The Rabbi would stand, leaning forward on his pulpit ('Shtender' in Yiddish) while I sat opposite him at the long table used for the Gemara lesson for community members. Very often I would read out a few lines and was about to explain them when, like an act of the devil, Feigele, the Rabbi's youngest daughter would appear in the doorway announcing: "Father there are people outside who wish to receive a Torah ruling." On another occasion a large woman came barging in holding the carcass of a goose in whose entrails a defect had been discovered, a situation that required the Rabbi's decision as to whether the fowl could still be considered kosher. Men and women would approach the honorable Rabbi for advice on almost anything.

The interruptions of our daily lessons grew increasingly longer. The Rabbi's repeated instructions to me to "continue reading the page and study commentary "X" until I return", was not always implemented in full. Sometimes the Rabbi would come back and find me gone. I would get bored and step out into the yard on my way to the 'Asher Yatzar' corner (i.e. the bathroom) and would run into some heder kids who were negotiating a trade - strings of carob seeds in exchange for "chips." Sometimes a disagreement would break out between the traders that was on the verge of turning violent when I arrived on the scene. Both sides were more than happy to have me act as arbitrator and in the heat of my passion to get to the bottom of the affair and see justice done, I would forget about my teacher and the Gemara tractate 'Ketubot' that I was supposed to be studying.

Father and the Rabbi soon realized that a change of scene was required, a step that was bound to have a positive effect on the level of my diligence. There was no alternative but to move the lessons to the Rabbi's apartment regardless of the frequency of the interruptions to which we would be subjected during the course of our lessons. In order to ensure I was not deprived of the Rabbi's tutelage, he and father agreed to cancel the regular two-hour morning session, replacing it with a more flexible arrangement that allowed for the Rabbi to summon me to his house whenever it was convenient.

It didn't take long for me to realize that I had gotten lucky and this change was definitely in my favor. Sitting in the relaxed atmosphere of the home of the Rabbi, where I had been taken on our first encounter, was far more preferable than the dull, hollow and intimidating atmosphere of the synagogue hall. The Rabbi's study was spacious with row after row of books lining the walls in all shapes and sizes. Within a short while, I could sense that the Rabbi had taken a liking to me. On one occasion while we were having a break, I plucked up the courage to ask him if I could look through the bookshelves and he generously permitted me to do so on condition that all books and pamphlets were returned to their proper place afterwards. As if I would do otherwise? I had been well trained by father every Passover eve when I helped him dust off the books and then return them to their correct places on the shelves. Father was excessively pedantic in this regard insisting that "just as each star has its rightful place in heaven in accordance with the will of the Divine Creator, so each book must have its correct place on the shelf in anticipation of the inquiring scholar when the time is right."

Readers may deduce from this that there was never a dull moment as a result of the Rabbi being called away. During winter months, we would sit together at a small table near the fireplace and in the summer, we would place the table next to a large window overlooking an expanse of land on which barren trees had sprouted providing shade from the midday sun. The Rabbi would listen while I read the pages of Gemara aloud. It was only when he wasn't sure that he would actually look at the pages of the book open in front of him before answering the question I had posed. From time to time, he would draw my attention to a couple of lines of commentary that were singularly pertinent to the text we were learning. Sometimes I would come up with an idea myself. The Rabbi made no secret of his pleasure at my progress. Such praise had been conspicuously absent during all my years at heder with my previous tutors. Not even father had a good word to say for me, his goal being to ensure that I did not become self-centered thereby abandoning, God forbid, the principle of humility as practiced by Moses and Aaron in their day. The Rabbi on the other hand did not hesitate to praise me even though he must have no doubt been aware of the commandment of humility.

***

The years I frequented the Rabbi's home were happy times. Things went like clockwork. I would enter the Rabbi's house with a cheerful "good morning" knowing that Feigele was pleased to see me and would silently greet me in return. I too was pleased to see her although we hardly spoke a word to each other. On one occasion, Feigele was asked to take a basket of fruit and food to a poor housewife who had just given birth, since the Rabbi's wife was indisposed and was unable to perform this Mitzvah herself. The Rabbi could see the basket was too heavy for her and without a second thought he asked if I would hold one handle. I needed no further bidding and lifted the basket together with Feigele.

Once we had stepped out into the street, a wave of mischief swept over us and we ran all the way up the street laughing all the while but still avoiding any direct conversation with each other. On the way back from delivering the basket we fell silent, I walked several steps ahead in keeping with the tradition of the men who would always walk ahead of the women upon leaving synagogue.

And so I became a permanent member of the Rabbi's household, initially out of lack of choice but eventually out of preference. Father appeared to have relaxed his constant vigil over me once I had been entrusted to the Rabbi's supervision. He had either placed his trust in the Rabbi's ability to positively influence me or given up on the idea of getting any satisfaction from me in the manner he would have liked. A few perfunctory conversations on Torah knowledge convinced him that I was not playing truant, God forbid, while at the Rabbi's house. The more he relaxed his grip on me, the more I made progress in my studies and consequently his outbursts and tantrums grew more infrequent. There was not much the Rabbi could do about the continuous irritating interruptions of our lessons by visitors while I was at his home. 'That which is frequent takes precedence to that which is infrequent' is the primary rule in all matters relating to Torah. Rabbinical duties were a permanent feature in the Rabbi's daily routine whereas my studies together with him were merely a passing phase.

To be perfectly honest, I was not terribly despondent over the constant interruptions, a clear reflection of the adage coined by yeshiva students: "Abi nisht lernen", (avoid Torah whenever possible). I would listen attentively to the claims, arguments and supplications of all those who frequented the Rabbi's house. As time passed, I became familiar with all the regular visitors. A woman with a question regarding Kashrut - such as a needle caught in the gizzard of a chicken - was of no interest to me.

If the Rabbi did not utter the magic word 'kosher' and instead began examining the fowl or looking through books by Rabbinical authorities on the subject, I would get up and walk out of the room leaving the Rabbi and the inquirer on their own. The free time created by such interruptions gave me an ideal opportunity to scan the selection of books on a particular shelf in the study. I would pick a work that aroused my curiosity, browse through it and then return it to its proper place on the shelf. Thus, I was able to put my spare time to good use, cashing in on an opportunity to broaden my interests.

Not so when the visitors were rival claimants who required a Torah ruling or synagogue wardens or other officials who came to discuss communal affairs. My curiosity was aroused the moment they walked through the door. I listened to the arguments of both sides or just the visitors' words and would silently form my own opinion even to the extent of making my own ruling too.

I was delighted on those occasions when it turned out that my train of thought had been similar to that of the Rabbi's. He in turn did not denigrate my intellect. Often when he was in a lighthearted mood he would encourage me to voice my opinions and give my interpretation of the Torah issue being discussed. On one occasion, he surprised me by saying, "Had this claimant adopted your argument, the ruling might have been completely different." Father smiled contentedly when he heard about this, cautioning that it was improper conduct for a Hassid to lecture the Rabbi on Halacha (religious law).

***

Those were glorious days but, like all good things, they eventually came to an end. War broke out, throwing the entire world into turmoil. The assassination of the heir to the throne (Archduke Franz Ferdinand) in Sarajevo and the resulting world war rained devastation down on the world, a state of affairs which affected me as much as everyone else. What's so special about that, I hear you ask and exactly how much does a ten-year-old understand about international conflicts? A claim, which is totally groundless. I was an expert in political affairs. I gained my knowledge from a variety of sources, one of them being the daily newspaper, "The Friend", which the postman Nachum Leib delivered every morning to the home of Getzil, a distinguished scholar well versed in Zionism, who had a subscription to the paper.

We always attended the same minyan each morning and Nachum Leib would place the bundle of mail on his seat, which was near father's alongside the eastern wall. I would speed up the pace of my prayers with the aim of finishing before Nachum Leib. By the time he finished folding his prayer shawl and removing his phylacteries, and had handed out letters to the congregation members who converged on him from all directions hoping to receive their mail on the spot instead of waiting for it to be delivered to their house, I had already managed to sneak a look at the front page of the newspaper, which I would carefully spread, making sure it did not get creased in the process.

I had a fixed ritual, which I religiously adhered to when making my daily perusal of the newspaper and order was strictly maintained. I would first absorb the telegrams on page one, being as they were, a synopsis that reflected events happening in the world at large. The importance of the news was graded according to the size of the letters in which it was printed. The most sensational items of all were printed in bold letters, the size of those used in the monthly prayer for the new moon with the rest of the news printed in letters that decreased in size until they were a miniature typeface. A seasoned reader like myself would be content just to scan the telegrams and the daily column by the editor, an individual who was well informed on current events.

As soon as Nachum Leib had stepped out of the synagogue, I would be surrounded by numerous inquisitive congregation members, all thirsty for information. "What do the papers say?" they would ask eagerly. These Jews, all of whom were father's age, saw nothing demeaning in relying on a kid of my age for their information on current political intrigues. I was flattered by the esteem in which I was now held and held nothing back from the discerning inquirers. I would divulge the contents of the 'Daf' (as the newspaper was known), throwing in some commentary and analysis of my own for good measure. Getzil's 'Daf' was written in the commonly used jargon, Yiddish.

Back at home I was able to gain access to another valuable source of information on politics written in Hebrew, a newspaper called 'Hatzfira' (The Clarion), which was shared by four partners in all. These were Ben Tzion Barak, who ran a gift shop, a former scholar with a pot-belly and a razor-sharp tongue; my Uncle Shmuel, who frequently traveled abroad on business and, to give credit where credit is due, returned a partial scholar but still had difficulty understanding traditional Hebrew vocabulary that did not appear in the prayers and Mishnah. The third partner was Rabbi Moshe Sanders, a reserved and somewhat reticent individual but a man of vision. It was he who passed on the crumpled and dog-eared issues to father, the last in line who was rewarded for his patience by getting to keep the papers which he read at his leisure.

Father also set aside some time for me to read the papers. Not only did I read its contents with abounding enthusiasm but I also obeyed father's request not to dispose of the papers after I had finished with them. I would smooth out the pages, fold them carefully and then stack them on the shelf that had been fitted specifically for that purpose in the new kitchen. The hurried look through the pages of the Yiddish 'Der Friend' was not the same as a relaxing read of 'Hatzfira' written in Hebrew; nevertheless, both sources provided me with a wealth of information on Jewry in other parts of the world and international events in general.

* * *

The truth be known, I was not the only political commentator in our community. My closest rival was a boy named Elke. He was the son of an affluent family and a character who was out of place in our small town. His parents lived in Germany and exactly how they earned their livelihood remains unknown. His father died young, leaving a young spoiled widow and her baby without any means of support. One of her uncles, a textile exporter based in our town took her under his patronage and gave her a job in his office.

She was called Sophia, not a typical Jewish name, and she supported herself by her work for her uncle. The stories circulated about her by the usual neighborhood gossips were, as always, blown out of all proportion. She was fundamentally different from the rest of the Jewish women in the community. Her uncle was an affluent and devout man and it was thanks to him alone that the 'aristocrat' (as she was called by all the gossiping women) was not tempted into leaving the fold and mingling with the select group of atheists and backsliders who lived in our town. This group included people like Dr. Zabadia, Motti Schlachter, the chemist; Potternick, the lawyer, and others. The uncle exerted a form of custodial influence over her, gradually bringing her closer to a traditional Jewish life-style.

Once Elke had reached bar mitzvah age, father took over his education. Father was more attentive to him, either because of his family ties or possibly because of his unique breeding as reflected in his German accented Yiddish, his trim and immaculate appearance and his good manners.

He became my friend and on many occasions would stay on after his heder classmates had gone home. We would talk and play together in my house. However, our opinions on world events and leaders were diametrically opposed to each other. In the standoff that was now developing between Germany under Kaiser Wilhelm II and Russia under the rule of the Czar, I took the side of Germany, not so much out of love for Mordechai but rather hatred of Haman. I loathed the local 'Straznik' (patrolmen) and 'Uradnik' (police officers) who were the Czar's henchmen and rotten to the core. They continually harassed the local Jews and the bribes they demanded in return for revoking the various sanctions they themselves imposed were increased regularly.

* * *

Were we to itemize all the sanctions imposed by the evil empire on local Jews, the list would be endless. They were subject to a plethora of nauseating schemes; all devised by the 'Priestav' (local administrator) together with his sidekick, the 'Uradnik'. This was in addition to the array of taxes and local rates set by the national government which deliberately discriminated against the Jews as opposed to the rest of the poor population.

There was also a constant stream of abuse to which Jews were subjected, the worst of all being the blood libel, perpetuated and disseminated by the national government that inflamed the peasants, namely that Jews used Christian blood in the preparation of Matzot for Passover. This insidious diatribe was to cost the lives of many of our brethren in the pogroms that took place immediately prior to the holiday. In principle, the sanctions and restrictions placed by the administration on the Jews were targeted at adults.

The 'chiestata', which inflicted suffering on entire families including children, was one exception to the rule. What exactly did this decree entail? Chiestata is an entirely innocent word in Russian meaning hygiene. In this particular context, it was taken to refer to the apparent 'concern' of the Czar's government for the health of the dirty Jews who were instructed to burn all the garbage and refuse deposited on the streets in the backyards of their homes and shops.

Thursday was the high point of the week as it was market day. This was a day of hope for Jews who sought to earn as much as they could from the trade with local peasants who would arrive on their wagons from both near and far to trade with local Jewish merchants. The peasants would offer a diverse range of produce grown in their fields and gardens and would purchase household goods and tools that they needed.

Residents from local and outlying villages would begin arriving in town early in the morning on wagons hitched to horses of a rather unusual breed. These creatures were small in size and ate very little yet had tremendous strength. The peasant would hitch one of his horses to a wagon that had a metal grill mounted on top of the paneling on both sides of the wagon to prevent merchandise from falling off on the way. These would be secured by wooden boards tied to the paneling and then padded out with sacks of ground straw.

Once this was completed, the peasant could load up his wagon with agricultural produce. This usually consisted of sacks of grain, fruits and vegetables, eggs and poultry, sheep wool, a few hogs that were ready for sale and other such items. Sometimes the peasant would also tether a milking cow or a kosher animal for slaughter to the wagon as well as a horse that he had no use for on his farm, which he would either sell for cash or trade for another horse in an equitable barter. After he had finished loading up his wagon with produce, the peasant would make a place for himself and his spouse who would come out of the house dressed in her finest outfit made from the best materials and sewn either by herself or a kind neighbor. The peasant couple would then hoist their children, if any, on to the wagon with the aim of showing them the sights when they reached town or, alternatively, using their help at the marketplace. Once he had arrived, the peasant would detach the shafts and unhitch the horse from its harness. He would then either lead it to a nearby water trough or tie an open bag of oats around its neck allowing it to champ away.

The peasant would usually park his wagon at a regular site in the marketplace whereupon he would be immediately surrounded by customers, all handling the merchandise and inquiring about prices. Both sides would then engage in a standardized bluffing ritual. The buyers would snort with derision upon hearing the initial price quoted by the peasant and then feign a sudden loss of interest in the 'bargain' on offer by moving on to the wagon of a rival trader. The peasant would scratch his forehead, indicating he was ready to negotiate. A familiar process of haggling would then ensue, the peasant lowering his price by a few pennies and the buyer improving on his original offer by a similar amount.

Finally a deal would be struck. The buyer would take a few silver and copper coins, or a note of currency and gold coin if a larger sum was involved, out of his purse, count them into the waiting hand of the peasant and then depart with his newly purchased goods. The peasant would recount the money and set some aside for the purchase of essential items that he needed such as tools, lubricating oil for his wagon, salt and sugar for cooking, a sickle and scythe, a flint for tool sharpening and other such items required for tilling the land and producing crops, as well as materials used for spinning, textile dyeing, darning thread and others.

Most of the peasants were poor and the handful of loose change they earned at the market was barely enough to live on. They were in no position to be able to afford a meal at one of the local cafes while in town. The peasant's wife would bring out a lunch box that she had brought from home, lay a strip of coarse cloth over the seat of the wagon and then serve the meal which usually consisted of some slices of smoked bacon, a loaf of black bread baked the same morning, onions and cucumbers, all of which were rounded off with apples, pears or other fruits in season.

***

Those who had money to spend would make their way to one of the many Jewish cafes dotted all over town. On market day, these would be packed with peasants and their families. They would huddle together on long benches and in display of magnanimity, the peasant would order a bottle of wine for himself and a bottle of beer for his partner. The proprietor was always more than familiar with his customer's indulgences.

The owner would then place a selection of appetizers on the table that usually consisted of chopped or pickled savories, chopped liver seasoned with a selection of herbs, and roasted goose drumsticks, which the peasant would eat together with chunks of bread, all washed down with swigs from his bottle of wine or mug of cold draught beer. In the meantime, a neighbor or an acquaintance from another village would walk through the doorway to the warm welcome of his already seated compatriot. Jonas would buy a beer for his friend Jurgis and they would drink to each other's health; Jurgis would then return the compliment and they would once again toast each other.

The proprietor would always be more than happy at his guest's show of generosity and as the drinking continued, new desserts were produced in the form of a selection of confectionery that melted in one's mouth. After the bill had been paid with the last few coins from the peasant's purse, he and his friend would shuffle out into the street, arm in arm with their wives in tow, singing and drunkenly lurching from one side of the street to the other.

***

Soon it would be nighttime and on market day this heralded the approach of the dreaded hour of 'chiestata', the clean-up of the main street. The peasants' horses would be stamping their hoofs with irritation and impatience by now, anticipating the arrival of their masters who would once again hitch them to the wagons that they were to pull on the return journey to their stables. One by one, the wagons would pull out, leaving a vacuum in their wake. Within an hour, the market-place would be completely emptied of all wagons, horses, peasants and neighbors.

This vast stretch of land had been paved by a second-rate workman with cobblestones that overlapped, the jagged and roughly hewn stones jutting out above the smooth and neat sections of paving. The one thing they had in common was that by the end of market day they were all soiled with horse droppings, animal urine, and the vomit of drunks, who had thrown up the meal they had recently consumed. This was reason enough for them to curse the Jew who had coerced them into stuffing themselves with all the garbage his satanic wife had baked, cooked, fried and steamed, for one purpose only: To rob decent Catholics of their hard-earned money.

This torrent of verbal abuse, as bad as it was, was nothing compared to the horror that followed when the 'Straznik' patrolmen would materialize from out of the blue, filling the market place with their odious presence. Their barked orders were not long in coming: "You over there, sleeping on the job are you? It's chiestata time! Grab hold of that broom, rake and rubbish pail and get cracking." The task of cleaning the street was to take one hour and not a minute more. The people responsible for cleaning up and gathering those mounds of refuse were not permitted to move them again and so they would stay where they were for up to two days until Vininka, the apostate, who had a concession allowing him to use manure as fertilizer on his lands, would turn up on his garbage cart. He was usually accompanied by his sons, all of whom were stockily built, with mournful eyes like those of their grandfather, Yankel the blacksmith, who died of heart failure the same week that Benzi, his stubborn and rebellious son turned his back on his faith and his God, changing his name in the process. In short, piles of animal fertilizer swarming with flies do not detract from the infinite value of hygiene and purity, according to the authorities.

When the hour was up, one of the patrolmen, Jurk Vertinski, a crafty and malicious individual who also functioned as the local 'registrar' and was thus well-versed in the art of filing reports against those rancid Jews who neglected their cleaning duties thereby endangering public health, would proceed with his all too familiar ritual. Out came the notebook and spitting a drop of saliva on to the tip of his thick pencil, he would produce row after row of bold Cyrillic letters. On a certain day at a certain time, the lot belonging to the Jew 'X' was inspected following the completion of the 'Chiestata' and had not passed the test. The owner of the lot had clearly been derelict in his duties and had failed to uphold the law requiring him to comply with the requirements of the 'Chiestata' in the interests of public safety and hygiene.

This protocol would be forwarded to the courts as a matter of course and they in turn would issue a summons for the offender in question to be brought to trial and punished. But things usually didn't reach that stage and the protocol would never see the light of day again after it had been written. Yankele Terper, a close associate of the 'Priestav', would find a way of placating the town's law-abiding officials. This usually entailed the remittance of a small gratuity in respect of such mediation. Two rubles would usually suffice, though sometimes the price rose to three. The 'Priestav' would take his cut with the rest being divided between the 'Uradnik' and his men. The mediator swore he never kept anything back for himself but his insistence failed to convince the usual band of skeptics.

***

One way or another, the whole 'Chiestata' business was sheer hell for everybody. In my home it was particularly hard on mother, worn out as she was after a full day's work and she needed all the help she could get from the men in the family in order to cope with this awesome chore. Father always came to her aid and I followed suit. Armed with the ultimate in cleaning and sterilizing tools - in this case a couple of brooms with tough bristles - we would set about cleaning up all the refuse and garbage that had gotten wedged in the crevices of the cobbled paving. Along with the brooms, there came the dustpan, rake, and shovel, all essential tools for the task of cleaning. The shovel, of course, complemented the work performed with the three previously mentioned implements, its role being crucial to the successful completion of the task at hand.

Father and I worked as a team. He would gather heaps of garbage with the broom and I would stand opposite him holding the shovel in readiness. However, the task of carrying the shovel filled with the recently collected filth over to the large mound of refuse could not be entrusted to children for fear of possible spillage en route, an event that would render all our efforts futile. We would converse with our neighbors who were also engaged in the same activity and together we would bitterly curse the hygiene loving tyrants whose sole aim was to persecute Jews to the point of total degradation in the hope of finding opportunities to file protocols against them whenever possible. The vindictive 'Chiestata' ritual was not one of the worse sanctions imposed on Jews but it was a weekly ordeal and each time father was subjected to public humiliation all over again. The sight of his prostrate figure, broom in hand with his gabardine tucked under his waistband caused me considerable anguish and I have never be able to forget this insult

***.

The hatred I bore for the authorities grew in its intensity and I prayed with all my heart for the downfall of this evil empire. In my wildest dreams, I imagined myself to be the supreme commander of the combined forces of Palestine and under my leadership we would wipe those 'Strazniks' off the face of the earth, with any remaining taken captive and put on trial as written in the book of Isaiah.

So it was only to be expected that when I became an expert in politics and diplomacy, I sided with Russia's enemies in accordance with the well-known axiom: 'My enemy's enemy is my friend'. Since the empire of the German Kaiser was one of Russia's enemies, I considered myself an ardent supporter of this country. It was as not as if I had ever seen a map of Germany with my own eyes. Elke was my only source of information and from him I understood that the people there spoke a form of bastardized Yiddish and the Jews were different from those in our town, in their speech, temperament and lifestyle.

In short, Kaiser Wilhelm had won the loyalty of Rabbi Meir's youngest son and I eagerly awaited the opportunity to prove this loyalty to my new-found allies and show my Russian enemies a generous display of brute force. Surprisingly, the one person who had nothing but scathing remarks to make about Germany was none other than Elke who had moved to our town from the land of 'Teich' (Germany in Yiddish). "The Germans, all the Germans, are anti-Semites", was his unequivocal verdict. I didn't know what the word anti-Semite meant but from the vehemence and contempt with which Elke uttered that word, I gathered it was not terribly complimentary towards the Jews. He chose not to elaborate on the subject, but I sensed that his reluctance towards Germans was born out of his own experiences at home.

His mother Sophia's earlier life in Germany was shrouded in a veil of secrecy. Later on when we were older, Elke confided in me and revealed her traumatic experiences. Her German husband, a dentist and a drunk, beat her regularly and finally walked out, never to be seen again, leaving her and her young child to fend for themselves. However, at this particular time in our lives I was still unaware of Elke's own family history and so we found ourselves disagreeing profoundly over our attitude towards these two empires that had suddenly become the focus of international interest and concern. By the time World War One had broken out, I had already left home and no longer had access to my sources of political enlightenment, namely the newspapers written in Yiddish and traditional Hebrew.

***

That year one of my older sisters came home for a visit during summer, departing from the usual custom of only visiting during the holiday season. It transpired that my two older sisters had dedicated themselves to pedagogical training and had successfully qualified as primary school teachers practicing the 'Farbel' method, used by Yechiel Halperin, a Jewish educator from Warsaw (who was the father of the author Jonathan Ratush of blessed memory) and the scholar, Uzi Ornan.

A new trend had begun to sweep the country at that time, childrens' nurseries. The Zionists, in their role of propagators of our ancient language, were at the forefront of this new trend and actively promoted the establishment of nurseries that would use Hebrew as the language of communication. Yechiel Halperin was one of the key figures in the movement and he founded a seminary for training primary school teachers who would use this particular method in the course of their subsequent employment. It was not long before a rival educator from within the same community, Alterman, father of the poet Natan Alterman, entered the scene. Since Halperin was promoting the method of nursery school education that had been devised by 'Farbel', Alterman opted for an entirely different method of teaching devised by a Mrs. Montessori. Farbel and Montessori both devised methods of nursery school teaching that broke new ground in the field and Alterman and Halperin, in their roles of rival protagonists, were the ardent exponents of these methods within the Jewish community.

Halperin had the good fortune of having Rabbi Meir's daughters choose to complete their vocational training at his institution. This should not be taken to imply that father deliberately chose to exile his daughters. Not at all! The decision to move to a location as distant as Warsaw was of their own choosing and in defiance of father's wishes. He had plans to lead them to the marital canopy and from there to a life of communal service but they had opted to pursue their education to the point of graduating with full matriculation. But it didn't end there.

The two daughters subjected their father to even more shame when they failed to return home after receiving their 'attestat zrelosti' (matriculation certificate), choosing instead to stay away for another year or two, eking out a meager living by giving private lessons. They cut back on their food and other expenses. At the Halperin school, they met other progressive minded girls like themselves, among them the future actress, Hannah Rovina. Thus, Meir had the honor of having his daughters' number among the very first Hebrew primary school teachers to work in Israel, an honor he would have gladly conceded.

Father was enraged by his daughters' rebellious conduct. Not only had they deserted their home in favor of exile to a place of Torah study but they also succeeded in corrupting their younger brother, a handsome boy of noble character with a sharp tongue and a passion for poetry. The eldest siblings had left their father's custody forever. They made do with the bare necessities and earned a meager living giving private lessons, but they did not flinch from physical labor either. Father never discovered that his educated and refined daughters also slaved away in a confectionery factory.

***

The factory in question was in fact nothing more than a long room with a small window that let in a limited amount of light. The atmosphere was stifling during both summer and winter. There were large urns filled with sweet contents which would stand on tripods under which a fire would be lit that would burn for hours causing the mixture inside to become a sizzling sweet mush that gave off a pungent aroma. The owner's wife, a buxom individual with a keen sense of taste, would stay in the room continuously since her particular role was twofold. She would regularly taste the bubbling mixture with a wooden spatula and add sugar or spices if required while keeping a watchful eye over the consumptive girls - whose eyes had become bloodshot from all the smoke - who worked on the production line. This was to insure they were not tempted to help themselves to some of the finished products thereby violating the commandment 'Thou shalt not steal'.

Usually, the girls singled out for supervision were the ones that worked at long tables covered with shining foil, rolling lumps of congealed sweet mixture into biscuit shaped pieces with their rolling pins. These would then be transferred to an adjacent table where another team of girls would slice them into small portions using a double-bladed cutting tool. These divine tasting sweets would be wrapped in foil covering only and this meant they were cheap. The wrapping on the better quality sweets would usually display the head of a pretty girl wearing a brimmed covering with a floral design on the sides. The benefit from the extra packaging was the fact that they increased the value of the merchandise, as opposed to home-made products.

The confectionery girls were all Jewish, a prerequisite that was essential to prevent Gentile hands coming into direct contact with the foodstuff in question, an act that would bring its Kashrut into doubt. They were from poor homes and their modest income helped their families make ends meet. The starting rate for the job was five kopecks a day, going up to ten kopecks as staff progressed in seniority and experience. Only a few girls reached the higher ranks and Rabbi Meir's two daughters were among them. In addition to their work on the production line, they earned an extra three rubles from the private lessons they gave.

As a result of their socialist leanings, my two sisters preferred hard labor in the factory in the company of their comrades to private lessons in the homes of wealthy executives. While rolling the sweet mixture with their rolling pins, they explained the theories of Marx, Engels and Lasalle - two of whom were Jews themselves - to the other girls, assuring them that socialism was egalitarian in nature and did not discriminate between people of different nationalities and faiths. The main task that lay before the proletariat from all countries was to rise up in unison and topple the evil and brainless Czar and his henchmen from power. The spirit of harmony and love would then prevail and the ignorant proletariat would finally understand that its real enemy was capitalism and not the Jews as the criminals in St Petersburg had continually claimed. On the day that occurred, the masses would awaken to the truth and as a result they would distance themselves from hatred of the Jews. This would be cause for celebration since the Jews were part of the proletariat themselves.

The weary workers were not able to understand all the eloquent vocabulary emanating from the intelligent Lithuanians but sensed it was all said with their best interests in mind. They liked the impassioned sisters and ensured that they came to no harm by making sure the factory owner did not hear of the fiery rhetoric they were uttering in condemnation of wealth and in favor of revolution by, and in the name, of the underprivileged of society. As soon as anyone suspicious would approach, a signal would be given and the seditious conversation would be cut short. It was found that the best way of giving the alert was by breaking into popular songs that warmed the heart. These were usually romantic melodies that sang of the love of a maid whose soul longs for reunion with her chosen mate who has been drafted into military service. He would respond in kind by singing of the woes and troubles inflicted on him by his anti-Semitic colleagues, and the power of his everlasting love for her in spite of all the hardships.

***

Suffering of this kind was not half as bad as that which my sisters had to endure in the course of the private lessons they gave. As a rule, my sisters' pupils were spoiled half-witted brats who were incapable of successfully mastering the art of proper handwriting using the Cyrillic alphabet, which is written from left to right and then read in the opposite direction. The lucky pupil would sit with his private teacher in the drawing room. The robust mistress of the house, key chain hanging from her apron, would make frequent appearances in the drawing room so as to ensure that the teacher was not wasting valuable time.

Every few minutes the mistress's offspring would find an excuse to interrupt the lesson, the most common reason being that he needed to use the bathroom. This would also provide the opportunity to pinch his younger brother, antagonize the housemaid with one of his infantile pranks, and then round off the brief adventure by scrounging something appetizing from his mother's kitchen as a bribe for agreeing to return to his teacher and the extremely dull 'Uchebnik' (textbook) from which he was supposed to be studying. The teacher would wait for her pupil's return and once he had done so the whole routine would begin all over again.

When payday arrived, the mistress would make a reckoning of all the time wasted during lessons as a result of the teacher's inability to control her pupil but ultimately she would back down and with a condescending air would make the sanctimonious gesture of paying the teacher in full. My proud and bashful sisters would endure the degrading ritual and on receiving the ruble note they would offer a muffled 'spasiba' (thank you) and take their leave, humiliated to the depths of their soul.

***

Still some teachers became deeply attached to their pupils. Anyone who was able to find a suitable position would consider herself fortunate but there weren't that many around. The majority of employers were nothing but a bunch of arrogant misers. As far as they were concerned those brought in to coach their children were nothing more than a servant over whom a constant vigil had to be maintained so as to be sure she was indeed working for her keep and not eating them out of house and home. Therefore, the mistress of the house would assume the task of verifying that resident tutor gave full value for money. The plight of those teenagers who gave regular private lessons was not as dire because no matter how bad the abuse they were subjected to during their course of their work, they could always walk away when it was over. Those engaged in "conditioning" work (a live-in arrangement) had no set hours to speak of and were condemned to a state of bondage day and night.

Many a pillow was drenched with the tears of "conditioning" victims, usually sensitive girls from poor families who were bullied and badgered by these foul-mouthed employers.

Sometimes the mistress in question would be jealous of her refined manners or beauty, qualities that she and her own children had not been endowed with. The odious creature would never miss an opportunity to insult the young teacher in her employ, even in the presence of her pupils. Under the circumstances it was hardly surprising, that those unruly children, having observed their teacher being ridiculed, felt free to make their teacher's life a misery.

My eldest sister, being the proud and passionate socialist that she was positively loathed the prospect of working in a "conditioning" position and would have preferred any form of hard labor to this job which she viewed as demeaning to the core. However, upon graduating from the Halperin Institute, she was left with two options: Either to return home or submit to the cruel regime that would most likely be her lot if she worked in "conditioning." Having developed an aversion for life at home under father's authoritarian guidance, she chose the latter.

***

Rabbi Meir's daughters survived on bread and water only, living in a decrepit little room on the fourth floor of an apartment block in a run-down neighborhood where pollution and filth reigned supreme. The two sisters were fortunate enough to have each other for support. Once a week they would sit down and write a postcard home, half in traditional Hebrew to father and the other half in Yiddish to mother. The primary rule of life is that experience is the best teacher of all and Rabbi Meir's daughters soon realized that the postcards were simply not large enough to accommodate a full letter from both of them, and so a solution was called for.

They established a routine by which one sister would write a letter with all her news and the other would add a one line greeting at the end. In the next postcard, they would swap roles but whoever was writing always took care to make her characters as small as possible so as to pack in as much information as possible about their activities in the bustling metropolis. Rabbi Meir's daughters, being the gifted scholars that they were, made sure the content of their letters was tailored to the interests of the recipients back home. The section in Hebrew that was addressed to father was full of praise for the pedagogical approach, illustrating how infants are taught good behavior and how songs and games are employed to make learning as interesting and as entertaining as possible. Father would read through the part of the letter addressed to him a couple of times and then relate it to mother, praising the flair of the letter while nevertheless disagreeing with its contents.

It was not a question of whether the matters raised were trivial or not, but rather there were more important things to be considered.

Although nothing was explicitly said, I realized that what was missing from my sisters' letters was not another theory on pedagogical methods, an important subject in its own right, but the good news that a decent match had been arranged for one or both of them by someone in the city, an event that would give their parents some satisfaction. Girls inferior to them in both education and family lineage were married and now had children. My sisters, on the other hand, educated and as unconventional as they were, had a dowry in property guaranteed as part of their inheritance from their grandfather, yet they chose to evade the entire issue. They were too busy putting the world right but when would they start putting their own house in order?

Once father had finishing airing his grievances he would pass the letter on to mother. Although well educated, she was not up to the level of reading traditional Hebrew written in minute characters and the section of the letter addressed to her was in Yiddish. In these lines, the daughters gave a frank account of their hardships. They wrote about life in the city in general, they told of their visits to the theater, and described the plays they had seen in great detail.

Occasionally more down to earth matters would be mentioned like food, clothing and shelter. There was no need to go into details since it only took a few well-chosen phrases to give mother a clear hint that her two daughters were living in dire poverty. From time to time she would make up a parcel containing several types of spread, sweet breads and two pairs of thermal underwear. It was only to be expected that she put aside such items to send to her daughters whom she was sure were feeling the bitter cold. It was no secret that the city had no shortage of greedy and miserly individuals and mother could not rule out the possibility that her girls were boarded with a vile landlady who skimped on wood for heating during winter, so some warm clothing would certainly be welcome.

Mother knew how much her daughters appreciated these parcels. So late at night, after father had fallen asleep over his book and finally retired to his room (it was better than this work be done without him around since they would only get embroiled in the same argument over again about whether they as parents were to blame for their daughters going astray), she would then fish out a well-padded cardboard carton which would be used to mail the package to the city. She would line the box with newspaper and packaging material and placed the underwear and other items of clothing at the bottom. Laying a strip of coarse paper on top of the clothes, she filled the rest of the carton with a few slices of dried cheese, a jar of cherry flavored jam, a jar of raspberry jam (which she hoped they would have no need for since this was mainly used for medicinal purposes) and a jar of fried goose fat which, after becoming solid, would assume an amber like color making it an extremely tempting sight. Last, but by no means least, would come the honey cake or 'lekech' as we called it, a traditional delicacy that was everyone's favorite. The following morning mother would take the parcel to the shop from where it would be collected by Nachum Leib, the postman who sent it off with the first delivery. The reason he went to all this bother was because he was something of a scholar himself and, as such, he silently applauded Rabbi Meir's daughters for the hard work they were investing in their future careers at so great a cost.

On receipt of the parcel, the weary young women would be overcome with joy and bless their mother for her thoughtfulness with mother receiving full credit for her handiwork. Father disassociated himself from mother's charitable activity, preferring not to get involved in any way. Mother kept him informed of what she was doing but he always feigned total disinterest as he was extremely bitter at his daughters' decision to go against his will.

***

Some conduct could hardly go without rebuke and the opportunity would present itself once or twice a year during Passover and the religous New Year when the prodigal offspring came home to their parents for a few days. When it came time to leave, after father and his daughters had argued, reasoned and remonstrated with one another until their voices were hoarse, father would closet himself in his room until he regained his composure. Finally, he would re-emerge with two ten ruble notes in his hand and with a somber look he handed them over to the youngest of my two sisters since the elder sister, being the dyed in the wool socialist that she was, took no interest in money matters and totally relied on her younger sister's discretion.

Although she was always reluctant to take any money from father, she did not really have any choice but to accept his helping hand. There were no kisses or fond farewells on my sisters' departure. Father would mutter a farewell and then follow it with what sounded like a prayer but might also have been a random observation, "There are observant Jews in the city as well." The hint having been dropped, father would hurry back to his duties clearing his throat noisily.

***

The fortunes of my other sister, Peska, took a different path. Perpetual illness had worn her down. When she arrived home on our neighbor Mendel's horse and cart together with two 'Karzinot' (wicker baskets) filled to bursting point, she was on the verge of total collapse. Apart from a few clothes and personal effects, her luggage consisted solely of literature, poetry and textbooks that she had purchased with her hard-earned cash at a second-hand bookshop at giveaway prices.

This constituted the spiritual enrichment that would support her during her stay in the 'province', ensuring the studies and skills she had acquired at the institute of the revered Yechiel Halperin would stay fresh in her mind.

Mother only had to take one look at her daughter to realize she had become emaciated to a degree that could prove fatal if not checked. This usually placid woman, who always deferred to her husband's will, took a firm stand now that an emergency had developed. The following morning while my sister was still asleep upstairs recuperating from the strains of her tortuous journey, mother addressed her husband in a clear and unequivocal manner: "Peska looks as thin as a rail and God only knows how ill she really is. As soon as Shabbat is over, God willing, I shall go to Shovitzei and rent a dacha for her in the 'gypsies' forest'. This was a forest with huge sprawling pine trees and small houses that were let to Jews who loved visiting the countryside during the summer months. It became known as the 'gypsies' forest' on account of the bands of traveling gypsies who set up camp there. They made a living by breeding horses and pilfering whatever they could get their hands on but they were careful not to accost visitors since this would result in them being chased off the premises.

Father was level-headed enough to realize that in announcing her decision regarding the renting of a dacha for their daughter, mother was not asking for his approval but merely appraising him of a decision she was determined to see through. It may well have been that father himself was horrified at the appearance of his daughter and did not object in principle to the idea of a dacha although certain key issues had to be addressed such as who would stay with the girl? It was improper for a daughter of Israel to be left all on her own in the forest and most certainly not within proximity of anonymous holiday makers. This was not considered respectable in our part of the world.

After failing to succeed in persuading her neighbor to allow her eldest daughter to join my sister at the dacha, dear mother came up with a rather unusual idea: "We will send the boy with his sister. He also looks a bit off color due to his constant studying." At first father was less than enthusiastic about the unsavory prospect of this protracted neglect of Torah study while the lad was in the charge of his educated sister. But the current emergency situation could not be brushed aside and he acknowledged the fact that on this occasion his will would not prevail. The issue of renting a dacha for his daughter was a matter of life and death and as far as the neglect of Torah was concerned, I was willing to solemnly promise I would take the Gemara volume with me and set aside a few hours each day for study. Father cautioned me that on my return, he would test me on the Gemara pages I had learned while on holiday. The dacha trip was on!

***

How many days of sheer unforgettable bliss does a person experience throughout his life? Very few to be precise and these are firmly entrenched in his memory like a heavenly gift to be remembered for eternity. Mother rented us a small peasant's cottage with a straw roof, situated in the depths of the forest on a bare patch within a cluster of pine trees. The cottage was new and it looked as if it had been specially built in our honor. When we arrived, the shell had only just been completed and the doors and windows fitted, yet in spite of this the building was incomplete and the workmen, apparently the peasant owner, together with his family, had yet to add the finishing touches. The glossy timber gave off a sharp pleasant aroma that mingled with the fragrance of the surrounding pine trees. The the moist perfumed smell of the earth, with black currants and blue berries sprouting in every corner of the moist and dusky landscape were waiting in anticipation of their being picked.

I had never been in a dacha before, and I had never enjoyed such total freedom in my life. I and could do whatever I pleased! Did I break my promise and abandon my Torah study now that I was not being supervised? Heaven forbid! Not only did I not neglect my Torah study but I even added on an extra hour. Every day as twilight approached, having already completed my quota of study time from nine in the morning until midday, I would sit down again with the Gemara volume and study a bit extra.

My sister did not deride my Torah study and even enjoyed listening to my melodious tones when I was learning. When she was feeling in a good mood, she would give me a surprise, which was usually a piece of the honey cake mother had sent us that week and would continue to send every week during our holiday. My sister displayed considerable proficiency in the Gemara, especially in those parts that dealt with Jewish folklore. Apparently, she was an expert on the book jointly written by Bialik and Ravinitski that had recently been published and was considered an essential textbook for all Yechiel Halperin's graduates.

On the face of it, my life had changed little over the past year. I was still studying the Gemara tractate 'Ketubot' plus commentaries for a set period every day. So did the dacha really make any difference? What had all the arguments and deliberations been for? What was so special about a dacha anyway? There was no shortage of food at home. Our cow produced a bucket full of milk three times a day, and this provided an ample supply of butter, yogurt and cheese. Our garden, which extended from the bottom of the hill all the way to the Kupka River, provided all the vegetables we needed. Our house and cellar were well-stocked with onions, radishes, carrots and potatoes.

So perhaps it was the fresh air that made the place so special? The forest certainly had air and fragrances that were known to be beneficial to health, especially for those people with lung complaints. We may not have had pine trees growing in our back yard but the surrounding area was full of shrubbery and plants, many of which were deadly such as the prickly nettle bush which was to be avoided at all costs and the chrysanthemum produced a form of sunflower seed that tasted great. So with all this in town, what business did I have leaving home for the gypsies forest?

The actual novelty of this trip boiled down to the wonderful time I spent in my sister's company alone at the dacha. She used the holiday to practice the Farbel method in its Hebrew form, i.e. children's games combined with Hebrew songs that had delightful melodies. My sister was an expert at getting programs organized and utilizing time to the full. "To every thing there is a season and a time for every purpose." These words from the Book of Ecclesiastes were the basis of a formula that I now apply to myself. A time for Torah and a time for prayer, and I never prayed so fervently as I did during that brief spell at the dacha.

Following the afternoon break, my sister assembled all the children of holidaymakers in the area and played several Hebrew games such as 'the shepherd's watch' Eventually after continuous practicing, even those girls who had not attended heder had mastered the words and melody of the song. I still remember the verses to this day:

> Around the bonfire the shepherds gathered
> Singing and dancing till morning, tra-la-la
> From midnight the soldiers will sing

We'll keep watch till the dawn of morning

Beware o wolf of the forest, stay clear of our flock

Do not come near, do not attack

Cause with our sailor's clubs

And our sheepdog

We'll keep driving you back.

Due to my relationship with the songstress and my mastery of the language, I was chosen to play almost any part and this won me the admiration of all the other children as well as the overt affection of beautiful Masha whom I came to love passionately like Jacob's love for Rachel, David's love for Michal, the daughter of Saul, and Amnon's love for Tamar. This did not refer to the cold and callous Amnon who slighted his sister Tamar, the king's daughter, but the Amnon who appeared in the book entitled 'The Love of Zion', a hero whose valor was matched by his handsome looks and noble acts. In short I loved Masha!

We played several different games. One game that comes to mind was called 'the tramp'. One of us would play the tramp and dressing up in rags, he would wander back and forth carrying his stick and backpack, looking for a place to stay. All the places would be taken and the tramp would rap his stick on the ground entreating all those present to give him shelter. Suddenly a wave of unrest would sweep over the children and all at once they would begin circling the area in a game of musical chairs. The tramp would see his opportunity and lunge at one of the vacant seats before the commotion had died down. The last child still standing would become the next tramp to beg for shelter in a wailing voice. We would join him in his song:

A poor man comes a knocking

tick, tick, tack

kind people open your doors to me

tick, tick, tack

day and night I've been wondering

tick, tick, tack

give me board and lodging

tick, tick, tack

through the valleys and mountains I've been traveling

tick, tick, tack

just for tonight I'll be resting

tick, tick, tack

and then gone with the wind by morning

tick, tick, tack.

And then there was the 'Ten Sisters' song that I found enchanting:

Ten little sister birds singing in the forest

One little bird flew away

And there were nine little........

I learned many songs throughout the course of my life but none of them compared with the delightful repertoire of songs that my sister brought with her from the Halperin Institute.

We were an odd bunch in that group; three and four-year-olds together with nine and ten year olds, boys together with girls, Chumash children together with Gemara pupils, a proper little Noah's ark. My sister was the one who made it all work, with games and songs in Hebrew that entertained not just us but all the fathers, mothers, brothers, sisters and casual visitors who gathered to watch our group at play and then found themselves joining in.

Fortunately, or perhaps unfortunately for me, I was unable to keep up my usual custom of reading the newspapers while I was away in the forest. During the first few weeks of our stay in the gypsies' forest, we completely forget what a newspaper looked like. These were holidays and were not to be encroached on by the political machinations of the outside world. In all, I received two letters from father addressed to me personally, which made me feel quite flattered. He asked how I was getting on with my Torah study and gave me the latest news about the minyan, as well as a few words of fatherly encouragement. No mention was made of the gathering storm of conflict between the Austrian empire and the strong men in the Russian Czar's camp over the murder in Sarajevo of the Austrian heir to the throne. The Russian Czar had taken Serbia's side and prevented Germany from coming to the aid of her ally, the grand old Emperor Franz Joseph who sought revenge for the murder of his heir.

I was totally oblivious of the conflict that was now brewing since I was far away in the gypsies' forest where I was more concerned with the business at hand than with articles, telegrams or arguments with Elke and other friends. Hence, I was unable to comment on the events that were currently unfolding. The turmoil was raging without my knowledge. When finally, on the day war broke out, a telegram arrived ordering us to return home, I rubbed my eyes in disbelief and was heartbroken. It was like someone being ordered to leave paradise, being blamed for other peoples' misdemeanors and taking punishment instead of them.

* * *

We returned home to a state of total mayhem. War had been declared in our country. On the face of it, this was a war between two Gentile nations and was no concern of ours. Although we were Russian citizens, we did not take any interest in public affairs, adhering to the rule laid down by the ethics of the forefathers: 'Do not consort with authority'. We interpreted this warning as meaning that it was best for Jews not to get involved in public affairs in their countries of exile, regardless of the circumstances. This time, however, we felt we were being dragged into a horrendous war against our will. It wasn't long before draft notices were issued to all those Jews who had served in the Russian army.

The number of Jews serving in the Russian armed forces was small, a situation that was largely due to the official hatred of and crude discrimination against Jews, deprived of their human rights, and an array of malicious sanctions aimed at curbing their personal freedom. In addition, there were numerous legal provisions guaranteeing benefits for citizens, which all had an addendum consisting of two vicious words in Russian: 'Krome Evre'ev' meaning 'Jews not included'. And as if that wasn't enough, the Jews had to contend with a string of blood libels and the perpetual abuse of Jewish soldiers who had to endure starvation throughout their tour of duty in the absence of any kosher food and were never allowed to rise any higher than the rank of private. The Jews felt nothing but contempt and utter loathing for their Russian counterparts and it was hardly surprising that on reaching conscription age, Jewish citizens did whatever they could to avoid military service. They enacted every possible relevant clause in the law that might effect a discharge and if there was no alternative, they moved to other countries before they were old enough to be eligible for conscription.

In spite of all this, there were still a few Jewish boys in each community who enlisted in the armed forces and spent up to four or five years away from home, bullied and abused from start to finish. They had barely arrived home after being discharged when the entire nightmare would begin all over again. They received a notice recalling them to active duty on behalf of the 'motherland', Holy Russia and the divine savior Czar Nicholas II. The sound of heartrending crying and wailing could be heard in the houses of the families of these recruits. They and their families would frantically run around from one official to the next hoping to get some help in saving them from the dreadful fate. Very few succeeded and most bade a tearful farewell to their loved ones and reported to the local recruitment offices from where they were shipped off to an unknown fate.

***

An atmosphere of gloom mixed with trepidation overwhelmed the Jewish community in our town. Every day, hundreds of young Gentile recruits from nearby villages would descend on the town where they were to report for enlistment at the local recruitment office. In keeping with the tradition set by their fathers i.e. drowning their sorrow and anxiety in drink, they would head for the local cafes which would all be packed to capacity. After having drunk themselves sick, they would go on a rampage through the streets of the town

The four 'Strazniks' and their commander the 'Uradnik' who were responsible for law and order in the town and were well-aware of the state of terror in which the Jews lived, would disappear from sight leaving the Jews exposed to the thuggery of the marauding visitors. Jewish community officials would immediately raise the sum that was required to flush out the inconspicuous law enforcers. Once all the 'king's men' had received their share according to their rank, they would reappear on the streets, resplendent in their dress uniforms, royal hats and swords tucked in their belts. As soon as they reappeared, the 'revelers' would instantly disperse and the Jews would breathe a sigh of relief. Once the new recruits had moved on to their designated postings, life in town would generally return to normal and those people who had been affected by the recent disruption kept their experiences to themselves.

Shabtai, the sexton of the local minyan, who had always put the fear of God in us boisterous children and stopped us from playing games inside the synagogue or even out in the yard, wandered around looking crestfallen. His recitals of the daily 'Shmone Esre' prayer had turned into one long wail. "Hear our voice o Lord, our God, have mercy and pity on us and accept our prayers with compassion and mercy." As he said those words, tears would stream down his face since his prayers were specifically for his son, Gershon, who had returned home from military service a year ago and was about to get married when he was conscripted once again and sent off to the front. There were other families who had also been forced to part from relatives that had been recalled to military service and were now piercing the skies with their emotional invocations.

***

My family had so far remained unaffected by the whole crisis. I returned to my Rabbi and my Torah study, and also resumed my daily perusal of the newspapers and my political analysis with enthusiasm. To give credit where credit is due, the thick bearded community members did not consider it beneath their dignity to talk to youngsters like me about either Torah or secular matters. I recall with no small amount of satisfaction, one elderly community member who frequently approached me in the synagogue with a query regarding the Gemara tractate he was currently studying. He would come across a couple of lines that totally stumped him and without hesitating he would ask me for my help.

And if it was all right to consult with a child on Torah matters, then there was certainly nothing wrong in asking him about current political affairs. I soon became famous for my expertise on the latest developments and was approached for information by everybody: "What do today's papers say Zalmenkeh? What's news from the front"? they would ask fixing me with an intense gaze. At first glance, everything looked crystal clear. According to the telegrams in our paper, the invincible Russian army under the supreme command of his royal highness, the valiant Nikolai Nikolaevitch, was making short work of the current offensive having crossed the Prussian border, and was now approaching the outskirts of Koeningsburg, a large city in the Prussian state in the course of its unstoppable drive towards Berlin.

The telegrams themselves were extremely brief. The official commentary from the authorities did the rest, describing the victorious advance of our glorious armed forces in great detail. The artillery, cavalry and infantry with their shining bayonets were sweeping through the land of the German infidels. Large numbers of prisoners and a substantial amount of loot had been captured. In short, the whole campaign was a runaway success. It wouldn't be long before the arrogant Kaiser Wilhelm would be on his knees begging us for a truce. Such wishful thinking! An optical illusion is always preferable to the truth.

As proof of the victories described in the telegrams, a carefully chosen selection of pictures designed to give the right impression began appearing in the papers. There one could see the heroes of the Russian armed forces on their trusty steeds chasing the pathetic Germans who were falling back in disarray in the face of the advancing armies. The telegram page was full of items like this and only the more discerning readers were astute enough to notice the ambivalent innuendoes contained in the reports, which were intended to ward off any unwanted interference from the censorship authority. Anyone who raised people's doubts by questioning the superiority of the Russian army was asking for trouble.

* * *

Elke, my political adversary with an anathema to Germany as a result of the manner in which his mother was treated by, was clearly delighted with the progress of the war and held great faith in the authenticity of the pictures of Russian heroes in hot pursuit of the retreating Germans. I tried to gently reason with him, suggesting that the news contained in the telegrams may have been somewhat overstated and the developments depicted in the pictures appeared to be one-sided. Drawings hardly constitute concrete evidence in their own right. To be perfectly frank, he was less than enamored with my commentary and assessment. In fact, I had great difficulty in convincing anybody to support my view that all the stories about spectacular victories and breaching enemy lines were nothing but utter nonsense.

As luck would have it, my salvation came from an unexpected source. My Rabbi and teacher, Rabbi Yossef Alperovitch, the leader of the Lubavitch community in our town, always avoided making any public comments on current affairs. "And the scholar shall fall silent at that time" was how he put it to me and the hint was crystal clear. However, when we were on our own, he would often take time off from our Torah lessons to impart his views on politics to me and I was pleased to discover we had in identical train of thought.

In his calm and collected voice, he explained to me that a corrupt regime like that of the Czar and his cronies was no guarantee of victory on the battlefield. It was highly doubtful whether there was a shred of truth in the telegrams describing all those supposed military triumphs. Even if the Russians had succeeded in crossing the German border, this did not mean the war was over. "The successful execution of war requires valor and wisdom, and the tactics employed can often be quite deceiving", said the Rabbi. "It could well be that the German minister of war ordered his forces to retreat so as to draw the Czar's army into a trap they have waiting. The Lord God moves in mysterious ways and we should certainly not jump to any conclusions. Time will tell." At the end of the conversation, the Rabbi warned me several times not to repeat anything he had said in public. I understood his intentions and honored his request. We kept such discussions to ourselves.

I was glad the Rabbi had now reached the end of the Gemara tractate 'Ketubot', which we had been laboring over for some months now. In accordance with the times, the celebration held at the Rabbi's home was low key. I read the final page together with several of the Rabbi's loyal followers and I gave a perfunctory explanation of the text we had just read. They recited the refrain and accompanying prayer after me and then, much to my surprise, mother came into the Rabbi's house carrying one of her honey cakes. Father then took a bottle of wine out of his coat pocket and the Rabbi's wife served tea and cherry jam, a clear sign of the nonchalant atmosphere that currently prevailed. The Rabbi broke out into song and we all joined in. Halfway through our singing the Rabbi opened the Gemara tractate 'Baba Batra' which had been chosen as my next project. He then gave a brief sermon in honor of the assembled guests, following which we departed, the spirit of Torah fresh in our minds.

* * *

The disaster that was to strike a few days later while I was hard at work on the first chapter of 'Baba Batra' was totally unexpected. Disasters strike without any prior warning, including those that take place on the battlefield. I was still bemoaning the alleged victories of Czar

Nikolai Nikolaevitch's uncle, the commander in chief of the armed forces, reflecting on the words of the prophet Jeremiah, "Why is the way of the wicked successful"?

I had begun to keep my political opinions to myself and was minding my own business that day when Mendel, the coachman, came into the synagogue for afternoon prayers with the latest news. He had just come from the railway station and witnessed a convoy of passenger and freight trains making their way east. These were all packed to capacity with wounded soldiers being transported from the front to military hospitals and pandemonium had broken loose. The soldiers were in desperate need of first aid and water and the medical orderlies were rushing from one carriage to the next, screaming, cursing and jostling one another, all powerless to help the wounded soldiers who were bleeding profusely and groaning in pain.

A few compassionate nurses were begging staff at the railway station for a little 'Kipyatok' (hot water) with which to wash the soldiers' wounds and, as if cursed by bad luck, the large boiler had broken down. To sum up, it was all one awful mess!

Mendel's news was in stark contradiction to the reports in that morning's 'Der Friend' which kept up the official line of reporting of victories and triumphant conquests. Something had gone wrong at the Prussian front and as yet we had no idea as to what had happened. It was only on the following day that the papers began to adopt a more reserved tone, providing a brief cursory report of Nikolai Nikolaevitch's decision to halt his army's advance and regroup at the front. The telegrams were carefully worded so as not to frighten the public back home, which until now had been fed with bombastic accounts of victory and glory on the western front. But the stark truth was now beginning to filter through.

The German high command had cleverly drawn the Russian armed forces away from their supply depots. The inept and now isolated Russian army, having fallen for the ploy, had charged forward leaving its rear completely exposed, straight into the trap the Germans had prepared for them. In the surprise counterattack that followed, the armies of Czar Nikolai were totally decimated. The German guns and artillery mowed them down relentlessly. Tens of thousands died on the battlefield and tens of thousands more were taken prisoner. The injured were ferried back east in a virtual stampede, and hundreds of thousands of riflemen, cavalry troops and their officers fled in every direction possible. Starving and dehydrated, they descended like plagues of locusts on provincial towns and villages, looting, pillaging, murdering and raping wherever they went. By the time a few more days had elapsed the situation became crystal clear. The Nikolaevitch army had been routed and the Germans were now massing forces on the border in preparation for a full-scale invasion.

***

Do not rejoice at thine enemy's downfall! There was certainly no cause for jubilation at the hated Nikolaevitch's downfall as far as the Jews were concerned. It was not long before the official propaganda machine began 'explaining' the reasons for the recent debacle to the people. It was the fault of the Jews living in the provincial areas that the heroic army had been so badly defeated. These Jews, the enemies of both Russia and Christianity as a whole, had conspired with the German enemy and in an act of betrayal of their native land, they had revealed the secrets of the Russian army to the Germans using the Yiddish language as their means of communication. It was only with the assistance of the Jewish traitors that the demonic Germans had succeeded in luring the Russian army into the trap that had been prepared. This was how the Jews repaid the Russian nation for its kindness and good will!

The Jews knew the fate that lay in store for them. Mediators immediately set about stemming the tide of seething hatred that was now brewing. They approached government officials and begged them to exercise clemency towards their clients, in return for a generous fee. The officials agreed to ensure the Jewish communities were protected from the retribution of the public at large who believed that the treachery of the Jews was responsible for the current catastrophe. However, they could hardly expect to escape without some form of punishment. And so the defeated commander-in-chief Nikolai Nikolaevitch issued an order, giving Jews 24 hours to leave their property and homes and go into exile in the east. Hundreds of thousands of Jewish families, who lived in the provincial towns and worked hard to make ends meet, had to abandon their homes and property and flee for their lives.

* * *

No concept is more abhorrent and demeaning to a Jew than the one embodied by the Hebrew word, 'Galut', meaning exile. This is a word which strikes terror in the heart of every single Jewish person until his dying day, because it is synonymous with desolation and deprivation since time immemorial.

Like every Jewish person, I became familiar with that dreaded word right from an early age, a sentiment embodied by the words of the poet Bialik: "I have been bound by Shaul and my distress runs deep." Father, whose doleful and piercing voice ensured his regular selection as cantor for the additional prayers (Mussaf), had a special tune when it came to the verse "and because of our sins we have been exiled from our land", with the words "we have been exiled" evoked with a sigh of despair. The congregation could clearly sense the agony in the cantor's voice as he intoned the words "and because of our sins", a fate that was all too familiar to our forefathers and would continue to afflict future generations until the coming of the Messiah.

I had fully internalized the gravity of the concept of exile as so vividly described in such stark realistic terms in the verses of 'Lamentations' and works of Jewish folklore which recounted the trials and tribulations of the Jewish people, from the first exile to Babylon right up to the second exile to Rome, both of which are commemorated on the Fast of the Ninth of Av. While rummaging through father's bookshelves, I also came across books and pamphlets which described barbaric atrocities that the Jewish people suffered throughout the ages in all the countries of the Diaspora.

I had also read about the expulsion of the Jews from Spain and the immense suffering that people endured throughout this period. I was in short, a typical 'galut' child and fully identified with the privations that had been the miserable lot of every generation since time immemorial. Still, I never dreamed for a minute that I would witness a latter-day expulsion of Jewish communities en masse in all its horror with my own eyes.

The Jews were blamed for the defeat of the invincible Russian army. It was not because of the contemptible regime of tyranny with all its obscene behavior and debauchery, nor was it the vacillation and procrastination of the administration headed by a sick and demented despot, nor was it due to the graft, bribery and nepotism that was rampant at every level of government, from senior ministers right down to junior clerks in God forsaken locations throughout the endless expanse of the Russian empire. None of these were responsible for the disaster that had befallen the country. Neither was it because of the drunken swaggering senior army officers who had command of thousands of men in battle and most of whom were overbearing, salacious members of the aristocracy who didn't know the first thing about soldiering and relied on their subordinates to coordinate the functioning of the entire military apparatus, a move which hideously backfired at the crucial moment.

None of this, of course, had any influence whatsoever on the outcome of the entire campaign. Neither did the shortages of ammunition, or the tons of arms and equipment abandoned at some remote depot on their way to the front, or the thousands of starving disheveled and demoralized soldiers whose food and provisions had been siphoned off by suppliers, agents and distributors, or the military hospitals with their acute shortage of first aid and drugs, that were full of wounded servicemen whose injuries became increasingly complicated through lack of proper treatment. None of these failures were given even a casual mention in the official military reports filed from the field headquarters at the crumbling front, and they certainly were not responsible in any way for the Russian army's crushing defeat.

All the Russian people knew was that their heroic army would have achieved a comprehensive victory had it not been for those lousy "kikes" who had stabbed it in the back, causing a disaster of such epic proportions. These damned Jews who had relayed signals to the Germans by way of their Sabbath candles and Havdalah candelabra and supplied the Russian army with blank ammunition, defective weapons, moldy bread and putrid water had sucked the lifeblood from the Pravoslavs during peace time and had bled them white now that a war was on.

By the good grace of the king of kings from the holy capital of St. Petersburg and by kind consent of the supreme commander of the armed forces, the sentence of the perfidious Jews was reduced from total annihilation to mere exile. They had no more than two days and in some instances as little as a few hours to pack their bags and head eastwards with their families to an unknown fate.

***

Thousands of displaced persons fled their homes in every direction possible, to avoid the seething hell of xenophobia that was now rampant everywhere. The deportation orders caught hundreds of thousands of Jews in provincial towns and settlements in Lithuania totally unaware. Local police, assisted by military police, served warrants with breathtaking speed. The regime was in a hurry to stifle any backlash from the more enlightened sections of Russian society who, despite being under surveillance and harassment by the authorities, were not afraid to ask difficult questions in public. There were those in St. Petersburg who felt that by blaming Jews and subjecting them to collective punishment, the authorities hoped to provide the masses with an outlet for their frustration and anger. The deportation of the Jews and the resulting opportunities for a wholesale ransacking of their property would, it was hoped, defuse any feelings of resentment towards the incompetent authorities for the time being.

The police launched midnight raids on the homes of rabbis and community leaders throughout provincial towns and escorted them from their beds to the offices of local government officials. There, the deportation warrant was read out to them in a raucous voice and they were entrusted with the responsibility for ensuring the order was carried out in full. The wording of the warrant was missing essential details such as who was to go where and when.

The assembled community heads were shoved out the door and told to get on with the job. Nobody knew whether this order was for real or whether just another scam run by the usual assortment of lowly civil servants to be rescinded at the last minute, as always, in return for a generous payoff. It would take a few more hours before people realized that there was no way of escaping this particular decree and time was running out. It wouldn't be long before the dreaded Cossacks turned up to serve the warrants on the Jews in person with their whips and cattle prods.

By noon those people who were still hesitating, finally realized there was no hope and that the only way they could save themselves was by taking to the road while they still had the chance. No one knew the extent of the territory encompassed by the deportation order. Not even local officials were able to throw any light on the question of exactly which settlements had been designated as relocation sites and which would provide temporary shelter until the nature of the deportation order had been clarified. In the commotion that followed, none of the assembled company could hear themselves speak. A cacophony of shouting, remonstrating, charges and counter allegations ensued and when finally the noise and tearful emotions died down, nobody had come up with any more ideas than they had before.

Towards evening, a rumor was circulated that the authorities would be providing extra trains to transport refugees to their destination. In those settlements that were not situated near the railway lines, horse and cart drivers would be recruited to transport the herds of Jewish refugees in return for a fee to be paid by the Jews themselves. This news provided precious little consolation since all the train stations were located out of town and nobody knew when the trains in question were due to arrive. Even during peacetime, the service was notoriously unreliable and it was only by the grace of God that there were no collisions between trains approaching from opposite directions on the same track.

With total mayhem looming large on the horizon and the threat of the impending arrival of the Cossacks, panic and desperation set in. Those who had money and connections cornered the few horse and carts that were available. They would hurry back and forth from their houses carrying a random selection of clothes, crockery, cutlery and personal effects plus some merchandise from their shop, if there was one, and sling it all on the cart in a heap. Scholars would rescue as many holy books as they could find while the women loaded up with sacks of flour and potatoes and pots of chicken fat, cheese and other foods in preparation for the indefinite period in exile. After the cart had been loaded up to the hilt, anyone who was fortunate enough to find a decent length of rope lying around would secure the contents of the cart to stop things falling off during the journey. Once the terrified passengers themselves had climbed on board, the coachman would crack his whip on the horse and the task of ferrying the damned Yids and their baggage out of town would get under way. Several times throughout the journey, he would stop at a crossroads and wait while his nervous passengers chattered on in the devil's language and began arguing as to whether to make a left or a right turn.

Only a small number of people were lucky enough to find a horse and cart to get them out of harm's way before the Cossacks turned up and sent them on a trip of an entirely different nature. Others paid huge sums to porters to wheel all their belongings in trolleys down to the local train station. Nobody was under any illusion as to whether there would be any room at all on the scheduled trains but it was felt that the best thing to do was to get to the station and hope for Divine Providence.

Up to this point, people still had no idea as to where they could go. Those who had family headed in their direction although relatives were not expected to provide entire families with accommodations and assistance they could ill afford. "Blood is thicker than water" went the famous saying. The people of Israel had always been imbued with the gift of compassion. Would they now turn their backs on their own flesh and blood, the victims of war and tyranny? Most of the displaced people had been born, grew up, married and had children in the same town; hence, they did not have a single relative or contact anywhere else in the country. Where would they go?

* * *

A sorrow shared is a sorrow halved and nearly everybody was affected by the recent disaster. A person's true character shines through when he is down on his luck and it appears that the current crisis highlighted the character traits of kindness and compassion for which Jews have been renowned. No widow was left unattended and many people took it upon themselves to ensure that the sick and elderly were also evacuated.

One of the best gifts bestowed by God on the people of Israel was the propensity for charitable deeds. This was a trait of character that had saved our forefathers and was now on full display during the course of the present crisis which saw so many people displaced from their homes and now huddled in one great mass on the platform of the train station. Everybody maintained their dignity and piety throughout the ordeal. The refugees waited on the station platform for days. Fortunately, it was now spring and there was no rain. Mothers managed to find shaded areas where they were able to lay a blanket on the ground on which their babies could rest in relative comfort. Children amused themselves by racing up and down the platform, playing with and teasing one another until their parents, frantic with worry came after them and returned them to the family fold.

Every now and then, the horn of a locomotive could be heard in the distance indicating the imminent arrival of a train. This would be the signal for the crowd to surge forward like an anthill disturbed by an outside force. Hundreds of families would make a dash for the platform edge with people shoving each other aside in an effort to reach one of the carriages as the train drew up. Not all the trains were carrying wounded soldiers and supplies back from the front but then not all trains stopped at all the stations along the route.

Sometimes a train would come through carrying Jewish refugees from another location and masses of people would rush forward hoping to board one of the carriages in which there was still room. Occasions like these provided railway staff with an opportunity that was too good to pass up and in return for a certain payment, they would delay the departure of the train to enable more people to pile on. Those who managed to find room on a carriage for their entire family were extremely fortunate. Occasionally screams of despair could be heard from mothers whose children had been wrenched from their arms in the horrendous crush.

Nobody had any idea where the trains were going or how far the boundaries of the deportation zone extended. Those who were unlucky enough to be left behind on the platform took consolation in the station master's assurances that, according to the telegram he had received, more trains would be made available to collect the stranded refugees. It transpired later on, that this philanthropic gesture on the part of the transport minister cost Jewish executives with 'connections in the right places' a fortune in payoffs to all those who had a hand in the dispatch of additional trains westwards to collect the deportees. By the time a few weeks had passed, the refugees had found temporary shelter with communities situated outside of the deportation zone.

In the meantime, the mediators continued to negotiate with the authorities over the reduction (as usual, in return for the appropriate remuneration) of the size of the provincial area in which Jewish communities would face deportation. As a result, several towns were taken off the list, thereby granting the Jewish communities there a reprieve. It was just as well that a settlement was reached since the whole traumatic episode of the deportations had taken people's minds off the fact that a war was still raging and it could very well spread in their direction.

The armies of the German Kaiser were unlikely to stop at driving the Russian forces back over the Prussian border and could be expected to pursue the campaign further. For the time being, however, while the current crisis was in full swing, nobody had the time to dabble in any form of speculation. Father and mother had begun the transfer of bundles of cash in readiness for the worst possible scenario but ultimately, by virtue of its hereditary privilege, our town was unaffected by the current misery.

It wasn't long before the news reached tens of thousands of refugees that had camped out in the small settlements located in the vicinity of our town. An endless stream of homeless people arrived at our train station. Each train stopped for an hour's break during which time tens of families with children got off, too weary to travel any further. Our town, whose Jewish community numbered, only three hundred, families, was suddenly filled with thousands of Jews that had no shelter, food or moral support. Only time would tell whether our community would be up to the challenge of opening their doors and hearts to their less fortunate brethren.

* * *

The saying goes that new troubles put old ones in the pale. If that's the case, how can I have any recollection of the horrors I experienced in my childhood years? The overwhelming majority of Lithuanian Jewry who lived in the country for centuries, having been traumatized by the deportations ordered by the 'defeated general' were eventually wiped out completely some years later. The Nazi Holocaust with its barbaric savagery made the harassment and expulsions of previous years look insignificant by comparison. What point is there in describing such in graphic detail?

Time heals even the deepest scars both in the collective and individual experience. We have endured untold suffering since we were exiled from our homeland centuries ago and in our lamentations over the destruction of Jerusalem we incorporate the anguish and distress over the disasters that each new generation experienced in its own right. What point is there in dredging up the past over and over again only to feel anger and pain once more?

***

The sweet taste of salvation can never be totally obscured by the bitter taste of the poisoned chalice. Although having sunk in the history of the past, its memory remains undimmed and its taste infinite. During the scant hours of respite, at a time of turbulent changes in the lives of men and nations, when seasons and stars come and go in a flash, when a person's word is no longer his bond, when sacred values are traded on the stock market at going rates, when the morally bankrupt purchase their stock for next to nothing and then parade it on walls of fragmented culture, 'on a day of mass killing when towers collapse and darkness covers the face of the earth' - nothing can provide more gratification than to retreat back to one's childhood days for a breath of fresh air and rejuvenation of spirit.

It is at such moments that I reevaluate the truth and commit myself to viewing objectively the lifestyle and values of my father's day. There can be no better time in which to assess qualities of character than in extenuating circumstances, when a person's true colors shine through.

***

During that summer I celebrated my birthday. In keeping with the dictate of the sages which determined that 'blessings do not abound in that which has not been concealed', it was not customary in our part of the world to make a person's age a cause for celebration as if that person was deserving of some sort of prize for having survived that long. Even bar mitzvah celebrations were, by definition, merely an opportunity for close family to celebrate their son's mastery of Torah and philosophy for the pleasure and benefit of relatives and guests.

Still, my older sister who instigated the arrangement of a birthday celebration of a more conventional kind for her younger brother to whom she had become attached during their holiday at the dacha in the gypsies' forest. The celebration was scheduled to take place at nighttime after mother returned from another long day at the shop. Business was pretty slow at this time of year as most peasants were busy working their fields and had no time to come into town to do business with local shops. This was still no reason for mother to close the shop before nightfall, an arrangement which suited her daughter quite nicely.

On her own in the house, she set the table with the Sabbath cloth and set out sparkling cutlery. Placing a milk frying pan on the primus stove (which, being the only one around, was the talk of the town and the envy of all the neighbors who saw it) she cooked a quantity of tantalizing cheese blintzes, usually eaten on the Shavuot holiday. These are pastry rolls filled with cream cheese and cinnamon.

In honor of father, she bought a bottle of cold beer from our neighbor, Malka, who sold goods from home rather than a shop, thereby avoiding the need to apply for a license from the 'acksisnik' (the local customs and rentals clerk) to run a stall in the market. My sister knew that father liked nothing better than a sip of cold frothy beer and a piece of black bread sprinkled with salt.

My surprise present came in the form of a small Torah scroll. Although made from paper (instead of parchment made from the hide of a kosher animal), it looked just like a proper full-sized Torah scroll with the Five Books of Moses and wound around two wooden shafts with the customary decorative heads. A real pleasure to behold! The breastplate for the small Torah scroll consisted of a lattice of silk and steel threads which hung on a red cover which had the words 'A tree of life to all those who hold faith in it' embroidered on the front. And if that wasn't enough, the Torah came packed in a beautiful cardboard box designed like the ark in the synagogue.

My sister had spent a fortune on this gift - almost one silver ruble, wages for four private lessons. There was a joyous atmosphere in the house that night. I came home from evening prayers with father to find the house lit up with a large kerosene lantern and the table set. Even my weary mother had been swept along by her daughter's enthusiasm and greeted us with a loud 'Mazal Tov'. Father acted startled at first but soon understood the reason for the mid-week celebration. He had been clearly caught off guard by the whole idea but saw nothing wrong in this festivity. A few swigs from the beer bottle put him in an ebullient mood and he was clearly impressed with the quality of the miniature Torah scroll.

As an expert Torah reader, he was able to examine the quality of the printing and upon doing so, he concluded that it was top notch. He hinted to me that he expected me to make good use of my Torah scroll for practicing the reading of the weekly portion of Torah using the proper intonation, in preparation for the period following my bar mitzvah when I would be legally able to perform this service in synagogue for the benefit of the entire congregation.

***

The conversation around the dinner table was generally upbeat with father relating amusing anecdotes, all in honor of my birthday. Although a bloody war was raging, it was still remote enough for us to be oblivious to its menace. 'Out of sight out of mind' is what they say. We were still sitting around the table enjoying the light-hearted atmosphere with father joining in the gaiety in a surprisingly unrestrained manner when the door opened and Uncle Shmuel walked in.

Uncle Shmuel was a relative from my mother's side; she and his wife were sisters. We were neighbors by way of the extended property that had been divided into two separate dowries bequeathed by my grandfather to his two daughters on their marriages. Two houses had been built next to each other on one of his lots on the horse trader's street and each daughter was given a shop in the block he had put up in the marketplace.

Two sisters who also happened to be neighbors, blood and neighborly ties all rolled into one. Sounds simple? Not quite! Father resented the fact that his brother-in-law had added an extra floor to his house, causing it to tower over the roof of our home and a dispute had broken out between the two. They even took their case to the Rabbi to receive a Torah ruling, although they exercised restraint at all times as befitting two senior community members and avoided descending to the level of trading insults in public. Nevertheless, the two brothers-in-law hardly spoke to each other and at family celebrations they would exchange a few pleasantries and then avoid each other from that point onwards.

The two sisters met outside in the joint yard everyday while putting the cows out to graze and also ran into each other outside their adjacent shops. Fortunately, there was no economic rivalry between the families as my uncle did good business selling fabric and mother had her haberdashery shop. However, relations between the two sisters were also tense. Every conversation ended with a snide remark by one side towards the other and both sisters were astute enough to understand what was being insinuated. This cold state of relations would take a drastic turn on Yom Kippur eve when the two sisters would embrace each other and ask forgiveness for all the harsh words that had been said.

The two sides were also capable of burying the hatchet when a member of the family had, God forbid, been taken ill. We children did not consider ourselves party to the dispute over the roof. We had a partnership that was sealed with an ever-increasing pile of sweet wrappers and together we secretly raised litters of kittens born to the cats living in the straw store room or in the shed where the firewood was kept. I knew father disapproved of my visits to my uncle, although the grounds for his objections had more to do with the possible neglect of Torah study than anything else. Any form of game constituted a neglect of Torah study regardless of where it took place.

You may gather from all this that Uncle Shmuel's unexpected visit that evening came as something of a surprise. Father stood up to greet him and they entered father's study where they were closeted in discussion for quite some time. Eventually father re-emerged with a worried look on his face. "Bad news from the front", he said, " a trail of Jewish refugees is heading in the direction of our town. The Rabbi of the Misnagdim (most of the Jews in our town did not belong to the Lubavitch community but to their Misnaged counterparts) has called a general meeting at the synagogue tonight. We are going over to the Rabbi for further consultations", and with that he and Uncle Shmuel walked out.

I felt totally deflated and my sister almost burst into tears. We didn't know any details of what was going on but I had the feeling something terrible was about to happen. The ongoing war was no longer just a matter for disagreement between Elke, the 'Poyena'. ('Poyena' was a derogatory term for Russians and I called my opponent Elke by this name because of his ardent support for Russia throughout the conflict).

I sensed that this evening was not just my birthday - an occasion of nominal importance only - but would also bring the curtain down on my contented childhood whose main elements had been the study of Torah and moral instruction by a strict father. I would now have to face the realities of a tough life, the life of a Jew in exile in an empire of evil that knew its crimes but was looking for a scapegoat on whom to place the blame.

***

Father returned from the meeting after midnight. After I had awakened and tasted the eggnog which father had prepared as always, we had a long conversation, man-to-man. I sensed that he too was now grasping the fact that my life was about to undergo considerable change and so he felt he could take me into his confidence. He described the unique atmosphere at the general meeting in great detail.

In an unprecedented move, the Misnaged Rabbi had dispatched one of the community leaders with a message to Rabbi Alperovitch, the leader of the Hassidic community, the first such communication between them since they took up their posts. Following the standard form of greeting, the Rabbi went on to say, "The situation is becoming intolerable and indeed this is a time of affliction for Jacob. We are now in need of Divine Mercy. Tens of thousands of displaced persons are about to invade our town like a swarm of locusts."

The Misnaged Rabbi of our town was a gifted writer. He had become renowned for his work written in fluent, traditional Hebrew script in which he railed against liberals, provocateurs and agitators, calling for a strengthening of religious roots. He was a hard-liner and a fanatic in all matters pertaining to the upholding of Mitzvot. It was the sense of communal duty that led to the acknowledgment that past differences had to be put aside and all sides were duty-bound to join forces in the effort to save our brethren in distress. The Misnaged Rabbi ended with an urgent appeal to his Hassidic colleague to attend the general meeting that night that was to take place, God willing, in the 'cold' synagogue.

This was a rather ostentatious building with no facilities for heating during winter months. It had been built by a landed aristocrat who was keen to have the Jews settle on his property, in the belief that they would enhance its value with their industriousness and diligence. As a token of his friendship and good intentions he spent a small fortune on the construction of a synagogue whose architectural design clearly resembled that of a church. Because of the size and draught inside the building during autumn and winter, the synagogue was only used for prayers on holidays and the High Holy days with the service conducted according to the Misnaged tradition.

The Misnaged Rabbi had chosen the 'cold' synagogue as a neutral venue for the scheduled meeting in order to avoid stirring up any controversy. He, himself, had never set foot in the synagogue since it was built since it was too cold inside and had no adequate facilities for studying Torah in comfort. Hence, the decision to convene the meeting at this particular venue was a way of highlighting the severity of the crisis that now faced the community as a whole.

The Misnaged Rabbi's suggestion appealed to Rabbi Alperovitch and, in light of the clear and present danger and the action that needed to be taken, he was more than happy to take up the challenge. He now felt that this was an ideal opportunity to extend the atmosphere of reconciliation to disputes that had broken out within his own community and this prompted him to come up with a great idea of his own. He summoned my Uncle Shmuel who was one of his closest aides and gave him an unusual task:

"Please go and see your brother-in-law, Rabbi Meir, and show him this letter from the other Rabbi and after you've talked it over, bring him here and we'll go to the meeting together. On your way back, contact Rabbi Getzil Hoffman and his brother, Hillel Zilber, and bring them too. They have been at loggerheads over the right to a bequest from their late father, Rabbi Zalman of blessed memory, namely the rights to the recital of the 'Maftir Yona' (the Haftorah read in the afternoon prayers on Yom Kippur) and have not spoken to each other since the mourning for their father ended. Now is an ideal opportunity for them to make amends and agree some form of compromise, an act which will credit them with Divine Mercy."

My Uncle Shmuel, being the adroit individual he was, grasped the significance of this errand. And so, after a long conspicuous absence, he strode into our house - much to our embarrassment - acting as if he owned the place and shook father warmly by the hand like he had just returned from a long journey, before retiring with him to the side room for their private discussion.

***

The meeting at the synagogue was the talk of the town for many days afterwards. The two Rabbis and wardens from the respective communities ascended the rostrum. On the Rabbis' bidding, the sexton of the big synagogue, 'Mendel der rupper' (Mendel the announcer) walked with halting steps up to the Ark, swept aside the curtain and opened the doors to reveal a row of Torah scrolls. As was the custom on fast days and High Holy days, this was the cue for the congregation to burst out in a flood of weeping following which the all too familiar verses of supplication were read out aloud: "The Lord God shall answer thee on the day of trouble, the God of Jacob shall shelter thy name, He shall send His help from Kodesh and from Zion He shall nourish thee."

The highly charged atmosphere caused any remaining inhibitions among the congregation to dissipate completely and the synagogue was filled with desperate cries and wails, reminiscent of the emotion evoked when reciting the psalm 'To the chief musician, a psalm to the sons of Korah' which is read on New Year's day prior to the blowing of the Shofar. The agitated voices reverberated back and forth from the huge dome shaped ceiling. Eventually the commotion quieted down and the Hassidic Rabbi invited his Misnaged colleague to give the opening address. Naturally the Misnaged Rabbi reciprocated by inviting Rabbi Alperovitch to do the honors.

Seated in the assembled congregation were community leaders, traders in holy artifacts, married yeshiva students who were being supported by their fathers-in-law as well as skilled tradesmen (who, although not scholars themselves, were by no means ignorant or illiterate and generously supported all charitable causes).

Also showing up that evening were several members of the educated elite or 'Yom Kippurniks'; a derisive term taken to refer to that band of individuals who made their living by providing services to the rest of the community but were non-believers themselves, preferring to dress, talk and act like their Gentile neighbors. Some of them went as far as to violate the Sabbath in public like Dr. Zabadia and Dr. Michleson who, as opposed to physicians in other towns, did not engage in any rivalry and went out for picnics together on summer evenings in their carriages just like the aristocrats. They would stroll in the woods behind the church arm in arm with their colleague's wife as if in a gesture of defiance.

They only attended synagogue on Yom Kippur eve for the Kol Nidre prayer, occasionally putting in an extra attendance on New-Year's-day around mid-morning when the Shofar was being blown, in order to show their children how a traditional service looked and sounded. The doctors came to the meeting looking as scared as everybody else, although they tried to show as much restraint as possible.

Also attending were the lawyer Schlechter, Reznik, the pharmacist, and the head bookkeeper at the office of the linen exporter, Luzovski, who declared himself to be 'secular' and wore a type of student's beret, claiming that prior to moving to our town he studied economics at some prestigious institute in Kiev. Nobody had gone to the trouble of verifying his claims and when referring to him the "town clowns" quoted the famous adage of the sages: 'He who wishes to lie will keep his evidence out of sight'.

The Rabbis kept their addresses brief due to the lack of concrete information and their inability to control their emotions for long. There was no way of knowing how events would turn out and one could not rule out the possibility that we would suffer a similar fate to that of our brethren, becoming victims of an updated version of the now infamous blood libel. For the time being, however, our community was staying put whereas thousands of men, women and children were on their way to us and we were duty bound to welcome them with brotherly love and compassion in compliance with the Mitzvah: 'Thou shalt not stand against the blood of thy neighbor'.

In practical terms, the Rabbis had several suggestions that were put to the congregation for debate. To start off with, the women involved in charitable work, assisted by the heder pupils would go from door-to-door with sacks collecting as much food and drinks as possible. The gifts would then be loaded on to wagons and several women and boys would escort the wagons to the railway station and then wait on the platform to welcome the evacuees who were due to arrive on the trains.

The groups responsible for this task would work in shifts changing every few hours to allow mothers and housewives to get some rest. Another group would start work on the organizing of temporary shelter and accommodations for the weary refugees who were expected to arrive on trains, wagons and even on foot.

No sooner had the Rabbis finished speaking, when a chorus of voices began babbling in unison. People exchanged views, made suggestions, examined ideas, voiced disagreement and made calculations. The two Rabbis, meanwhile, were engaged in serious consultations, with other eminent scholars, both Hassidic and Misnaged, who were in attendance answering the Rabbis' questions, their faces sober and fearful.

***

It appeared that the Rabbis and scholars were deliberating over a very serious issue that would require an extremely problematic verdict. Finally, the consultation ended and the sexton once again ascended the rostrum holding a unique implement known as the 'Faatsher' (gavel). This was a form of rattle with two lacquered wooden boards held in place by a strap and was used to call the congregation to order during services when the noise of people talking got out of hand. Clasping the leather grip on the handle the sexton would bring the implement down hard on the rostrum with the resulting clap echoing through the hall. The implement was used at various junctures throughout the service such as the reading of the Torah or the calling up of a bar mitzvah boy or bridegroom to read the Haftorah.

Now that silence had been restored, the two Rabbis ascended the rostrum once more, followed by several prominent community members. The Hassidic Rabbi was once again invited to speak first and this time he didn't refuse. With his voice quivering with emotion, his body trembling and his eyes closed as if reciting a Hassidic liturgy at the Shabbat afternoon meal he said:

"With the consent of the Divine Presence and the consent of the Rabbis and Torah sages, we hereby announce and declare that the current situation is one where the Shabbat may be broken in order to save a life, this being in accordance with rulings made by the leading authorities. Therefore, we permit, and even command, the women to perform any kind of work on Shabbat that may be required to assist our displaced brethren on their arrival in our town. All persons are permitted to light fires for the purpose of preparing food and caring for children and sick people."

The Rabbi's voice was unsteady to begin with but became more authoritative as he continued speaking. This was not just another didactic rabbinical ruling but an order binding on Shabbat observance in our town. We were now being called on to publicly violate the commandment of Shabbat observance whenever necessary.

The Misnaged Rabbi, who was well-known for his fanatical adherence to mitzvot, adopted a similar line in his address.

"This is a time to do the Lord's will by violating His Torah. There is no greater mitzvah than the saving of a Jewish soul as it is written: 'He who saves a single soul is considered to have saved the entire universe'. Now that we are being tested by the Lord God, whose ways we can never aspire to comprehend, we must submit to His will and transgress on His commandments. Through the merits of this deed, God will show mercy and revoke all sovereign edicts. The oppressed shall return to their homes and the Redeemer shall come to Zion and let us say Amen."

The Rabbi then signaled the orphans present to recite the mourners Kaddish whereupon they all broke out in a chorus: "Yitgadal Veyitkadash shme rabba." The meeting ended and the crowd dispersed, numb from the proceedings that had just taken place.

***

The crucial test was not long in coming. The very next day Jewish families began arriving in town on horses and wagons. They recalled the details of the deportations and described the mayhem and heartbreaking scenes they themselves had witnessed. Soon, more wagons bringing families from other settlements were arriving in town.

The first thing the refugees wanted to know was what had been decided regarding our town and whether it had been included in the deportation zone or not. The truth was that nobody really knew the answer to that question. Community leaders were given a plethora of differing replies from various government officials. It all depended on whom they talked to. The one thing they all had in common was the speed with which they shoved the proffered ruble notes in their pockets in return for testifying to the loyalty of the town's Jewish community to his royal highness the Czar and confirming that no one was under suspicion of committing espionage, heaven forbid.

To be perfectly honest, none of these individuals knew a thing about the extent of the deportation and it was highly doubtful whether any of the staff officers on the ground had ever seen a map. The 'supreme general' and his cronies, the military high command, kept a considerable distance between themselves and the front. They were quite happy to issue orders from afar, which were then relayed by telegram, telephone and principally by cavalry dispatch riders who made long journeys from place-to-place on racehorses with orders from the general secured in a leather pouch hanging from their neck.

Sometimes the rider would get lost and find himself asking direction from local peasants who couldn't understand a word he was saying and gave him some approximate instructions in order to get him off their backs. Sometimes the rider would arrive at his destination to find that the entire camp had been disbanded and moved to a safer location. On other occasions he would reach his destination to find it had been captured by advance German forces following which he would either be taken prisoner or, if less fortunate, face a firing squad.

There was no source of authority whatsoever that could throw any light on the exact scope of the deportations and until such time as information to that effect was forthcoming, the rate of refugees arriving steadily increased. Trains packed to capacity continued to arrive at the station and hundreds of families that had squeezed into the crowded carriages together with their children and sick relatives stepped down on to the platform, too weary to travel any further.

During this time, I kept up my Torah study as usual. Every morning I turned up at the Rabbi's house carrying a large volume containing the Gemara tractate 'Baba Batra' under my arm. Both the Rabbi and I viewed our sessions as an ideal opportunity to escape from the bitter reality outside but these periods were always short-lived. We would manage to study for an hour at the most after which community officials on refugee business would barge in with questions, suggestions, requests and complaints.

The fact that I was still young did not stop the Rabbi from consulting me on crucial matters and he often called on my help to settle disputes. He also gave me the job of supervising food distribution down at the train station on Shabbat. I never knew whether he genuinely trusted me or whether he merely found it expedient to give all the chores that entailed breaking Shabbat to a minor who had not yet reached bar mitzvah age. Either way, I tried to be as meticulous as possible when carrying out the tasks I had been given.

He even allowed me to organize a group of friends my age who would be given jobs providing assistance and care as required. Father took his lead from the Rabbi and consulted him over his ideas and plans, all of which were aimed at providing relief to the displaced families that were heading our way. And so we were able to get father to agree to clear all possible space in our home and yard in readiness for the provision of shelter for refugee families should there be no more vacant rooms in the synagogues and other people's homes.

***

Two completely incongruous individuals took upon themselves the difficult task of finding more accommodations, the iron merchant, Rabbi Mendel Rabinovitch, one of the community leaders and an eminent scholar, and Motti Schlechter, the pharmacist, one of the local comedians with an aversion to religious affairs. Together they walked the streets, knocking on the doors of every single suitable home, asking the occupants to provide shelter. Such an unusual duo could hardly be turned away empty-handed and when they had finished, they handed the list of potential hosts to Rabbi Alperovitch.

Under an agreement reached between the two rabbis, Rabbi Alperovitch took charge of all the arrangements for accommodations for the homeless while his colleague, the Misnaged Rabbi, went from house to house asking for donations that would be used to purchase food and clothing for the refugees. Rabbi Alperovitch was accompanied on his rounds by none other than Dr. Zabadia who, in deference to the Rabbi, left his carriage at home and undertook the Mitzvah of charity on foot. He and the Rabbi walked the streets together, engrossed in deep conversation to the disbelief of onlookers who had never seen anything like it before.

The square outside the train station and the main roads leading out to neighboring towns were a hive of activity. Estimates of the exact number of families arriving by train or wagon differed. Those who tended to exaggerate, put the total number of families in thousands with as many as ten members per family. The Rabbi estimated the total number of families to be around one thousand, three times the number permanently living in our town. It was positively mortifying to observe on that first turbulent Shabbat, religious Jews breaking the Sabbath in public by stoking up fires with more wood, on which hot meals were being prepared for babies and the sick and elderly.

Were it not for the gravity of the moment, I would have probably doubled up with laughter at the sight of my former Gemara tutor, Rabbi Moshe Mordecai, trailing behind a scruffy looking woman with a toddler on either side while he carried a baby girl in his arms that was screaming her head off despite his best efforts to calm her. Father, on the other hand, was a stickler for order and personal initiative. He took charge of all the refugee children of heder age whose parents had found shelter in the town. He placed me at the Rabbi's disposal for the first two days of turmoil and, as mentioned earlier, I organized a group of my friends who worked at temporary stands on the station platform, handing out food and hot water to the weary and thirsty refugees. The doctors had ordered that all water be boiled so as to prevent outbreaks of dysentery among them.

* * *

One of the families arriving on the trains stood out among the rest due to their exemplary conduct. Although refugees themselves, they did not panic or become agitated like the rest of the unfortunate masses, but instead they calmly took down a few elegant looking suitcases and found themselves a secluded spot under a large tree. There, the mother spread a blanket and placed a beautiful three year old girl down to rest.

The father, a trim individual with a pince-nez perched on his nose, busied himself giving instructions to the children who were doing their jobs and offering help wherever possible. He came towards me and alongside him I saw a handsome child, smartly dressed unlike the local kids. The father offered me his hand and gave his name - Yaakov Epstein - and asked mine.

Then he brought the boy forward, introducing him as 'Yossef', not Yossi or Yossel as children with that name were known in our town. The boy offered his hand in a cordial manner and asked if I needed any help. The father said they were only stopping over for a few hours until a more comfortable passenger train came by that would take them east to Vitebsk where his brother lived. During the last part of their journey, which they caught in the nick of time, their daughter had felt ill and so they decided to get off and wait for a passenger train before continuing their journey. The son had watched what I was doing and was interested in joining in. I was excited at hearing the father and son converse in

Hebrew in the same manner that father used to talk with me when we were out walking on Shabbat. For a moment I forgot where I was and what I was supposed to be doing and blurted out with enthusiasm *"atta medaber ivrit?"* (do you speak Hebrew?).

Our joy knew no bounds! Yossef spoke Yiddish with a somewhat different accent, rolling his 'r' in a distinct fashion. We immediately became bosom pals and in all the excitement I almost forgot about my local friends who were awaiting my instructions. Yossef was clever and enterprising.

Barely an hour had passed when an old woman, who was standing near our stalls, fainted and collapsed with exhaustion. With all the activity going on, none of us had even noticed her lying prostrate on the ground. I had never seen a person faint before and froze with horror. Yossef, however, did not lose his composure. He instructed me to throw cold water over the woman while he ran off towards his family's camp site. In the meantime, onlookers had gathered round, exacerbating the entire commotion even further while I stood over the unconscious woman whom I had just doused with water, my hands shaking with fear. She started to move her hands and emitted a groan.

At that moment, Yossef's father made his way through the crowd and bending down he took hold of the woman's wrist. In the meantime, the surrounding crowd had swelled even further. We soon learned that Yossef's father was none other than Dr. Yaakov Epstein, a physician of repute whose patients held him in the highest regard. He was also famous for his ardent support for the Zionist idea, a rare occurrence among the upper classes. I wasn't to learn of this until later.

In a firm voice, Dr. Epstein requested that the crowd disperse, and people immediately responded. The woman needed to be moved indoors and nursed in bed until she recovered, he explained. The patient's daughter and son-in-law arrived on the scene but, being helpless refugees themselves, they were of little help. The daughter began sobbing hysterically as if her mother was already dead, "Mamale, Mamale!."

***

As luck would have it, father himself came to the rescue. By an act of Divine Providence, he happened to walk by and saw what was going on. The volunteers had given him a good account of my work so far. He was indeed the right person at the right time. He took control of events and welcomed the doctor. A local coachman volunteered to transport the patient and her family to his home where they could stay until more suitable accommodations were found and the woman had fully recovered. I told father about my new acquaintance's fluency in Hebrew.

Although not a Zionist himself, father was a keen user of Hebrew and educated his children to carry on the tradition. When he invited Dr. Epstein's family to stay on in our town for a few more days, I felt as if my prayers had been answered. "The two doctors we have can barely cope with the vast number of patients we now have among the refugees here", said father to Dr. Epstein. "Perhaps the good doctor would be willing to join them and be an assistant rather an emigrant", he added in a jocular manner. "There is no problem as far as accommodations are concerned as we can make a room available in our house. The boys can sleep in the empty shed and use the haystacks as bedding." The guest talked briefly with his wife and accepted father's offer.

It would have all been perfect had it not been for the misfortune that had befallen all of us. I couldn't have wished for better company. The Epstein family turned out to be extremely friendly and cultured people. I found Mrs. Epstein's Yiddish rather amusing. Her mother tongue was Russian and she had been born in Kharkov. She married Dr. Epstein when they were both students at Dorfet University in Estonia and cut her studies short when their eldest son, Yaakov, was born. She continued to work as receptionist in her husband's clinic and picked up her Yiddish from his many patients.

My sister, who was fluent in Russian, found her company delightful. They got on well together and had long and frank discussions on current affairs including Zionism and socialism. My sister tried to interest our guest in socialist policies and in response our guest tried to convert my sister to Zionism.

The men, on the other hand, tentatively avoided discussing such issues. Father busied himself with teaching Torah and traditional Hebrew to his pupils while Dr Epstein became renowned as a specialist. His only condition was that a local doctor accompany him on his rounds to ensure that his local colleagues were not deprived of their livelihood while he was in town. His brother kept sending him telegrams from Vitebsk urging him to move on, to which he replied by saying he would only leave town once his services were no longer required. Nothing is stranger than having a calamity trigger an event with positive, even joyous consequences. Within two weeks things had calmed down. Not that the Jews had anything to celebrate about by any means! As the saying goes: 'Troubles don't look that bad once you've had a chance to sleep them off'!

Gradually most of the displaced families moved on, leaving behind a hundred and fifty of the poorest of the recent exodus, who were more than happy with their sorry lot as refugees in our town and were reluctant to continue wandering in unknown territory. At least, here they had a roof over their heads and their children were able to join the local heder thereby ensuring they kept up their studies. Even the local 'Ocielazi' (school), which specialized in teaching Jewish girls to read and write Russian, opened its doors to girls from refugee families who had already started their schooling before being deported. Tradesmen found work in their professions with local employers while the few people with capital entered the real estate business and prospered. The Rabbi was introduced to the family of Dr. Epstein and father gave his permission for Yossef to join me in the study of the tractate 'Baba Batra'.

Yossef was a year older than me but I was still ahead of him in knowledge of the Talmud. Luckily for him, his father had ensured that he had received the basic grounding in Torah and Jewish studies in his education up to this point. He attended the "gymnasia" (or high school) in his hometown, whose population was overwhelmingly Jewish, yet was nevertheless limited by the gymnasia management to a pupil quota of no more than fifty per cent of the total school population. Jewish parents who wished to send their child to the gymnasia were required to find him a Russian Gentile classmate whose school fees would also be paid by them. And if that wasn't enough, the Gentile classmate, who in some cases turned out to be a complete dunce, would also have to be taught Torah by his Jewish counterpart, a venture which did not always prove successful.

***

My life changed beyond recognition after Yossef came to stay at our house. I was glad to be of help to him in his Gemara studies and he, in turn, although not a great student himself, was methodical and thorough when applying himself to his studies. He encouraged me to do the same, much to the satisfaction of father who observed a tangible improvement in my level of diligence when studying.

We had a lot of spare time for intimate conversations and we exploited it to the fullest. He revealed all his secrets to me, including his fervent love for a girl who was in his class back at the gymnasia but who was several years older than him. This was not a drawback as far as he was concerned. He had not yet had an opportunity to confess his love to her, but would do so in good time. For the time being, he was willing to settle for some form of illusion which was extremely vague in nature.

Her name was Nora, a non-Jewish name, but when they were older and the romance became mutual he would convince her to change her name to Shulamit. This was a name taken from the book 'Song of Songs' and all Zionist girls had adopted it as their own.

Eventually, Yossef's parents would move to Palestine, or Eretz Israel, where his father would purchase some land and divide his time between two occupations. Half the day would be devoted to cultivating and planting crops as well as harvesting and treading grapes in the wine pit - in accordance with biblical tradition - with the other half devoted to his medical practice.

Yossef hoped to follow in his father's footsteps and be a doctor as well. He had not yet decided what his beloved wife-to-be, Nora, would do following her immigration to Palestine. They had not had a chance as yet to discuss their future together, so he still had no idea as to the profession she wished to pursue in their new home. Naturally she would be free to make her own choice but it was more than likely that she would want to assist him in the tending and shearing of their flocks of sheep, a true Zionist vocation if ever there was one.

I was unable to reciprocate by telling Yossef about my own secret love. The trouble was of course, that the object of my affection was merely a figment of my imagination called Tamar, whose adulation I shared with another story-book character called Amnon. I had never had any experience of being lovesick up to this point, save for the brief encounter with Masha who left me heartbroken during my stay at the dacha.

The stories I told Yossef were complete fabrications of my own design and had more to do with bravery than romance. This should not be taken as inferring I was ignorant in such matters. A boy like me with three Gemara tractates under his belt, namely Kiddushin, Gittin and Ketubot, all of which deal with relations between the sexes, could be relied on to know a thing or two about virginity, proper conduct, nuptial agreements and suchlike. These were Gemara tractates whose contents I had learned until I knew them backwards. Of course, this didn't really have the slightest thing to do with romance and courtship! The daughters of my neighbors that were my age were all irritating and slovenly individuals and I kept well away from them. It was during the difficult period of deportation that I had an experience that was quite a novelty for me.

A refugee family was staying with Uncle Shmuel next door to our house. The father was a Shochet (ritual slaughterer) by profession and had seven children, one of whom was a girl my age. Her name was Yochebed and she always looked for excuses to mingle with the boys. When we were putting our cows out to graze each morning, she would turn up and give us a hand. She was always eager to help us put out straw and feed for the animal's evening meal so that it would be able to chew its cud thereby reaffirming its own kashrut.

One evening while visiting our shop, mother asked me to put out some extra hay for the cow since she had forgotten to feed it earlier in the day. I came home and headed straight for the shed. No sooner had I entered and begun laying out the hay when Yochebed followed me in. I felt two soft arms encircling my neck and then a wet kiss was planted on my cheek. The horrified cry 'oy" that involuntarily escaped my throat scared the brazen girl away and like an alley cat she slipped out the entrance and was gone in a flash.

For some reason, I never ruminated over this incident during the following days. I didn't tell my loyal friend about it either. Yochebed kept out of sight for the next few days and then reappeared in the yard as if nothing unusual had happened. Several days after that, the entire family left town on their way east. Yochebed, or 'yellow Yochebed' as we called her because of her ginger colored hair and pony tails that flapped in the breeze as she ran, soon faded from my memory completely.

* * *

According to the Russian newspaper that Dr. Epstein received, some form of cease fire was holding on all fronts and in Switzerland initial contacts were being made in preparation for possible peace talks between the warring sides. I held a deep-seated yearning for revenge on the Russians and hoped for their downfall. Yossef also hated the Russians but, unlike me, he was happy to see a peace deal struck since the trauma of deportation had left him mentally scarred and weary of the war. He was not looking forward to the planned journey to stay with his uncle who for some reason, he was not fond of at all.

Our friendship gave both of us a great deal of satisfaction. With our parents' permission, we went swimming from one end to another of the crystal-clear waters of the Lavina River. My sister would take us out for 'evening conversations' which were held in simple straightforward Hebrew. Father found the Zionist doctor extremely interesting although he did not attempt to hide his reservations regarding the Zionist movement which could, heaven forbid, go the same way as the movement of Shabtai Zvi.

Dr. Herzl may have sported a beard as long as those usually seen on the faces of distinguished clerics but he always appeared bareheaded in photographs; hence, it was doubtful whether he had been chosen as the oracle through whom news of the Divine Salvation would be delivered.

Our studies at the Rabbi's house were making good progress with Yossef taking an avid interest in the material we were studying. I remember those few glorious weeks as some of the best days of my childhood. Was this to be the period of calm that preceded the storm? We had just about forgotten that only a few kilometers away, two armies were camped out, armed to the teeth and were ready upon being given the order, to drown the evergreen fields in a sea of blood. The war was a frequent topic for discussion and argument among us, with sardonic jokes made about the contemptible Russian regime of the Czar.

***

The turbulent atmosphere during this period resembled the erratic tide of change in the opinions, queries, theories and commentaries contained in a chapter of the tractate 'Baba Batra'. At least father was now more relaxed, no longer expressing any concern over the relationship between me and my sister, whom he feared would lead me astray, God preserve us, in the same manner that she and my eldest sister had influenced my older brother. My sister's attitude towards our parents also took a turn for the better. She listened with interest to father's lessons on the Lubavitch Hassidic philosophy that he gave to a few close friends during meals on Shabbat.

* * *

My sister's opinion regarding mother's shop, which she had always viewed as taboo, changed considerably. Young Jewish militants had always viewed shop keeping with utter contempt and saw it as a form of bourgeois lifestyle, to be expunged on the day of socialist emancipation and revolution of the proletariat. The young Jewish socialists found themselves having to direct all their fire at the enemy from 'within', namely Jewish shopkeepers with their middle-class mentality, who were unable to identify with the oppressed and underprivileged and, as a result, would be incapable of pulling their weight when the class struggle began.

My sister looked at things in an entirely different light, once she witnessed mother slaving away in the shop from dawn until dusk, in addition to finding time to crouch on her knees in the garden weeding, hoeing planting and gathering onions, carrots, cucumbers, turnips, radishes, beans and a sack full of potatoes whenever they were in season. Mother did all this in addition to baking, kneading, cooking, milking, making cheese, and the rest!

And if a housewife just happened to give birth there was always time to drop in with a bowl of soup, as the shop wasn't going any place in the meantime. The bowl of soup was but a by-product of the chicken mother had put on the stove that morning and on her way to the shop, she would make a detour which, as luck would have it, took her right past the door of the home of the new mother. With the usual greeting: "Mazal tov, and all the best for the future", she would make her way to the shop before the bewildered mother had managed to get a word in. So it was difficult even for a die-hard revolutionary like my sister to see her mother as a middle-class snob.

* * *

These were days of high expectations, interest and pleasure for me. I was in demand at home like I never had been before. One day while father was expounding on his own interpretation of the hymns recited on the High Holidays - a pastime we both enjoyed - Shabtai, the sexton, came to summon us to a consultation at the Rabbi's house.

I went along with father and Yossef came too. On our arrival, we were surprised to see twenty community members, all participants in the minyan, seated in the Rabbi's study. They were chatting in earnest with one another, filling the room with the smoke from their cigarettes. The Rabbi came in last and invited his guests to move to special benches with arm-rests that had been brought in specially for the meeting. Once they were all seated again, he began his address.

על קבר אימי בקופישוק

My sister Dina z"l at my mother's grave (left) and my father's grave (right)

It now transpired that the 'Koropkas' (the community fund financed by a self-imposed tax placed by the Jews on kosher meat, the proceeds of which were used for community expenses such as Rabbis' salaries and other regular costs), both that of the Hassidim and Misnagdim had been completely used up. They were never in any surplus to speak of at the best of times and the recent crisis had been a considerable drain on reserves, in spite of the impressive philanthropy and charitable pledges that had been forthcoming from the community as a whole.

Out of lack of choice, the wardens responsible for the 'Koropkas' had to resort to soliciting for funds and borrowed any money they could lay their hands on. At first they stuck to asking for charitable loans and took money off anyone who had a couple of rubles to spare. Then, when the crisis deepened, they found themselves borrowing off local money lenders. These were Jews who made a living by lending money and were granted a special dispensation by way of a Torah ruling that allowed them to charge interest on loans. These individuals had contributed vast sums to the central charity fund and, in waiving their rights to any interest they were due, they had left themselves completely broke. Traders, street vendors and others were all in need of assistance but there were no funds left.

The Rabbi forgot to mention that neither were there any funds left to pay his or his colleague's salary and as a result their wives had been buying Sabbath groceries on credit for two months now, a situation that was intolerable. The required sum would be another form of 'Maot Chitim' (the charity fund raising money for the purchase of Passover groceries for the poor, which operated according to the principle of being willing to be either a donor or recipient), only this time the figure required ran into the thousands rather than hundreds and nobody had the faintest idea as to where the money would come from. The Rabbi did his best to soften the blow he delivered by incorporating verses from the Torah and quotations from the sages and Lubavitch ideology in his speech. When he finally finished, he sat down, stroking his beard pensively.

As expected, an uproar broke out with the entire gathering shouting one another down in one long deafening racket. Rabbi Getzil Hoffman, a wholesale dealer and a keen scholar who also had a penchant for Zionism and secular education, was asked by the Rabbi to conduct the meeting. Getzil knew whom he was dealing with and so he let the members shout, heckle and castigate one another for an entire hour until they were all completely hoarse and more than willing to let him take charge. He had been waiting for this opportunity and with the Rabbi's permission he analyzed the ideas that had been discussed so far. It had all been a lot of rhetoric with very little substance. Rabbi Getzil went over the ideas one-by- one, discreetly commending the individual concerned for his ingenuity so as not to cause offense but at the same time exposing all the flaws in the suggestion he had broached.

It was, of course, possible to increase the 'Koropka' on beef and in addition place a new 'Koropka' on chicken. This would entail a charge of five kopeks for each foul killed by the slaughterers. 'A Gedank' (good thinking!). But this tax would only bring in a limited income since chicken was the staple food of the community's poorer members and they could barely afford to buy a sizable amount of meat even for the Sabbath. So that idea was not much help.

One could, of course, sell burial lots in the new cemetery, perish the thought (words which one must always add when talking about such matters). But even at the best of times, land was going cheap and it was always possible to close a deal for the purchase of several lots at a bargain price, even more so during these days of total mayhem. Everyone had enough on their plates worrying about the trials and tribulations of everyday life; who could possibly have time to worry about investments in the after world?

The same verdict applied to the suggestion to auction off the franchise for the sale of yeast for baking. Several communities had already adopted this idea but people in our town were reluctant to use this method of raising community generated revenue due to the opposition of shopkeepers. They demanded that no measures be taken which might have an adverse effect on their income. It was not just the sale of yeast that was at stake but rather a whole range of accompanying products such as flour, spices, raisins and other items used in the preparation of Shabbat foods (such as gefilte fish and challah) that would be at risk if this proposal was implemented.

To sum up, all the ideas broached were good on paper but little more than that. Now it was Rabbi Getzil's turn to broach an idea he had prepared in advance, as he was accustomed to doing in such instances. He was the last person to speak and as a rule his ideas were usually accepted by the majority. He never held himself back and always spoke his mind when addressing the community. He recalled the phenomenal success of the last fund-raising campaign for the 'Sofit' that our minyan had undertaken a few years earlier. Everyone remembered the special Sabbath on which our minyan held an 'Ufrufen' (special invitations to the reading of the weekly portion of Torah).

"We needed a total of five hundred rubles back then", said Rabbi Getzil, reminding the assembled company that after deduction of costs they had been left with a surplus of a hundred and fifty rubles which had been used to buy a new curtain for the ark and a copper basin for the priests to wash their hands in prior to the communal blessing. And there was still money left over to have a Hassidic style celebration in which the entire congregation had been invited to a sumptuous afternoon meal with a guest speaker on Hassidic philosophy to top it all off. The wine had flowed like water and the honey cakes were in abundance. All in all, the 'Sofit' had been a runaway success. Why not try the same thing again?

The requirements were considerably larger this time but what of it? Everyone knew what was at stake, that this was a time of trouble for Jacob and the funds were needed to keep the community afloat. There was no doubting the willingness of all the members to economize on their own expenses and contribute as much as they possibly could to save the community from falling apart, heaven forbid.

The problem was that with a war on everybody had difficulty making ends meet and those who could, saved all their spare cash for contingency purposes. Under these circumstances one could not expect to witness any magnanimous acts of philanthropy from anonymous donors. The sages interpreted the verse 'And thou shalt love with all thy heart' as referring to both the good and evil spirits within man. Pride was not a trait of character synonymous with the Hassidic way of life but, when there was no choice, one was required to use it to advantage in mitigating circumstances.

The declaration of a pledge made upon being called up to the Torah is about as public as you can get. The congregation would always listen carefully to the pledges being made by the benefactors and then render their verdict accordingly. A generous contribution would be greeted with a long "pshhhh" which indicated the congregation was clearly impressed by the splendid display of benevolence.

A miser on the other hand, whose miniscule contribution clearly indicated his reluctance to part with his money under any circumstances, would be greeted with a long "paaaa" upon stepping down from the rostrum, indicating the congregation's contempt and disgust at observing the individual giving in to his evil inclination that had prevented him from performing an act of charity of the highest order. This was the only way to get any considerable sum of money out of the congregation as pledges made on the Sabbath were always realized the following day when the wardens came around to the houses of the individuals in question to collect their payments.

Rabbi Getzil suggested that a repeat of the 'Sofit' fund raising campaign be launched as early as the following Shabbat. All through the coming week, Rabbi Shabtai would make the announcement three times a day following prayers that the coming Shabbat would be a fund raising drive aimed at meeting the phenomenal costs incurred during the refugee crisis. Everyone would be required to make their pledges in hard cash that could be collected the next day, in order that the clearance of debts could commence immediately. Rabbi Getzil was confident that the generosity of the Lubavitch congregation of the minyan would more than match that of other congregations in our town.

It had now become apparent that the meeting that had just taken place was nothing more than a token gesture to placate the community members so that they would not feel they were being sidelined before the planned fund raiser was officially launched. The actual decision had been taken two days earlier at an emergency meeting attended by the two Rabbis and leaders of congregations from all the synagogues in town. Rabbi Getzil's proposal, backed as it was by the proven success of the 'Sofit' project, was unanimously adopted.

Unlike the previous 'Sofit', however, this fund raising campaign would not be limited to one synagogue only but would encompass the entire community. Each person would be called up to the reading of the

Torah in his own synagogue and the members of synagogues and prayer houses throughout town would be vying with one another for the ultimate prestige, inherent in pledges made in public. This was what Rabbi Getzil was getting at when he said we should not feel inferior to other synagogues when we came to make our pledges since we were the pioneers who first thought of the idea and the 'Sofit' project was an example that would now be emulated by all the other synagogues in town.

The mention of the word 'Sofit' aroused renewed feelings of contempt and anger towards father over the shameful ordeal he had put me through by sticking to his principles that Shabbat. I had long since forgotten about that awful day and now, just when my relationship with father had taken a turn for the better, it had come back to haunt me all over again. I stole a look in father's direction when Getzil mentioned the 'Sofit' project and expected him to blush with embarrassment or contrition, or perhaps raise an objection but no such response was forthcoming.

He stood near his usual place at the minyan leaning against the prayer pulpit, browsing through a book that was open but was still following the entire proceedings without missing a word. Father did not get drawn into arguments unless it was absolutely necessary. He would listen without making any comment, which was what he did on this occasion even when he was cornered by some of the intellectuals involved in the debate who urged him to take a stand in their favor. In reply, he brushed them aside with a brief remark, reluctant to get embroiled in the acrimonious discussion.

Father maintained his silence on the way home. Mother, as usual, did not question him as to what had happened at the meeting since he would say his piece when he felt the time was appropriate. A wise woman

was what she was! I almost forgot to mention that our former tenant (
who was now renting a spacious apartment for a few weeks), Dr. Epstein
also attended the meeting. Unlike the other doctors, he came to the
Minyan every Shabbat and was considered a pillar of the community, but
not by virtue of his knowledge of Torah and Hassidic life style.

He too kept quiet on his way home. I didn't tell my friend Yossef
about the degradation I had been put through a few years ago when we
were talking later on but he could sense my agitation. As Shabbat
approached, I became ever more disoriented, distancing myself from my
friend who clearly did not understand what was wrong. And although I
may have been mistaken, father and mother were acting as if they had a
secret which they could not disclose at any cost.

That Shabbat eve, mother busied herself with the usual preparations
for the weekend break. Aside from our friends the Epstein family, father
had, as always, invited a traveling guest to join us for the Shabbat meal.
Mother, who had grown up in a home that was always filled with guests
(although my grandfather was particular about what kind of people he
entertained and Misnagdim were quite definitely unwelcome in his
house) used to say that the Shabbat table should always be decorated
with extra guests. The guest joined father in the singing of Zemirot
(Shabbat hymns) and then we followed suit. In deference to his doctor
friend, father did not object to the men and women singing together in
unison. As Dr. Epstein had a traditional Misnaged upbringing, his songs
were different than those of father's.

Our Shabbat meal proceeded in the traditional atmosphere of song
and exhilaration. Yet if anybody could have read my mind they would
have uncovered what could only be described as a 'split personality'. I
took part in the singing of Zemirot as usual yet inside I was dreading the

ordeal that would be my lot the following morning when the calling up to the reading of the Torah in the synagogue commenced halfway through the morning service.

On this particular occasion, the reading of the weekly portion would be interrupted after every three verses so as to call up as many people as possible. Each time, the person that had been called would step on to the rostrum, recite the opening blessing: "Blessed art Thou, the Lord God who hast chosen us from all other peoples etc.", and then the reader would fire away. Three verses later, the person would recite the closing blessing: "Blessed art thou the Lord God who hast bestowed on us the Torah of truth etc.", whereupon the sexton would announce the name of the next person to be called up.

While the individual named was making his way to the rostrum, the reader would recite the following prayer: "May He who blessed our forefathers, Abraham, Isaac and Jacob, may He bless 'X', the son of 'Y', in honor of his calling to the Torah and in honor of him donating the sum of 'Z' rubles to charity." At this point, a deathly silence would ensue while the congregation waited with bated breath to hear how much the individual had pledged. Once a figure had been named and then repeated aloud by the reader, a fracas would spread through the synagogue pews like wildfire, with the congregation emitting sighs of "psshh" in admiration or grunts of "paaa" in contempt and disgust as appropriate.

***

Although it had been a long time since the appalling spectacle of father exposing himself to ridicule during the course of the 'Sofit' project, it still felt like it happened yesterday, with me looking for somewhere to bury myself through the shame of it all. I relived the scathing mockery that my classmate Hirsch Leibke had subjected me to in front of everyone.

God only knew what might happen tomorrow morning. I lay awake in bed for ages thinking that if father repeated his pathetic posturing by once again donating the token sum of Chai (18) kopeks, I would never be able to show myself in public again nor look my friends - including Yossef - in the face because of the shame and disgrace he had brought upon me.

Hopefully, the omnipotent God almighty will forgive me for those wayward thoughts that pervaded my mind throughout prayers that morning. My mouth was reciting the words of the Shabbat morning service in a mechanical fashion while my heart pounded away inside, sending those two dreaded words thundering through my brain, "Chai agorot, Chai agorot, Chai, Chai, Chai, Chai!"

The moment of truth had finally arrived. The cantor ended his recital of the first half of the morning service, whereupon the person chosen to perform the mitzvah of opening the ark proceeded with his task. Once the Torah scroll had been removed from the Ark and placed it on the rostrum table, a yeshiva student was summoned to remove the scroll's silk cover embroidered with gold lettering which had been donated by the childless widow of the late Ben Tziyon, the one-eyed builder.

Yudel Cohen, was first to be called up, not by reason of his status and wealth but because of the upcoming 'Yaarzeit' (memorial anniversary) for his late father. The congregation greeted his donation with the usual round of vocal applause. His pledge, when he was finally called upon to announce it, was quite substantial for a person of his means - half a ruble, the equivalent of his weekly income if not more. Next up was Leib Kreizek, a Levi, who was also quite well off; his contribution was three rubles, a fair sum for such an occasion but not one that would tax his resources by any means. And so it went on, one after the other, each person pledging as much as he could, in the spirit of compassion and good will that Jews are known.

Apart from two or three exceptions, the sums pledged were more or less the same, since everybody knew what was expected of them. Rabbi Getzil Hoffman donated ten rubles. Yaakov Terper, the travel agent, raised the stakes to fifteen rubles. Opinions about him differed; there were those who thought he was genuinely wealthy and those who felt he was merely trying to show off. It was only after his death that it turned out that the latter were proven right. Since it would have been in extremely poor taste to heap scorn on a deceased person at his funeral, the person making the eulogy was discreet enough to deftly sidestep any controversy by praising the deceased for rallying to the cause by contributing a lot more than he could actually afford.

To be brief, the figure kept mounting up. By the time we were approaching the end of the proceedings with generous contributions having been pledged by all and sundry, it had reached the impressive total of one thousand silver rubles with still more to come. Then the moment came and my heart ground to a standstill as I heard the sexton announce: "Arise Rabbi Meir, son of Rabbi Yitzhak, number six!."

I hid my face in the Chumash pretending to follow father's recital of the blessing and the subsequent reading of the Torah verses word-by-word. Any minute now Rabbi Zalman, son of Rabbi Yoel, the last person to be called up would begin making his way towards the rostrum. The reader, Meir Motis, began reciting the set text: "May He who blessed etc. etc., may He bless Rabbi Meir, son of Rabbi Yitzhak in honor of him donating", and then bent his head sideways to allow father to whisper in his ear.

But instead of repeating the sum out loud, he again tilted his head towards father to make sure his ears had heard right. Surely Meir Motis the reader wasn't going deaf? But after father repeated the sum, he stood upright and in a jubilant voice, slowly and deliberately made the announcement, emphasizing each syllable as it left his mouth. "In honor of him donating to the charity fund, the sum of Chai rubles times two!!"(36)

He mouthed the astonishing figure and then looked around him triumphantly as if he had been the one who donated all this money, or at least played a pivotal role in convincing father, a modest and unassuming individual, to make a pledge that exceeded even those made by the wealthiest people in town. Throughout my childhood so far, I had never been able to relate to father on a emotional level in private nor in public. We had always kept our sentiments pent up inside. But on that Shabbat morning I came to love father like I never loved anyone else in my entire life. I didn't have any time or patience for my friends or the motley collection of individuals who were now singing father's praises to the sky. I wasn't even interested in by my best friend Yossef anymore. I wanted father all to myself and was not willing to share him with anyone else in the whole wide world. Even when I was hiding myself away in the straw shed, those magic words kept running through my mind, "Chai rubles times two to the charitable fund!"

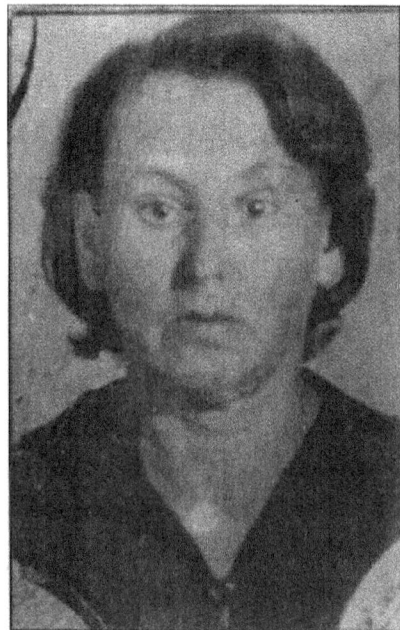

Reisel, my father's Meir sister   Chaim, the only son of my aunt Reisel

The family of my uncle Chaim Kodesh from Hanashishok (Onuškis, Lithuania) with grandmother, my father's Meir mother, the rebbetzin from Ponemunok (Panemunėlis, Lithuania)

The Kedushah Prayers of My Mother

I have told a great deal about my mother and those stories remind me of a perennial spring. Her body was tiny but the Creator took care in granting her a beautiful soul. Occasionally, when reflecting on her memory, I try to compare my mother with the greatest and most famous women in the world.

I suppose it was she which the Proverbs meant by saying, "The daughters of Israel are plentiful, but you have risen above all of them." (Proverbs 31, free translation.) From time to time, I see her in the tough days in all her greatness when she was hard as rock, not compromising on her faith, righteousness or kindness. Dozens of stories arise from the oblivion of long-gone days of my childhood. I present here a story which portrays the high moral soul of my mother, may her memory be blessed.

I left her in the provincial town of Kupishok as I departed to far away destinations in order to acquire an education and disseminate Zionist ideas among Lithuanian Jews. For most of the year, I contented myself with occasional entertaining letters in good Yiddish to my mother and received an emotional and usually eloquent reply.

From time to time, I enjoyed surprising her by sending a sum of money for covering the shop's debts. Of course, it was accompanied by a cheerful note which was supposed to eliminate the embarrassment that she might have felt when getting such gifts from her youngest son. I loved my mother and missed her a great deal. Twice a year, for Passover and the High Holidays, I used to visit her; those were the weeks of her peacefulness.

At the crack of dawn, she would leave the house for her store and wouldn't come back until midnight. When she entered the house, she was utterly exhausted from her constant efforts to persuade the stubborn customers to buy the merchandise. She was freezing in the winter and sweating in the summer. Only the Creator knows how her fragile body bore all the suffering, fatigue and hard labor.

As a matter of fact, she did not always benefit from my respect and good behavior at home. She found it difficult to understand how I followed the sinful concepts of a secular education. I was partially the reason for her tears that dropped on the prayer book "Kurban HaMincha" which I have preserved as a priceless treasure. She perhaps asked the 'Father of Orphans and Protector of Widows' not to treat her son too severely, to forgive his mistakes and return him to the right track.

My mother's time was limited and she could not spend endless hours sitting with me at home. For the sake of truth, I wasn't always at home either. The days of my visits coincided with the visits of my Kupishok friends who had been scattered all over Lithuania. We were delighted to see each other and enjoyed pleasant evenings together.

Mother was understanding and did not complain too much. Nonetheless, from time to time, the good inclination in me awoke and I felt as if I were hurting her virtuous heart by my constant absence while at home in the few days which we could be spending in each other's company. In those hours of regret, I hurried towards her store.

But good intentions and devil's deeds sometimes go together. Every time I set out for my mother's shop, I bumped into an acquaintance willing to exchange a couple of words with Hannah Kodesh's successful son, who was almost a lawyer. At the time, I taught in Jewish schools all over Lithuania and traveled to various towns delivering thrilling Zionist speeches. Many people in town were anxious to talk with me and I, naturally, didn't want to make an impression of being a stuck-up character by ending the conversation abruptly. Therefore, I kept it going and once again, to my regret and sorrow, did not reach the shop.

Our conversation would eventually end and I plodded to the store. As I went up the wooden staircase, I often found the door locked. Not locked with a padlock but shut down in haste. I turned back in despair thinking about my bad luck – precisely at the moment when I came to purify myself, mother did not assist me in doing so.

Working hours were not over yet, people were still buying at the marketplace and my mother, normally so responsible in everything that concerned her modest living was not there! Actually, I knew where she would be. Most likely she had popped over to one of the local synagogues in order to catch a 'Kedushah' which is sung by the cantor during the 'Amidah' prayer.

The synagogues were fairly close to the stores and the prayers could be heard by the shopkeepers. The holy sounds of prayers reached their ears from the open windows of two synagogues – Shul Hoif for Mitnagdim (the ones who were against Hassidism); the other one called 'Minyan" which belonged to the Hassidic part of the community and was located in a magnificently built wooden house.

Besides, there were several other 'shtiblach' (smaller shuls) which were adjacent to a big synagogue called the 'cold' synagogue since its size did not allow heating, so the place was in use only during hot weather. The holy sounds of prayer and Torah study were bursting forth from all those buildings and mixing with each other. Here the prayer starts, there it finishes, from minyan to minyan the holy sounds were rising to Heaven.

***

My mother had a very sensitive ear. At first glance, she was busy with her customers discussing various secular issues. She was loved by people since she had her own opinion on everything and they wanted to hear her fascinating stories. Despite that, she was invariably aware of the sounds coming from the synagogues.

She had a deep passion and was never content with three prayers during the day and used to attend an additional prayer in the women's section. She was accustomed to sitting alone or in the company of two or three women like her. For instance, ten males would be praying since one of them needed to say Kaddish. As they finished and left, somebody else started with a new minyan and so it lasted forever. Amazingly enough, the sounds of the cantor's chants reached the ears of my mother in her shop and she hurried in time for Kedushah which is said by the entire congregation.

No, she didn't consider that her absence might harm sales because the psychology of her customers was: If the shop is not open, we will come back later.

"The ones who perform a commandment are not harmed" was her philosophy.

***

The pattern was constantly repeated by my mother. As I bumped into the locked door, I didn't always have the patience to wait until the shop reopened. Late in the evening, when I returned home from a party with friends, I used to preach my mother about her actions at work which would not bring her success. I recall a heartfelt conversation with her concerning my arrival at a closed door. Time passed by; the days of my presence in Kupishok were about to end. In a short while, I was supposed to leave and was determined to talk to my mother.

"Mother, where do you disappear to during working hours? You are constantly complaining about your poor livelihood, pressing debts, and lack of merchandise. How can you increase the profits if the store is closed seven times a day?

She thought my words were reasonable; she shrugged and said, "The store is locked? The store is open from 9:00 in the morning until 9:00 in the evening, thank God, but my eyes are tired from seeing the place empty. I have virtually no work like all the other merchants." "That still does not explain your absence, mind you," I replied.

"What absence are you talking about? I just went for a Kedushah." "You actually left many times since I knocked on the shop's door at different hours during the day. And why, for God's sake, are you so keen on Kedushah? Other shop owners are also religious; they too pray a lot but don't overdo it. Even Shulhan Aruch does not demand that a woman like bring the business to a halt so often. Why do you bother Him so much?"

She smiled at me and sent a loving glance in my direction and calmly said, "How do you want me to behave if I have a request from the Lord and await His mercy?" Naturally, I understood what kind of wish my mother meant by the hint but pretended to be naive and asked, "What is this request that you have to repeat it seven times a day? Will you be so kind to reveal the secret of your pleas?"

"By no means is it a secret," she said with her clever eyes directed at me. "I am asking the Father of Orphans and Protector of Widows to turn your heart in the direction of commandments and faith following the tradition of your righteous father, may his memory be blessed, and the entire chain of your holy forefathers."

Although this was not the first time that I deciphered the wishes of my mother, I still tried to display my understanding and asked, "Is this the only desire that you have? Think of something else to ask the Creator, something you have never asked before. For example, apply to Him concerning your livelihood; maybe He will send you more customers and more satisfactory profits."

This was when my mother found time for a bit of preaching wile peeling an apple for me. She told me with a forgiving smile, "Listen, son, I can see that the Gentile wisdom in which you have immersed yourself makes you forget the teaching of your ancestors. Have you forgotten the meaning of a vain prayer which is a grave sin?" My mother was indeed educated in the field of Gemara, Torah, proverbs, etc., since she had always been present at her husband's lessons at home. She continued, "Shall I remind you of the significance of a false prayer? The person must not ask the Lord about something unreal. For instance, a man enters a town and hears that there is a fire. He must never say, 'I pray that this fire will not reach my house.' It is a vair prayer since the fire is already in his house."

"So, tell me then, Shlomo, why pray for a better living? As if this is something to be accomplished? Have you seen anyone in Kupishok who earns good wages? Our entire community lacks material means and I am obviously among them. The faith in God is a different matter altogether. This is why I am saying to our Lord, if I ever committed a sin, remember my and my husband's holy forefathers. Why don't You open the eyes of my youngest son and teach him to love You and perform Your commandments?"

"I know, my son, your deeds are righteous and the love for Eretz Israel is also a commandment. There is no one like you in relationships between people since you are so kind. But if you could enrich your life by more holy commandments, I would surely be happier."

דודתי בתיה אחות אימי
הדוד הילל זילבר מקופישוק הי״ד

בנות הדוד - בילה חצקביץ - הקטנה
טילה קודש - הגדולה
קרבנות השואה

Top: My aunt Batya, my mother's sister and uncle Hillel Zilber from Kupishok. May G-d avenge their blood

Middle: Cousins- Bela Chatzkewicz (younger), Tilla Kodesh (older); Both were murdered in the holocaust

Bottom: With my cousin David Pinskoy

הדוד שמעון לייב קודש
ומשפחתו סריגה
בחתונת בנס שלמה

הרב דודי ישראל נח
חצקביץ, אשתו
חנה רבקה אחות אבי,
בתם בלה - עלו במוקד
בקופישוק

1921 - בני הדוד: לייב קדישביץ, דוד פינסקו

Captions on Next Page

Top: Uncle Shimon Leib Kodesh and his family from Riga at their son's Shlomo wedding

Middle: My uncle rabbi Israel Noah Chatzkewicz, his wife Chana Rivka (my father's sister) and their daughter Bela. All murdered in Kupishok

Bottom: 1921 – Cousins Leib Kadishewicz and David Pinskoy

A group that participated in the rebellion against Tsar Nikolai II: Mina Kodesh –
standing far left, Pesia (Pnina) Kodesh standing second from right

Me and my sister Dina z"l in Kupishok 1919

My brother Shmuel with our sister Pnina and his young Fiancé Dora (1913)

Standing Reuven Kodesh; Seated (R – L): Shlomo Kodesh from Riga, his sister Tilla, May G-D avenge their blood and the author on the left

קלוב "הרצליה" קופישוק
ניסן 1931

שריד אחרון מדורנו
עומדים : נחום יחילביץ,
גרשון גרשוני,
יושבים : יעקב הופמן,
שלמה קודש,
הירש גפן

Top: "Herzliya" club, Kupishok Nissan 1931
Bottom: The last of our generation. Standing: Nachum Yechilewicz,
Gershon Gershoni. Seated: Yaakov Hoffman, Shlomo Kodesh, Hirsch Gefen

The Fateful Ticket

It was not a lottery ticket which determined my destiny but a simple train ticket – though not altogether simple. For the train itself was an innovation.

Lithuanian independence stunned me enormously. Amazing! How was it possible that I hadn't envisaged such a major change? I, who had been interested in current affairs since childhood, who was such an expert about politics; I, who thoroughly perused the first Hebrew newspaper, 'HaTzfira', which was edited (if I'm not mistaken) by the Zionist writer Nachum Sokolov.

In addition, I carefully read 'The Moment' in Yiddish which was the main source of the Jewish public's knowledge of world politics and Jewish affairs and was peppered with all kinds of entertaining supplements. It had some humorous sections, a little about health, and finally the famous serialized romances which thrilled the readers' imagination. The story was invariably cut at the most dramatic moment and everyone was longing to know what would happen in the next episode.

All of this was very much a part of my teenage years. In fact, current affairs attracted me much more than the endless philosophical arguments of Gemara which tired me. My well-developed imagination allowed me to change the world events which were not to my liking.

In 1914, when the Frist World War began, I was about eleven years old but already felt deeply involved in the world of politics of the time. From the first days of the War, I supported the German Emperor Wilhelm whereas my eternal rival, Hirsch Leibke – a shrewd and persistent individual who aroused my envy – stood by the Russian Czar Nikolai II, the persecutor of Jews.

I was a born politician! So how come, I thought, didn't I pay attention to the change of flags, to the numerous meetings at the Market Square, and the general revolutionary atmosphere around me. I was almost sixteen by this time and should have been aware of the crucial moment in the country's history.

One day the German occupation forces disappeared completely and Kupishok was suddenly flooded with red Lithuanians – bolsheviks. These were craftsmen, peddlers and even tradesmen who had decided to be Communist revolutionaries. They were dressed in short leather jackets with a gun stuck in their belt and were the people who embarked on fixing the world in the Marxist spirit.

Adversity makes a man wise and we knew already that each new attempt to correct the ways of the world or the borders of our small country with the neighboring powers started with the robbery of the local stores.

These plunderers acted in the traditional way! The soldiers took over the stores, grabbed anything valuable for themselves, mixed up the merchandise, spoiled more than they took and were off. As the storm passed, the Jewish merchants, who were quite accustomed to the procedure, would peek out of their shelters, count the damage, repair the lock and put everything in place again. All of this was considered natural.

But one Sabbath morning, however, things were somewhat different. For one thing, these were not hungry and shabby soldiers who had escaped from the battle and vented their anger on anything that was in their path. Instead, the Kupishok Jews were ordered to open their stores. It was not a robbery, God forbid, but a perfectly legitimate confiscation.

In other words, a few local apprentices, coachmen and peddlers who had now joined the red militia appeared to fulfill the holy mission of confiscating the goods from the shops of Kupishok bourgeois who exploited the working masses. It was a little bizarre to see Yankel Terpido, just a little older than me, in the role of the local commissar giving orders to his fellow revolutionaries what to take and how to pack the goods. All the merchandise was transferred for the sake of the Socialist Revolution, whatever that meant.

Bourgeois stood for my mother, Aunt Tzippi and Aunt Gittel, the widow who pawned her candlesticks for half a ruble every Sunday to pay for her children's heder. (We shouldn't forget, however, the virtue of the moneylender's wife who ran to Gittel's house every Sabbath eve to bring the candlesticks back.)

The Lithuanian Bolsheviks disappeared as quickly as they had come since the new leadership called 'Tariba' pushed the 'reds' out of the government with the help of the Church. The winning powers – America, Britain and France – forced a peace treaty on the defeated Germany as well as their allies, the Russians who, after the October Revolution, liberated the Poles, the Baltic peoples, and Lithuania from occupation.

Lithuania was one of those newly- born republics which emerged on the remnants of the Czarist empire. As I have said, I wasn't actively involved in those upheavals so the only thing I remember from that period are the sudden assemblies in the middle of a market day, flags in the air, fierce debates between the speakers and curses of Jewish shopkeepers about the waste of precious market time.

***

The new Lithuanian state appeared as if out of the blue. It began to recruit young men into the army and started some state services, the railway being one of them. The train operated between 'Abeli' – the last station in the north-east and 'Eidkoon' on the east -Prussian border.

In those days, I had a feeling that my Kupishok had disappeared and wandered around town having no idea what to do with myself. I dreamt of the 'Gymnasium' (a German high school) although Kupishok did not even have a secondary school. There was one in Ponevitz, about half an hour by train, and my sister Peska (Pnina) taught in one of the schools there.

As a center for education, the city did not particularly attract me. There was a different reason for my strong desire to go to this neighboring town. I was deeply in love with a girl I had never seen before. She was a cousin of my sister's colleague, Abraham Kessin, and what I heard about her urged me to leave everything, discover a new place, and prepare myself for a proper education.

Although I was quite good at Hebrew, German, and arithmetic, I hardly knew any Russian, the main language of teaching at the Gymnasium. Still, the incentive of being in Ponevitz overcame all barriers. My distraught mother packed some pillows and clothes; I filled my suitcase with all kinds of books, put a few marks in my pocket and these were all my belongings when in 1919 I arrived in Ponevitz.

Having rented a small room at the Lipshitz's, I tried to find ways that would lead me to an education and a future living. Both of these aims led me to the same Abraham Kessin, a sharp, handsome man who had captured my sister's heart. There I met the young lady who was the hidden reason for my coming, Shira Miller. She was about fifteen, pretty, and arrogant, especially towards a provincial type like me who didn't even speak Russian. I was totally infatuated with her but she rejected me with one hand and cunningly beckoned with the other. Shira agreed to help me with learning Russian. In the meantime, I met some local young people and learned that there was a Jewish youth party called 'Tzeirei

Tzion.' There I felt like a fish in water since the Zionists considered Hebrew a significant language and I was quite an expert in it.

Soon I was elected Secretary of the Party's Ponevitz branch and one of my tasks was to write circulars. I then duplicated them on the amazing machine which copied manuscripts on wax. I also taught Hebrew privately and thus earned a few extra marks.

My mother used to send me food parcels as she did when my father had studied at the famous Slobodka yeshiva during their first years of marriage. I spent some months torn between all kinds of political activities, private lessons to earn a living, and preparatory Russian classes with Shira, who continued to treat me in a reserved and slightly condescending way.

***

These lines may not be precise chronologically since my memory betrays me occasionally, but I remember that my Ponevitz period did not last long. Shortly after my arrival, my sister moved to Kaunas, worked as a teacher for some time and then started her career at the national 'RAT' – the Jewish National Council which was an active organization in the few golden years of Judaism in Lithuania.

It was a period of Jewish cultural independence. There even was a Minister of Jewish Affairs, Dr. Menachem Soloveichik (Sulieli, in Israel), an educated and respectable man who ruled with violence as a minister until he was sacked.

In short, I was abandoned by my sister with virtually no chance of entering the Gymnasium and my Russian teacher did not reveal great interest in me. I was active in the Party, awaited a miracle which would show me the way out of the dead end and, as it usually happens, time did what the brain could not do.

***

Life in Lithuania acquired some order. The Jews grew accustomed to the new rule by ignorant Lithuanians. (We called them 'Klompes' for the wooden shoes they wore in contrast to the leather ones which were a symbol of status.) Schools opened, businesses functioned, and the Jewish political life prospered under the aegis of the National Council. The mess in the government did not interfere with daily life for several reasons.

The disorder was no greater than it had been before and in any case the adaptability of our people to any chaos is famous. But most importantly, the Polish and Lithuanian Jews who had established themselves in America began to send money to their remaining relatives.

There also was some financial assistance from the Joint Distribution Committee (JDC) and other public organizations so that Jewish life somehow took its course.

***

One evening I entered Shira's room to find her with a train ticket in her hand. The railway was already in existence at the time but valid tickets had not been produced yet. Instead, there were special forms filled in by the few literate people.

She gave me a sheet of paper and jokingly said, "You've got a sister in Kaunas, so take it and go," which seemed to be the answer to my prayers. I didn't hesitate for a minute! I took Peska's address (the Little Vilna Street 19), separated from Shira and some friends at the Tzeirei Tzion Club.

A small coach was loaded with my scarce belongings and I set out for the railway station. I arrived in Kaunas in the evening. It was the first time that I had ever been to a big city!

There were buildings of three and even four stories high! But I was even more surprised when I saw that the streets were decorated with

Zionist flags – white and blue with the Star of David. I naively believed the entire city belonged to the Zionists – a path to the Land of Israel...

I later found out the reason of that festivity; the Kaunas Jewry celebrated the day of the Balfour Declaration, the second of November 1917, and many believed it was the beginning of redemption. It was explained that Zionist demonstrations were held on that day and the flags were the remains.

Eventually I reached my sister's home. She wasn't there but her landlord was kind enough to let me into her room. Peska hadn't really expected me in Kaunas and despite her affection for me had little reason to be excited by my arrival. She was lonely herself and could not do much to help a provincial, uneducated and penniless person like me. Had I waited for her invitation, I would never have reached the capital at all. With hindsight, I understand that she had made quite an effort to show her hospitality and was deeply impressed by adventurous behavior. I fell asleep in the city of my dreams!

The next day found me alone in the room. My breakfast was on the table with a note in Hebrew, "Will be back at noon." What should I do until then? I stepped outside and began to walk from the house constantly turning back in fear of getting lost and entered the main street called Liberty Avenue. Its beauty astounded me!

I felt very lonely in that great world when, all of a sudden, somebody touched me on the shoulder. I can't recall the language the man spoke but it was with a clear Russian accent. He was a student who I remembered from way back in Kupishok. Here is the story.

***

It all happened at the end of the First World War when some Kupishok people, and I among them, decided to get together and spend some time singing, reading and even acting. We rented a big room in the house of Bentzi, the moneylender, and organized a club called 'Locale."

The girls decorated it with taste so that the place became a real cultural center for the local youth. Each one of us contributed his own talent to the venture. One of the girls was a good singer and I had some aptitude of reading in public so we combined the two abilities and created a successful duet which had romantic consequences for both of us.

In general, I didn't have much success with girls so the club was an opportunity to correct the injustice. I was good at reciting Hebrew texts and that dramatic skill of mine was appreciated by the listeners. The place became a kind of spiritual shelter for the growing youngsters of Kupishok since everyone of us longed for human warmth in the harsh reality of the times. Our pleasant evenings contrasted with the horrors of the past war, occupation, and pogroms which we had all experienced. Our future was not paved with gold so the Locale sweetened the heavy feelings we had.

One winter evening as we were enjoying ourselves in the warm room, the door opened and a young man burst in. His outfit, a hooded jacket, showed he was a Russian student. He started in Russian, a language few of us understood as it wasn't taught in Kupishok even in the days of the Czar so we absorbed only the names he pronounced with his heavy accent – Palestine, Gerzel (Herzl), Tel-Aviv, pioneers and many other words which we had heard before but they did not really penetrate.

However little we understood, he spoke with such vigor that we wanted to hear more and more of his excited Zionist speech. In fact, I had encountered the words he mentioned in the Hebrew magazine, 'The World,' which was my secret reading material hidden on one of my father's bookshelves. Still I had never heard Zionist propaganda before so the entire event impressed me a great deal.

As he finished, many of our friends left but my cousin, David Pinskoy (Pinsker) and I remained to show him the way to the local hostel. It turned out that his name was Eliezer Perelson and he was involved with transferring Jewish refugees from Russia to their hometowns. As he happened to stay in Kupishok for one night, he naturally searcahed for youth and that was how he found our Locale. I told him about myself and we parted.

The club members discussed his performance for some days after he left until the event was forgotten.

***

Curiously enough, that same Eliezer Perelson (later Perry, an important figure in Tel-Aviv, and one of the first managers of the publishing company Am Oved) was the first person I met in Kaunas. I willingly shared my ambitions with him and was stunned when he offered me a job at 'HaHalutz,' (The Pioneer), an organization which started to act in liberated Lithuania. It united groups of Jewish youth who wanted to build and to be rebuilt in the land of their forefathers.

The HaHalutz movement was inspired by three outstanding figures: Eliezer Perelson, who was an energetic leader and Dr. Moshe Shwabbe, a young scientist who fled from Germany during the war and never went back. He was married to a German-Jewish girl and they had two children. His house was open to anyone who wished to hear about Zion and it became the center for many gatherings. Later he founded the Hebrew Gymnasium in Kaunas, whose students left their mark on the Jewish Zionist society of Lithuania. When he came on aliya, Dr. Shwabbe was Professor of Greek at Hebrew University until he died.

The third leader was David Cohen, the son of one of the famous Hassidic rabbis in Lithuania. He became a well-known writer, father of 'HaNoar HaOved,' (The Working Youth) and served as editor of the weekly 'HaMa'aleh.'

Perelson introduced me to the young Zionist leadership and I quickly became very much a part of their society. The HaHalutz building was situated opposite my sister's house but as far as I remember I soon found some other arrangements and moved out of her room.

I spent nights and days either at the Movement's office or at Dr. Shwabbe's place. My first occupation was installing small silk white and blue insignias to the jackets of our members as well as making donation boxes for the activists.

***

This is the story of my unusual absorption in Kaunas and all had been due to a memorable train ticket!

The Rebellion

Had I been a truly pious person, I would have had to atone for my sins after my behavior at the Jewish Secondary School of Exact Sciences in Kaunas. It was founded during the German occupation by Dr. Joseph Carlebach, a German Jew from Frankfurt-on-the-Main with a religious Orthodox background.

This community, which carefully preserved its identity despite the general tendency of assimilation, was highly educated, had patriotic feelings towards Germany and fiercely opposed the secular Zionist ideas of Theodor Herzl. In the course of the First World War, they even volunteered to serve in the German army and some of them reached high military rank. If I am not mistaken, Dr. Carlebach was a major. Moreover, Emperor Wilhelm II, who was determined to win the war and annex Lithuania to Germany, considered the Yiddish-speaking Jewish population loyal to his country.

The first attempt was the establishment of the Jewish Secondary school whose main language of teaching was German. Religion classes were conducted in Hebrew. Dr. Carlebach, still in officer's uniform, was appointed headmaster. He was supposed to create a high-level education institution – a task which he successfully performed as he was an experienced and tough educator.

Finding staff was not a problem since German teachers of Jewish origin could be found in the German army, some of them of the same Orthodox background as Carlebach himself. He also invited some Gentile teachers in uniform, so the school had a mixed German-Jewish character.

Subsequently, the Germans were expelled from Lithuania and even lost a part of their east-Prussian territory. Thus, an end was put to German occupation and the Baltic states became independent.

***

Kaunas remained with two major Jewish schools: The first was the 'Russian Gymnasium' and the second – the above-mentioned German school. The headmaster and most of the teachers saw no point in returning to the defeated, hungry Germany. Presumably, some of their reasons were idealistic. Most importantly, the school continued to work and the classes were full, many of the students were expelled Lithuanian Jews who had returned from Russia. Dr. Carlebach's prestige was not impaired after he changed his military uniform for civilian clothes.

The subjects were countless: German language and literature, Russian language and literature, the Bible and Hebrew literature, Latin, mathematics, physics, chemistry, geography, Jewish and general history, art and sports were taught. In other words, practically all domains of human knowledge were covered. Most surprising was the fact that there were quite a few students who were good at virtually all subjects. It was that school which I entered in 1920.

I remember the interview with the Deputy Headmaster, Dr. Schlesinger from Vienna. He spoke Hebrew with a Sephardic accent (which I heard for the first time in my life that day but got used to it during our conversation.) He asked me to read a Gemara page with Rashi's commentaries. I read it fluently and Dr. Schlesinger allowed me to choose the class I wished to enter but prudently suggested the sixth form because of my complete ignorance of secular subjects.

My school education was limited to fluent German, some elementary knowledge of arithmetic and a little Russian. The sixth class was just three years before the demanding matriculation exams.

***

I entered the boy's class (girls studied at the same level but in a different group.) Gradually I became integrated and even excelled in Judaism, history, and German literature. Except for math, I coped with studies with relative success and passed all the sixth year examinations.

For whatever reason, I received an exemption from the school and was never asked to pay. Mr. Halper, the school's treasurer, was laughed at by the students for his careful attitude to money, but he treated me extremely well. He invited me to his home where I met his daughter who was my age, spoke fluent Hebrew and even wrote poetry. He also recommended me as a private Hebrew tutor to a family with two spoiled girls, a part-time job which was my livelihood during my gymnasium years. So the question remains: Why did I rebel against the management and ruin the school's discipline when everyone supported me so much?

***

The element of rebellion had been inherent in me since childhood. I was a well-behaved boy though a little spoiled by my mother. She occasionally indulged me with a sweet or two which was a rarity among the poor Kupishok children. She also protected me against my father's wrath which I caused frequently with my mischievous behavior. Complaints about me reached him and he could be severe in his punishment but, at the same time, cared about me a great deal.

He was anxious about my health, feeding me with all kinds of foods which were supposed to strengthen me. In fact, in all my ninety-five years, I have not been able to find out what he meant by the dangerous disease called 'skruplitzni' for which eggnog and fish oil were the best remedy. The fish oil, called 'lebertran,' was thought to be the source of health. Every morning I was sentenced to swallow a spoonful. After that, I was compensated with an apple or a peeled pear. Eggnog was an altogether different matter as I have already described in a previous story.

***

As a student, I was good at humanistic subjects, German in particular. I somehow muddled through geography and Russian and wasn't successful in math – a subject in which I lacked basic knowledge. One subject which I especially hated was Latin! But most of all, I couldn't tolerate the teacher who was an arrogant German officer and one of the few Gentiles who remained in our school after Germany's defeat.

He was a Prussian 'junker' who always wore officer's boots. When he took off his uniform, he continued his dictatorship in our class. His manner of teaching was condescending. He even slapped the students' faces but did not touch me – not out of kindness but due to absolute contempt. He might have heard something about me from the school's management and possibly decided to keep his distance from the 'cheeky Jew.'

After each lesson of Latin, I attempted to arouse my classmates to action. I claimed that the teacher had no right to physically punish sixth level students. "We must protest against the teacher and his shameful actions," I vehemently preached. And little by little, my speeches took effect. The class somehow accepted my leadership and I only had to wait for the right moment which was soon in coming.

One morning our violent teacher failed to restrain himself. When checking the students' homework, he perused the notebook of one of my classmates named Kalverisky, the son of a well-to-do fur merchant in Kaunas. He was a quiet boy, slightly spoiled and not particularly bright but he had a good reputation in class.

Unfortunately, the Latin teacher looked at the wrong page in Kalverisky's notebook. He stood up and slapped the boy's face. When the boy showed the right exercise, the teacher mumbled in German, 'Ach so,' (Ah, here it is) and turned to another student as if nothing had happened.

The boy returned to his seat with a disappointed look. The class became silent. All of a sudden, I raised my finger. "What is it?" asked the teacher. I stood up and said in correct German, "Sir, you forgot to apologize for the punishment which Kalverisky did not deserve. And besides, I do not think that you have the right to beat students in our level." I then spoke to my fellow students in Yiddish and declared firmly, "We are leaving the class!" With those words, I walked to the door.

A few others rose and followed me energetically. Miraculously, the classroom became empty in a few minutes as the other students joined us in the yard. Two or three cowards remained but the teacher did not pay any attention to them. He stormed out of the class, passed our group without looking at us, and entered the management department.

"To the synagogue!" I exclaimed. We began to walk towards an old and neglected building in the vicinity of our school. Some of the boys were hesitant, others were excited as we filled one of the synagogue's rooms. More than seventy-five years have passed since that memorable incident and I still cannot understand the source of my courage.

I must give credit to two of my friends – Zevadia Levinson and Jacob Retzko. The first lived in Panmolis, a wealthy Kaunas suburb which was linked to the city by a shuttle. Zevadia, who came from a well-off family, always had pockets that were full of the coins he received from his caring mother. We stuck together from my first day in class. I even let him stay in my rented room from time to time, provided my landlady agreed to ignore the unknown tenant.

The other friend, Jacob, also originated from a well-established family and was not thrilled by school. So the three of us would miss some particularly boring classes and saunter to the Kapulsky Cafe where we devoured 'pirozhne' – absolutely delicious cakes.

* * *

We decided not to go back to school – either now or later. Our parents would not know! We agreed, instead, to continue our lessons when each subject would be taught by a student who was an expert in it. Thus, Jacob Dambo, a born mathematician, taught math; Jacob Sachs taught Latin and, or course, Israel Bernstein from Yorbourg conducted Russian classes.

It was my responsibility to teach Hebrew literature and the Bible, knowledge which I had gained at home. I had experience in teaching the subjects and had served as a private tutor. (The more renowned students of mine were Chief Justice Aharon

Barak's father who survived the Holocaust and became a successful economist in Jerusalem, as well as Michael, one of the famous Lithuanian Communist leaders, who was eliminated by Stalin in the years of terror.)

Having filled the teaching roles, we agreed to follow the rules and appear for the regular classes. It was not a planned riot but eventually we developed ideas which perfectly reflected the dilemma of Jewish youth in Lithuania at the time. It was a new trend in Jewish culture for it combined elements from the Orthodox religious tradition with the new wind of Zionism expressed by the Balfour Declaration.

The excitement quickly disappeared and we had to find a place where we could organize our classes. My idea was the soup kitchen on Mapu Street 7, where one could find a basic meal for a symbolic price. Mrs. Verblovsky managed the place with two of her daughters and her older sister, who was my landlady. She cared for me like a mother and I believed she would not refuse the request.

***

We were faced with the difficult decision how to continue the rebellion. Someone suggested that we produce a document in German which would outline our reasons and demands. When the class dispersed, four of us were left: Jacob Sachs, Eliezer Leipziger, Mattiahu Arnovitz and myself. This group was supposed to write the decree whereas the others would sign it the next morning.

Since signing the decree could mean being expelled, our classmates' fear was understandable. So someone suggested a brilliant idea – the signatures would be in a circle so that there would not be first and last ones. I was given the privilege of writing the document. Some friends approved, others disapproved what I wrote.

It contained four demands:

- Teachers will use no physical punishment from the 5th grade onward.

-Students will be allowed to sing 'HaTikvah' and other Zionist songs (which had been until then forbidden.)

-Students will be allowed to conduct a dance once a year with the participation of girls from the parallel class.

-No student will be punished for the rebellion.

We copied the text several times, drew a circle and left space for the other classmates to sign. The next morning virtually everyone turned up with a feeling of dignity and put his signature on the paper.

A suggestion was made to share our misfortunes with a member of the Parent's Committee. It was a good move as he was a gentle person who understood our feelings and even encouraged our struggle. Having calmed us down, he took the decree and presented it at the next meeting of the Committee. It turned out that the Headmaster had known about the Latin teacher and presumably made his decision for we never saw him again.

When on the morning my classmates turned up for the lessons conducted by their fellow students, I had a message to convey. "We must go back to school," I said. "Dr. Deutschlander, a former German officer and a professional educator, is the new Headmaster." As we later learned, Dr. Carlebach was about to leave Kaunas and to become Chief Rabbi of the Altona community in Germany.

I saw him again a few times but he never expressed a desire to talk to me even though he had heard about me from his colleagues. Dr. Deutschlander, however, displayed some interest and sent me to teach in a small town during the summer holidays that year.

Five months remained until the end of the school year. The teachers pretended that nothing had happened but there was something in the air which signaled a change of attitude. Our Bible teacher, Rosenson, a young and likeable man, had revealed his Zionist ideas back in Carlebach's days and was not fired since he was the husband of Chief Rabbi Kook's daughter.

***

The regime of punishments left over from the German occupation period eventually disappeared and, in any case, the old-fashioned 'Carlebach method' was no longer popular in the city's Jewish community. Our childish rebellion had its practical effect for us but also symbolized the other impending upheavals in our school and community.

As for me, the event greatly increased my popularity. Many more people strove to be on friendly terms with me and I was invited to their homes. But the peak was the dance at the end of the school year, when I finally received some attention from the girls. The 'flying post,' the then way of courting, brought quite a few notes in German and Hebrew addressed to me, some of them were signed, others weren't.

It was a good sign for the future.

Shlomo Kodesh, as a high school student, 1920 – Kaunas (Kovno)

Tenth grade in the Hebrew Reali (a school leaning towards the science/math) high school in 1920 in Kaunas. Standing: From right – Yaakov Dambo, Shlomo Kodesh, Seated: Israel Bernstein, Israel Kopilow

From a Stool in a Tavern to a Zionist Stage

A gathering of Kupishok youngsters. A 16-year-old orphan, none other than myself, was standing on a stool speaking excitedly.

The meeting took place on a Saturday night in a tavern at Moshe's house, a teacher and merchant. His spacious home also served as a meeting room for German soldiers in the days of the Occupation (during World War One.) On Market Days, it was a tavern for Lithuanian peasants.

On that particular Saturday, the place turned into a general ideological assembly of two main streams. The first was the 'working class' as the left-wing partisans called themselves. They consisted of simple workers, craftsmen and some shop-keepers.

The other stream called itself the 'intelligentia' (although their rivals used to refer to them as the 'rotten' intelligentia.) These were the sons of the local bourgeois, merchants and religious officials (rabbis, slaughterers, cantors, and beadles.) Some of the latter discontinued their religious practices as a result of the upheavals during World War One: The expulsion of Jews from the border towns in Lithuania, the Russian Revolution, the fall of Germany, and the destruction of religious institutions including townships like Kupishok.

There was an atmosphere in the country of rebellion and liberation. Even the uneducated Lithuanians from the villages would gather at the local marketplace opposite our store and make patriotic speeches in favor of an independent Lithuania which had been enslaved for hundreds of years. So this was the general ambiance of the day. It obviously influenced the Jewish youngsters, mainly males at first, who also decided to hold a meeting at the local tavern.

I was usually quite shy and soft spoken with strangers but on this day I uncharacteristically climbed on a stool and produced my first public speech. Although I cannot remember the exact contents of the presentation, it seems that I supported the ideology of the intelligentia.

The different opinions were similar at the gathering since everyone spoke about the sunny future awaiting us, about liberty, enlightenment, and a better world. What I never forgot was the storming applause which accompanied me as I descended from the stool. On that day, my reputation as a speaker was born!

***

I must point out that during my early childhood when nobody was at home, I would wrap myself in my mother's headscarf as if it were a tallit and imitate wandering preachers, called 'Magid,' who used to give pious talks at the Mitnagdim synagogue. The preacher accompanied his speech with a heart-breaking tune and would tell the gathered crowd all sorts of stories, fables, and anecdotes. The listeners would place coins on the plate which stood at the entrance since the preacher was often extremely skillful, eloquent and either had a good voice himself or appeared in the company of a local boy who assisted him during the musical selections.

During my rehearsals, I would try my hand both at preaching and singing and also invented stories, tremendously enjoying this solo appearance. But this was all a result of my childish mischief and playfulness. This time, however, I found myself on a real stage, albeit only a stool, with an audience in front of me. To this day, I haven't stopped speaking publicly although the thrill of it is partially lost as the years go by.

It was shortly after this memorable experience that my Zionist beliefs took shape and I turned into a well-known 'tribune' or to be precise 'tribune number 2' among Kupishok Zionists. I was not half as good as

Yankel'e (Jacob) Hoffman, the youngest son of Getzil Hoffman, a flour merchant and an outstanding scholar who would eventually become a respected Zionist leader.

Yankel'e was near-sighted, with ginger colored hair, and charismatic since birth. He already had some pioneer experience behind him since in Russia he had been a member of the Zionist group called 'Mishmar HaVolga.' Until today, I am convinced that he was a born orator. When this competitor of mine left Kupishok for Eretz Israel, I naturally took his place as head of the big mouths in town.

***

During our turbulent youth, we used to organize cultural balls. A typical program consisted of a Zionist speech at the opening, songs, and readings in Yiddish and Hebrew. Then came the romantic correspondence called 'flying post,' where boys and girls would exchange anonymous letters, and finally dancing. At the end of the evening, the boys respectfully accompanied the girls home. If one happened to be lucky, he might even have succeeded at giving a girl a quick kiss. These were typical romantic evenings of the early twenties in Lithuania.

I was very involved in the organization of those evenings and would recite extracts from Bialik, Frishman, Frug and other Hebrew and Yiddish writers. I read with great excitement, often receiving loud applause from the audience. I even tried my luck in acting as well as in producing although the latter field was dominated by an old bachelor, named Hair Kreichek, who did not have good looks but possessed a great sense of humor.

***

The disease of public speaking got a firm hold on me even after I had left my hometown. Already in my first days at the Kaunas Gymnasium, I was noticed as a talker. There I had tough competition from my classmates. One of the best was Eliezer (Leizke) Leipziger from Yorbourg, the brother of Aliza Porat from Kibbutz Afikim. He was the same age, same height, and we looked like brothers. Leizke excelled at math and painting and possessed charismatic qualities. In the skill of oration, however, I perhaps surpassed him due to the comprehensive Jewish education I had received at home. Still, the girls preferred him!

During my university years in Kaunas, where I studied law and economics, I became increasingly involved in the Socialist-Zionist party. Eventually I took over the task of spreading the party's ideas to the provinces. Having gained some experience, I was often invited to various communities, travelling widely throughout the entire country on a voluntary basis. I even paid the expenses out of my own pocket as I couldn't think of deriving material benefits from sacred ideals.

***

I received the nickname 'Kraft' which meant 'strength' in German and Yiddish because of my ability to give impressive speeches that excited the listeners. I have often wondered about the secret of an orator's ability to thrill the hearts of his audience. What is the reason for that unseen link which is created between the speaker and the public? And how is it created?

A person might flatter himself foolishly but being liked by others is a subject that has not stopped troubling the mind of the social man. The impression a person makes on others has remained one of the most important aspects of life.

What was my secret? I have no intention whatsoever of praising my talent as an orator who struck others with his eloquence or revolutionary speeches. Not at all! Not once did I bore my listeners chatting aimlessly about this and that. Moreover, I was never excited by my own presentations, exercised self-criticism, and tried to improve for the future.

I have never been fond of relying on a script. Instead, I tried to focus on someone in the audience and watch their reaction. That allowed me to assess the degree of interest among the listeners and only on a few occasions did I need an auxiliary sheet of paper.

More important than anything, however, was my unequivocal love for the people I spoke to and my strong belief in the ideology I represented. In my childhood, I was invariably attracted to people and to human matters. The education that I received at home was based on Habad Hassidism which was characterized by an extremely human approach to life.

Unfortunately, my father did not provide me with an insight into the sophisticated philosophy of Hassidism as it was formulated by the founder of Habad, Rabbi S. Zalman from Liadi. Not one single hour, among the numerous lessons I had with my father was dedicated to 'Tanya,' its central teachings. Instead, I had absorbed countless proverbs, cognitive stories, and colorful sayings which I used extensively in my speeches, preferring them to dry analytical explanations.

I have always felt that it was easier to speak to the hearts of an audience than to appeal to their intellect. The reason is simple: The human mind is structured to cope with intellectual challenges whereas the heart is open to emotions. It is enough for a speaker to show the audience his sincere affection for them and his desire to share this knowledge that the listeners will immediately react positively to the presentation.

There is nothing worse in public relations than telling the audience inaccurate information. The speaker's reliability is lost forever and any effort to correct the impression will be in vain. Knowing this, I have never separated myself from others; I mingled with everyone regardless of their age or status. The certain popularity which I have acquired over the years stems from this.

***

A few years after Lithuania attained independence, there was a sharp increase in Jewish awareness. Numerous Zionist organizations were established, conferences held and the Lithuanian Jewish community temporarily enjoyed some cultural freedom. The end of that short period marked the beginning of an era of hatred towards Jews and a drastic decline in economic well being.

The reasons for this sudden alienation had always been present in Catholic countries in general and particularly in Lithuania. The fanatical priests considered Jews to the 'assassins of the Messiah,' and believed in the eternal curse of this people. The churches were constantly preaching against Jews by exploiting all the primitive accusations and blood libels. During Passover, the attacks would become particularly vicious using all the anti-semitic techniques, especially the one accusing Jews of using the blood of Christian children for the Matzot.

Although the libels had existed for a long time, the issue was now complicated by the fact that the Catholic fanatics received a majority in the Lithuanian parliamentary elections in 1917. They immediately embarked on limiting the opportunities of Jews in commerce, state offices, and the army.

Only due to our people's ability to cope with great difficulties, many nevertheless retained their positions as doctors, lawyers, engineers and scientists. They worked in conditions of constant persecution by their colleagues and youth who desired to occupy their places. That "Lithuanian intelligentia" was the one to collaborate with Nazi Germany during the Second World War in their horrible task of genocide.

***

In the 1920's, for reasons which have remained unclear to me, the Lithuanian government did not hurry to completely destroy the scheme of autonomous Jewish education although it used all possible techniques to limit it. During those years, about twenty Jewish secondary schools operated in the country providing thousands of Jewish students with high-quality education and a widely recognized diploma, which gave the Jewish teenagers the opportunity to enter university.

The only practical remnant of the long-discussed Jewish autonomy was the national Jewish education. It involved four years of primary education at the government's expense and another eight years in a 'Gymnasium.'

The students completed their education by taking matriculation exams, usually supervised by a superficial Lithuanian official. At that stage, most youth prepared to enroll in universities which were still liberal enough to accept Jewish students. Medical careers attracted dozens of applicants. Despite the tough entrance conditions, many Jews studied medicine.

The faculties of Law and Economics were another popular option among young and ambitious teenagers like myself. The rest received BA degrees in philosophy, history, mathematics and natural sciences. The result was an influx of highly educated Jewish students into a limited Lithuanian job market. This fact naturally aroused a great deal of frustration and anger among their Lithuanian peers who hated Jews even without having to compete with them.

***

In general, the situation was not favorable for young East-European Jews. Many of them began to search for immigration opportunities. There were the 'ideal' destinations like the United States. Because conditions were generally so difficult, even poor and devastated countries like Argentina, Mexico, Brazil and Paraguay seemed a possible destination.

Palestine was another possibility but it was problematic. Many felt a great deal of patriotism but the harsh life-style of pioneers and the seemingly incurable disease of unemployment was not particularly attractive for the ambitious white-collar professionals.

The publication of the Balfour Declaration provoked a great deal of excitement in many European Jewish communities. Some people even believed that Zion was finally revived by a supernatural force. Zionists attempted to attract settlers to the barren land and called for donations. Very few responded positively to the request although there were some emotional Jewish women who readily contributed their valuables to the Zionist enterprise. Alongside them, some impoverished home-owners also donated their last resources and finally there appeared young excited boys and girls willing to go to Palestine to build and to be rebuilt. The message of the kibbutz particularly impressed them and some made attempts to reach the Promised Land against all odds.

As for the well-off part of the Jewish population, very few gathered enough courage to make aliyah – the majority abstained from places with limited investment opportunities.

***

The British Mandatory Rule did not look forward to receiving new immigrants, gradually becoming more and more hostile to the building of a national Jewish homeland. Simultaneously, the nationalistic Arab movement did everything in order to torpedo the return of Jews to their historic land: The horrible bloodshed of the late 1920's in many Jewish settlements in Palestine provided the British with another 'good' reason to limit the return of Jews. All of these events together contributed somehow to the negative attitude of east-European Jews towards aliyah.

***

The appearance of Dr. Theodor Herzl caused a great deal of embarrassment for religious Jewry who awaited the Messiah, the Lord's messenger, to liberate them and bring them to Eretz Israel. They could never come to terms with an envoy in the form of a polished diplomat who was secular and ignorant in matters of faith. Traditional tales had predicted the arrival of the Messiah in various ways but none of them foretold of an Austrian journalist, unknown to his own people and famous among the Gentiles.

Naturally, not all Orthodox rabbis openly criticized Zionism. They preached against the secular tendencies of contemporary Jewish society, against religious ignorance, and the mixture of boys and girls at public events. Still, generally speaking, the hearts of many of them were also directed towards Zion.

Quite a few rabbis declared themselves as Zionists, in particular the members of the newly established party 'Mizrachi,' which was under the aegis of Rabbi Jacob Reinish. As the leader of the Jewish community in Lida, he established a Zionist yeshiva which became very popular among the Jewish youth. His center succeeded in combining Torah learning with open support for Jewish settlers in Palestine.

Still, the vast majority of east-European rabbis did not back the Zionist enterprise although they expressed interest in everything that was happening in Palestine. They would listen attentively to the news and mourn those who perished there in the struggle for Jewish revival.

***

I must mention here a horrible story about my relative Rabbi Israel Noah Hetzkevitz, the rabbi of the Kupishok Habad community. Being a great scholar in the field of Jewish mysticism and Hassidic literature, he was involved in studies and community matters. Although the hot debate between Zionists and their opponents did not interest him, he was thirsty to hear any news about the pioneers and national rebuilding. He would yearn for the High Holidays when I used to visit my hometown and fill him in on all the news about Palestine. As a sign of gratitude, he sang some of his splendid Hassidic tunes at the end of our conversations and overwhelmed me with his immense spiritual wealth.

Adjacent to his house lived a 'Shabbat Goy,' the non-Jew who solved technical problems on Shabbat that Jews were forbidden to do. Many years later that same man spoke to Israeli visitors about the horrors of the Holocaust in Lithuania. He told them that the entire family was caught by the Germans and together with some other remaining Jews was put in the wooden town synagogue. The Nazis and their collaborators set the synagogue on fire with the people inside.

To everyone's astonishment, a voice was heard singing from within. It was one of the Sabbath tunes which the man had heard so many times from the Rabbi. It was the old Hassidic song composed by the Alter Rabbi Zalman, and is sung to this very day every Saturday and once a year on the 19th of Kislev in his memory.

***

The Orthodox rabbis were not our main rivals in the struggle for Zionist ideals. We did not witness any fierce antagonism on their part; our differences of opinion were felt only in election propaganda. Even then, the argument did not go beyond agitated but civilized discussions. Our parents had the opportunity to enjoy the eloquent talk of their offspring who would constantly add some Biblical and Talmudic expressions to embellish their speeches.

Our real political enemies were the left-wing, anti-Zionists who increased Jewish autonomy in Lithuania with the foundation of schools in Yiddish, the unofficial Jewish language. Their success was limited to a number of primary schools with Yiddish as the language of instruction but they never outnumbered schools that taught in Hebrew.

Then there were the Jewish Communists and their supporters. They were a particularly hostile group who hated Zion and detested any attempt to build a national Jewish homeland in Palestine. The Communist Party was outlawed and anyone who was caught was sent to prison and savagely tortured.

Despite the efforts of Yudel Mark, a prominent educator whose ideology was split between a love for Israel and his belief in Yiddish as the Jewish unofficial language, his students turned into extremists. They were glad to hear any bad tidings about Palestine which proved their case. They would hold dozens of fanatical demonstrations all over Lithuania calling Jews to look for liberation in the Diaspora instead of distant Palestine where Jews persecuted poor Arabs living in their historic land. Jewish children, they screamed, should not be educated in the obsolete Hebrew but in Yiddish, the living and colorful language of Mendel'e 'Mocher Sforim,' Shalom Aleichem, I.L. Peretz and others. Regardless of whether they succeeded in elections, the Communists harmed the Zionist enterprise a great deal.

***

During the thirteen years of living and studying in Kaunas, I was active in local politics which combined my passion with my studies. In our socialist rigor, we even tried to teach the illiterate Lithuanian peasants by organizing secret talks in their villages explaining to the people their rights and calling for a united struggle against employers, most of whom were Jewish. We did not receive proper gratitude from our 'students' in the days of slaughter. They paid us with blood and smoke, but this is a theme for a separate story. We may or may not have learned our lesson.

***

I might remind the reader of that talented 'ginger' boy whom I mentioned at the beginning of this chapter, Yankel'e (Jacob) Hoffman. He left Kupishok for Palestine but, as it later turned out, did not reach the Promised Land. He arrived in Paris and was fascinated by the Communist dream which occupied Paris at the time. Jacob held a leading position in the Communist movement and became a newspaper editor under the pseudonym 'Spero.'

It so happened that in the 1950's I was invited by the French government to Paris as a specialist in bi-lingual education. I decided to meet Hoffman. After locating his address and telephone number, I called him and introduced myself. There was no excitement in his voice, and he refused to me. Nonetheless, I pressed on.

We met. Although we both had changed, we felt that our Kupishok past united us. He and I overcame the ideological barriers when we spoke of our childhood. He confided to me that Communism and all its high ideals were nothing in comparison to the strength of our Jewish roots, to good old Kupishok with its values and people where he would have loved to return to even for a minute. He had long before returned to Zionism in his heart, he said, but could not free himself from the obligations to his Party which was the source of his livelihood.

***

The above chapter is dedicated to my grandson Avi on his demobilization day.

The family of my aunt Tzippa, my mother's sister from Kupishok.

Holocaust martyrs

Zionism on Wheels

The house of Beinish, the director of the Keren Kayemet office in Lithuania, was one of the households which was open to me in Kaunas. I cannot remember whether it was a friendship through my own merit or my sister Peska who was acquainted with some families during her activities at 'The National Committee'. In any case, I used to visit quite a few households of this sort in the course of my Zionist work in the city. Meanwhile, I acquired a certain status as a promising young Zionist, an exciting speaker at meetings and a generous contributor to national funds (when a coin was found in my pocket). Being an amicable partner in living-room conversations, possessing all the social graces of a young man and, above all, a bachelor. I was well-received at the Beinishes.

It was the time of the 1929 events is Palestine: Jew were massacred in Zefat and Hebron; there were bloody clashes in settlements, and the Mandatory Government continued its negative policy towards the National Home banning aliya and land purchases. After each conflict between Jews and Arabs, an objective investigation was underway, but it heard mainly the Arab claims and there could be no illusions as to the final recommendations – always hostile towards the Zionist enterprise.

All of this served as a topic of endless conversations in Jewish households, mostly left-wing, i.e. Communist. The anti-Zionist Labor party (Bund) was not particularly active in the then Jewish Lithuania. The Lithuanian Communist party, invariably led by Jews, acted in conspiracy since the authorities forbade its existence; many of its members were arrested, thrown into prison and suffered from terrible torture. Consequently, these left-wing activists penetrated into anti-Zionist parties and became extremely popular there.

The general distress in Palestine served as oil on the lamp of the anti-Zionist camp. The national Party published a daily newspaper Folks Blat which fought against Zionism and the Hebrew movement in Lithuania. It even had a special correspondent in Palestine called Abba Goutass who was based in Haifa and each week produced a defamatory article about the situation there. The most unimportant incident was painted in the gloomiest possible colors. The anti-Zionist rejoiced at calamity, the Zionists were furious and denied the libels, where one word as most Jews were embarrassed and hoped for good news from the land of their dreams.

It is worth mentioning the phrase 'nothing will stand against money'. That same Abba Goutass, who slandered Zionism and caused such wrath and depression in the Diaspora, was no other than Leible Rabinovitz, a Haifa resident. Years later we met and became friends; he was a warm person, member of Haganah and brought up his children in the best Zionist traditions. Not once did we talk about his evil correspondence and understood the suffering he went through when producing those shameful articles.

***

That was the state of affairs in the Zionist community of Kaunas in the days of the struggle for Jewish existence in Eretz Israel and the general cultural awakening in Eastern Europe. Lithuania was an integral part in the list of changes concerning the Jewish population and the future of our people was one of the major topics in the living room conversations of the time. We discussed all these matters endlessly during my Sabbath visits at the Beinishes.

During one of the debates, Mr. Beinish expressed his opinion about the poisonous Bundist propaganda and those words of his were to affect my life for the next few years. And this is what he said, "The nation is in turmoil and loses hope. The extremist left-wing propaganda is often successful and causes despair among Jewish youth. The Zionist movement seems to have lost its core with Herzl's death and cannot cope with the aggressive Bund on the one hand and the religious Orthodox on the other. The hatred towards Zion that both of them spread among the people shows itself in the income of Keren Kayemet, the Redeeming Fund. What we lack is a young Zionist activist with a sharp tongue who would go out to the most faraway villages and tell the Jewish people about the lofty activities of the Zionist movement. Despite all the attacks and difficulties, Jewish settlements in Palestine do make progress, each year more and more land is possessed by the pioneers either openly or secretly and the land of Israel is craving for working hands."

At this point, Mr. Beinish got so excited by his speech that he turned to me directly and asked: "Actually, Shlomo, why don't you fulfill this task? You have just returned to Kaunas from the post of headmaster in Neishtot and intend to embark on building your reputation as an independent lawyer. Several years will pass until matters have been settled and you open your office. So why not accept my offer at this tough tome for Zionism? I am looking for a 'propagator' who will travel around rural Lithuania and get the message of Keren Kayemet across to the nation. I am familiar with your abilities and think the mission is built for you. Come to my office tomorrow and we will see how this idea can take shape."

Those words fell on fertile soil indeed; I loved being on a stage and had a few successful presentations on my record. I hadn't yet finished all the bureaucratic arrangements which preceded the official lawyer's license. I had saved some money in Neishtot in spite of my extravagant lifestyle but still needed more in order to rent an office. Moreover, I had no particular desire to look for a job in somebody else's office, neither did I want to remain in the realm of teaching, nor did I have any family obligations. Going back to Kupishok did not occur to me and, thus, the idea took shape and I accepted the offer.

Until today I cannot remember whether the enterprise was purely voluntary as during my previous Zionist activities or was it for a symbolic salary. I was promised to be reimbursed for travelling expenses and was thoroughly instructed by Beinish, who was acquainted with the smallest corners in Lithuania. He reminded me of the famous notebook of Menahem Mendel from the stories of Shalom Aleichem. I also organized a notebook for myself and included there all the possible details about my destinations: Names of local activists and the address of the person responsible for Keren Kayemet donations. In addition, I was equipped with brief information about the leaders of communities, rabbis and their attitude towards Zionism, youth movements, school headmasters and details of just righteous Jews.

***

Dressed up in an impressive fur coat (used, but in good condition), which I purchased for the occasion, fur hat to prevent freezing in snowy Lithuanian forests, two large suitcases full of books (my custom since boyhood) and various brochures of Zionist propaganda, I was ready! Obviously, I didn't forget the photo album, an effective method during meetings with youngsters, especially Jewish girls who got stuck in the provinces, whereas their heart longed for a more active life. In other words, all was prepared for the journey.

***

My future destiny did not prevent me from travelling, mainly educational missions in the Diaspora. I invariably did my utmost not to disappoint either those who sent me or the Jewish public I reached.

However, the impressions of all those trips could never be compared with the experiences of that memorable Keren Kayemet tour. I do not exaggerate if I say that some fresh Zionist spirit was then blown into the dry bones of Lithuanian Jewry before the great destruction.

***

Some sixty-four years that have passed since then have not darkened my sheer excitement at the offer of Mr. Beinish.

One Saturday morning my friends and I attended an anti-Zionist gathering which shocked us tremendously. It took place in a hall opposite the City Garden in Kaunas and the topic was 'The Zionist Disappointment', the lecturer being one of the most talented and sharp-tongued anti-Zionist speakers of the time. His name has unfortunately escaped from my memory but I perfectly remember his eloquent highbrow Yiddish, yet with a lot of colloquial expressions. He did not bless the pogroms in Palestine, did not rejoice at calamity as his fellow Bundists and Communists. He even found a few good words for the young idealistic pioneers who risked their lives for the sake of a dream invented by their leaders.

These 'Dortikes' (from the German 'dort' which means 'there' in contrast to 'Doykes' who believed the solution of the Jewish problem is 'here' in the Diaspora) did not understand that the Jewish minority had the future of a cultural autonomy in the more and more liberal Europe. He spoke to us in a condescending tone and described the hars reality of Palestine full of aggressive Arab extremists. "Who can ever cope with them, closed the gate in front of the Zionists, etc."

"Eighteen million Jews" he went on "the choicest and best of contemporary humanity have the opportunity of being a respectable minority wherever they choose. It will be a minority linked to the rest of the Jewish nation by common cultural values in the national Yiddish language and a prosperous Jewish life. True, some outstanding pieces were written in the Holy Tongue but what does the Judaism of tomorrow and the obsolete language have in common?"

It was an impeccable lecture indeed, spiced with fables and jokes, based on facts and numbers. Our group, who deliberately occupied the gallery in order to disturb the hostile speaker, was spellbound by the lecturer's words lacking any provocation or hatred. The stormy applause depressed us greatly and we left the hall quietly and frustrated. The speech came as a blow! At the Beinish's on Saturday they had discussed the sad situation Zionism was in among the provincial Jews. The lecture confirmed this viewpoint.

***

Having served as a teacher and youth guide in several towns around Lithuania, I felt deeply involved in the Zionist struggle for the soul of youngsters. An enthusiastic young man as I was, I could not ignore the political arguments that arose. In the capital, however, the situation was different. During the seven years of my absence from Kaunas some new speakers had flourished and only a few of them remembered me on my return. I felt strange and alienated.

At moments of confusion, I tried to keep Zionist ideas out of my thoughts and concentrate on the law career which awaited me. Some of my acquaintances left for Palestine and thus realized their dream. One of them was Jacob Abel, a close friend of mine, whom I was often in touch with. At the same time, I applied to a relative of mine, the famous writer Alter Droyanov, author of the book "The Joke and Sarcasm", who cooled my enthusiasm.

***

I was to visit virtually all Jewish towns according to the following schedule:

Weekends at larger cities, weekdays in towns and villages.

My task was purely explanatory without any connection to raising money. I tried my best to keep a good standard in conversations with local leaders but made the emphasis on meetings with youth.

***

Transportation in the Lithuania of the early 30's was most primitive, one national railway track with a few branches crossing the entire country from East to West. Many towns were at quite a distance from the main road and could be reached only by coach. Buses almost didn't exist at the time so I traveled by rented coaches which often provided me with a bit of adventure.

On trains I met all sorts of people; during coach trips I enjoyed the fabulous forest views and breathed the fresh frosty air.

Normally I tried to reach my destination in the afternoon. There I was expected by the Keren Kayemet representative and a few Zionist activists, usually youngsters. After the initial meeting with the local community, I was led to a small hotel where I had a short rest before the evening speech at the synagogue or a special hall.

My speeches were long enough to satisfy those seeking new ideas and hope which was important in may folorn communities. Some of the talks continued for two to three hours spiced with Biblical verses, sayings of our Sages and Zionist songs. All in all, I succeeded in exciting the audience. Applause was not practised in synagogues so the talk was followed by a Kaddish DeRabanan prayer, the traditional custom of the community. The more liberal congregations allowed women to listen to the speech with men as if it were Simcha Torah festival; there were others who insisted on strict division. In the latter case, the girls approached the men after the program and joined them on the way home, with me leading the procession.

A delicious meal awaited me at my host's and served as a break between the official presentation and meeting with the youth which took place later in the evening.

Those spontaneous Zionist evenings became more and more exciting from place to place and there was no limit to our exhilaration.

***

The gentle twilight under the summer sky or even the warmth of a hall in the winter added to the feelings of togetherness and inspiration for a better future. Everyone felt delighted to escape for an hour from dark reality to the world of dreams and hopes. With the youngsters as with the adults, there was an exchange of opinions and ideas until we reached the main part. And that was the happy Zionist songs; also Hassidic tunes and Yiddish folk-songs were equally welcome. In every community there were men and women with good voices who kindly agreed to lead the public singing which continued until very late.

***

My departure was a difficult experience for all of us. For about a year, I rushed from one township to another and thus visited dozens of them.

Zionism on wheels

Me on a Zionist mission to encourage Jewish communities in Lithuania after the 1929 riots (in Palestine). I traveled by train and horse drawn carriages to many towns, villages and little settlements. There were sermons in synagogue and meetings with youth. Here I am in Telz (Telšiai) that had a famous large Yeshiva.

A Zionist Sermon at Dawn

In the State of Lithuania, which gained its independence immediately after the First World War, there were about a quarter of a million Jews. The Jews of Lithuania had been renowned for their love of Torah, prominent and wise religious leaders deeply attached to Jewish heritage, and the hope for redemption.

The soil was poor as were its Jews. They were settled in hundreds of large and small communities earning their living by hard labor. Only a few of them achieved an adequate economic status. The vast majority of the Jews worked in trade and commerce trying to keep their and their family's heads above water. The Balfour Declaration of 1917 and the news of young energetic people building our homeland excited the members of these communities.

Our longing for Zion was engraved in our hearts from childhood. Each person absorbed this attachment to Judaism from Biblical stories, Sages, tales, sermons of story-tellers and the Zionist enlightenment of the previous generations. Zionist envoys who reached Lithuania after a long journey from Palestine were warmly received by their brothers in the Diaspora. If he was a young person, he would find himself among his local peers who were thirsty to hear what the envoy had to say. The youngsters clung to him, organized parties in his honor, and they were elated by the good tidings from Eretz Israel.

If he was an adult, he enjoyed the hospitality of the middle-class Zionist members and was respectfully invited to the synagogue where he would give a speech to the congregation, informing them about the various events in the Land of Israel, about the brave actions of the pioneers ploughing the tough soil, about the Hebrew speaking guards whose weapons were on the ready against anyone intending to disturb the well-being of the pioneers.

As the guest departed, he would leave some Israeli songs and melodies behind which were happily sung by the youth. These songs aroused a great deal of emotion among the members of the community since they concerned the country of their eternal dreams. As a matter of fact, the envoys did not always arrive from Palestine itself. Occasionally, they happened to be the local Zionists who were talented orators who volunteered to make their contribution as well.

***

After the bloodshed of 1929 in Palestine, deep sorrow descended on the Jews of Lithuania whose eyes were directed towards Zion. The victims of violence in Hebron, Zefat and other places; the helplessness of the British mandatory rulers in defending the settlements; the anti-Jewish sentiment which was frequently expressed by British officers – all this depressed the Jews in the Diaspora who were extremely sensitive to whatever occurred.

A number of students who studied at the University of Kaunas joined the army of Zionist envoys at that difficult time.

It was a Thursday. The young activist hired a coach in order to go to one of the remote towns in the thick forests. All the residents of that area earned their living from a variety of forest trades: Lumberjacks, wood experts, and the agents and owners of carts who brought the products to the place for distribution. The work was extremely hard and not very profitable either. The workers who were both Jews and Christians carried their burden, desperately trying to make ends meet.

Before he arrived, the head of the Jewish community had prepared the groundwork for the envoy's visit. The members had been waiting for the Zionist representative. Like in many other places which he had visited before, he stayed at the house of the community leader. After an hour's rest, the emissary would head for the synagogue where his listeners would be awaiting him after a day of hard work, eager to hear what he had to say. The next morning, the visitor would awake early and proceed to the Jewish community nearby where he would spend an enjoyable Sabbath.

***

It so happened that one cold Thursday my hopes were dashed! All of a sudden, a heavy snowstorm started. The harsh wind was blowing large heaps of snow into the air; the tracks from the horse had disappeared. The wretched animal was trying its best to struggle against the weather. I found myself inside a deep forest where no way out could be discerned. The curses of the driver did not improve the state of affairs, neither did his nervous hits on the thin back of the horse. The peasant was irritated by everything and obviously by the fact that the bloody Jew had talked him into the risky enterprise of going through the storm. There was no point in arguing with him.

I wrapped myself into my long fur coat and patiently waited for the end of the storm. The day is long, I calmed myself, and I will reach my destination before dusk. However, the wind grew stronger and apparently the storm was going to continue. Hours rolled by and the wintry sun began to set.

My serenity enraged the coachman who began telling all sorts of horror stories about predator wolves and forest robbers. These stories obviously were not particularly encouraging but they were the least of my troubles. What will happen to my mission in the community was the main reason for this anxiety. Night was approaching rapidly and the Jews were waiting for my arrival. As a matter of fact, not all volunteers among the students were excited by the opportunity to spend their time in some forsaken hole but I understood the importance of my duty and was not frightened by wolves or robbers.

Darkness descended on the forest. I knew from experience of traveling that as dusk fell it would be easier to see houses since they were lit. On the other hand, there was no guarantee that we would reach the right town. It was clear that I wouldn't get there on time. The following day, Friday, I was supposed to be in a different town with a larger community where I would spend the Sabbath eve.

At a very late hour, we finally arrived at the house of the local Zionist leader. Although most of the people of the town had already sunk into a deep sleep after the long working day, a few had remained awake and they were sitting inside worried about the envoy who had gotten lost.

As the 'lad from the center' stepped in, the household became jubilant. Hot tea was ready in a minute's time; the long-expected guest drank some anti-cold syrup. Large amounts of previously cooked dishes were put on the table. Hearing the noise, the older kids woke up and their bodies appeared from the beds in the corner. Their curious eyes were directed towards me, who was apologizing for the inconvenience caused by the storm.

"Oh, it's just as well," said the host, "as tomorrow is the Sabbath, you will have a good rest. We will be delighted to have such a respectable visitor here. There will be no end to the excitement of our congregation which is invariably deprived of a proper Sabbath cultural activity, especially of a speech given by a Zionist activist."

I felt that the misunderstanding should be cleared up and explained that I had to be on my way to another community the next morning. The host and his fellow activists started to ask for mercy. "Don't deprive us of the pleasure of having you here for the Sabbath. The Jews of this town hardly survive. The poverty is unbearable, the families are large, and some even suffer from lack of food. Despite all the difficulties, they are not short-armed and donate a bit of money to the Jewish settlements in Palestine. The news about your arrival has spread over the town. People spent an hour waiting for you after the evening prayer and dispersed with great sorrow. If they find out that you had been in town and we let you go, they would eat us alive!"

All that was undoubtedly reasonable but the schedule could not be changed. It actually was the activist's wife who made a suggestion. She saw that the dispute had gone too far and her husband had become more and more disheartened, so she hesitantly said, "Maybe we should leave our guest for an hour's rest. In the meantime, we can gather the crowd." Her husband signed and thoughtfully responded, "It is almost midnight and everyone is already in bed." His wife insisted, "We don't enjoy such visits every day. The public will never forgive you when it turns out that the envoy was in town and not everyone met him. You'd better let people know and whether to come or not is their problem. Let's go and wake up the synagogue attendant; he should open the doors and light the heater."

As she was talking, she got dressed into winter clothing which was hanging on a nail. That probably persuaded her husband and he joined her. The other people in the room left the house in order to interrupt the sleep of the local Jews. I was the only one left in the room and fell asleep at once, though not for long. About an hour later, a freezing wind burst into the room and I was up. It was the young people who were sent to accompany me to the synagogue.

***

My entourage and I entered the synagogue. Two candles were lit and burned steadily. They produced very subtle light which allowed me to see several bearded men sitting around the table with their heads resting on their folded arms. Loud snores filled the room.

A number of young community members were huddled in the corner. A group of girls were sitting in front of them wearing large headscarves, their eyes filled with expectations. Some of the people raised their heads and smiled at me.

One of the community leaders opened the proceedings with several general blessings and told the people about the tribulations of my trip. He praised my perseverance in fulfilling the Zionist mission against all odds. The speaker finished and I stood up in order to give my speech.

***

There was something amazing about that room. It was in semi-darkness and the shadows of the people standing or sitting were moving slightly as a result of every little movement in the audience. That bizarre atmosphere puzzled me and my talk was a bit quiet and I even stammered.

But when I mentioned Eretz Israel, I recalled the miraculous deeds of the pioneers. I imagined those morally strong people defending their towns and villages and my voice was restored to its formidable power. At once, my brain was full of verses, tales and stories since I felt as if I had just left the settlements in Judea and the

kibbutzim in the Jezre'el Valley in order to tell that frozen Jewish community about the heroism of the pioneers.

My words were encouraging but did not involve any euphoria. Eretz Israel expects her sons to return back to its borders and the nation must prepare the ground for newcomers. The pioneers are building cities and villages thinking that their brethren in the Diaspora will provide the material and bricks for the future buildings. I touched on many other topics using some humorous remarks and unusual stories. The tense atmosphere in the room lessened and the people were captured by the speech.

I spoke with my heart and the listeners felt it despite their sleepy mood. Not all of my eloquent speech was clear to the listeners, but it made them feel proud and they sat up and straightened their backs!

The speech lasted for quite a long time as speeches always did in Lithuania where audiences loved to listen to more and more. The congregation was overjoyed to hear about the Jewish shepherds in the Homeland. It seemed to them that Jacob and Rachel had stepped out of the Torah and walked on the Holy Land. They loved to hear about the big city, Tel-Aviv, whose policemen and judges were Jewish, and Jews walked there without any fear.

***

The sounds of roosters crowing reminded me that dawn was approaching, and the people didn't even have time to rest before the working day began. I ended the speech with a lovely story and finished with the verse from the Torah, "The one who comes to Zion brings the redemption closer" (free translation.) The synagogue attendant said "Kaddish DeRabanan" and as he finished the last sentence, the youngsters in the corner sprang to their feet and began to sing 'HaTikvah.' The older generation did not quite understand the meaning of the words but everyone in the room knew that something significant happened in their empty lives that night.

The public returned home in order to start a new day which was breaking from behind the heavy clouds that covered the frozen land.

***

Many years later the envoy came to the Land of Israel. When I have plunged into my memories of those turbulent times, I have always been deeply touched by this extraordinary story.

A Yiddishe Tate (A Jewish Father)

This phrase is not as renowned as the phrase 'A Yiddishe Mame' (a Jewish mother) which became popular due to the American song.

The Jewish mother has always been the symbol for self-sacrifice – giving of herself for the sake of her children's well-being and happiness. She was rewarded with a song that became a hit. The most popular singers, Jews and non-Jews alike, sang it all over the world. Is the love of a Jewish mother more passionate than that of an Italian, Arab or English one? I just don't know.

The Jewish experience has confronted the Jewish mother with such exclusive experiences that they merit research of their own. However, there is no similar phrase for a Jewish father who illustrates his devotion to his offspring.

***

In 1930, I embarked on a Zionist mission under the auspices of Keren Kayemet LeIsrael (KKL.) My task involved reaching out to Jews in various Lithuanian townships in order to revive their faith in modern Zionism, a faith that was weakened after the appalling massacre of Jews by Arabs in 1929.

Among the towns included on my list was a remote place called Salant, a township in upper Lithuania which was known in the Jewish world for its Rabbi, Israel Salanter, who founded a stream of spiritual Judaism called Mussar, meaning moralism. His followers, called 'Mussarniks,' excelled not only in their studies but also in their elevated moral behavior. Therefore, I was particularly curious when I noticed Salant on my list of destinations.

***

A Lithuanian Jew like me invariably breathing in the aura of Torah and Hassidism in childhood could not remain indifferent to a visit to the cradle of the Mussar movement, even though I had abandoned their teachings. But to my regret, I was disappointed by the reception I received in the town.

Normally, the Zionist activities, i.e. the activities of the KKL, were entrusted to the local youth, in particular to the excited and lively girls who took care of the guest. The envoy's name usually reached the destination before his arrival. A letter was sent from the Zionist center in Kaunas depicting the upcoming speaker with unlimited praise and appreciation. This was not the case in Salant.

The promoter, a volunteer who was responsible for KKL donations, was an established individual Jew busy with his work and family. Upon my arrival, he received me amicably at his store, while negotiating prices with his customers at the same time. He then directed me and the coachman to our accommodations, where I would eat and rest after the long journey, one full of broken roads. According to the promoter, I would give my speech later in the evening following Mincha when I would then meet with the local Jewish community.

Everything went according to plan. I reached my accommodations, went upstairs and found myself in a small room with a cozy bed, pillows and warm blankets. I was offered a substantial meal resembling one for the Sabbath, although it was only a regular weekday. It included chopped liver, a plate of a greasy boullion with floating 'eyes' of fat, a quarter of a well-cooked goose and a fruit salad for dessert. The ambience was extremely hospitable, but I kept wondering where the active and excited youngsters were. Either they did not exist in Salant or possible would come later.

Having devoured the delicious meal, I sank onto a comfortable featherbed and took a refreshing nap. When I woke up, I felt as if I were born anew. I felt refreshed and energetic. A large wash-tub near the opposite wall and a piece of soap and towel caught my eye. After I had changed my clothes, I sat down to have a look at the numerous brochures, newspaper clippings and other auxiliary material that served me during these Zionist missions. Basically, I knew the entire program by heart but, as the Sages say, "A prayer said one hundred times is different when said the 101st time."

***

In reality, the success of a speech depends on the mood of the speaker and the way he expresses himself. Most of all it depends on luck, as do so many other things. If a speaker creates an atmosphere of ease and social comfort, he will enjoy agreement and positive feedback. In this case, the speech usually flows by itself. I suppose that the key to success in public presentations is the emotional aspect. Information should come from the heart and be directed to the heart of the listener.

I was not afraid of failure. And I was not familiar with stage fright since I believed in Eretz Israel then and I still believe in it today! The more I have had the opportunity to know the simple people, the ones we used to snub, the better I understood that the shopkeepers represented the Jewish nation in the Diaspora. I felt that I had come from among the people and was now sent to encourage them, to strengthen them, to open their eyes to reality, and urge them to change their way of life.

***

I was sitting in the room, looking forward to seeing the activitists who would accompany me to the synagogue where I was supposed to give a speech. The promoter and two other Zionists arrived. I remember neither their faces nor personalities. It seemed that Salant was not a Zionist center in the way that other towns were, although it was not anti-Zionist either. It was a perfect example of a Lithuanian town which worried about financial survival and believed in miracles.

***

On my way to the synagogue, I learned that because of a request from the 'Gabbai,' my presentation was postponed until the end of the Maariv prayer. Why? The official explanation given to me was because they didn't want me to have a time limit. This excuse was convincing enough since in those days Jewish speakers were not limited in time like today. On the contrary, the speaker could ramble on endlessly. So anyone who made an effort to speak before the evening prayer was extremely welcome since he saved the congregation from an enormous waste of time and ensured the proper audience for the guest speaker. As he was not a rabbi, he had no intention to return the hearts of the listeners back to commandments and good deeds.

Naturally, a legitimate question arose: What connection does he have with the synagogue? The reason for the envoy's presence was the new direction of Judaism in Lithuania. It was called Zionism.

In reality, not just any Zionist speaker received permission of the local rabbi to speak in the synagogue. But since it had been granted, there was no better time than before Mincha or between Mincha and Maariv. Invariably, some would grumble about the new idea, others would accept it with an open mind. There was no choice – new times, new tunes.

Before the evening prayer was supposed to start, the speaker would finish his presentation, and everything would end calmly. It didn't matter to me whether I spoke before or after Maariv. The hosts hurried to assure me that whatever the reason for the delay, it would work out fine. They repeated that I would not have any time limit. Those who remained after the prayer would be willing to hear what I had to say about Eretz Israel and the economic and political situation in Palestine. I could speak as long as I wanted and the longer the better. Having no choice, I accepted the sketchy explanation.

The man who told me about the postponement of my speech hinted that the local activists were not being idle. Three of them went house-to-house inviting the audience to the synagogue. They promised that the guest speaker was worth listening to.

***

We reached the synagogue shortly before the evening prayer. Scattered about were a few Jews sitting, reciting the Psalms. Several others were spread over the room reading in solitude. The entire house sank in the dusk.

The rabbi was sitting in the corner near the Holy Ark with a large book of Gemara open in front of him. My host led me closer to the Rabbi in order to greet him. The Rabbi measured me with an inquisitive eye, as if asking, "What kind of speaker is this?" True to my nature, I found several appropriate words in order to open the conversation with the Rabbi who apparently was not excited by Zionist ideas as many of his contemporaries were. Still, he did not reveal hostility towards Zionist activists. Perhaps the polite sentences of mine succeeded in warming up the atmosphere since the Rabbi shut the book and, to my delight, began a conversation.

As we were chatting, my eyes did not stop wandering about the hall. It seemed that there were only about twenty people. Who could guarantee that even those few did not intend to slip off after the prayer and head for their home and Shabbat meals? I feared having to remain with a bunch of depressed Zionists full of sadness and frustration.

Meanwhile, the Psalm readers finished and the synagogue attendant knocked on the table marking the beginning of Maariv. The Rabbi, his eyes closed, opend the prayer with vigor. The congregation followed. I also behaved piously, directing my face to the wall and praying. As the Service progressed, I contemplated the splendor of Jewish prayers.

After the prayers finished, I turned to the audience. The synagogue was slowly becoming packed. The efforts of the local Zionists were not in vain. Dozens of men and women had already managed to return home, grab a quick bite to eat, and hastened to the synagogue where the 'eloquent Zionist speaker' was supposed to 'preach.'

The younger members of the congregation thrust themselves forward and immediately caught sight of me. From that minute on, I was inundated with warmth. The synagogue attendant introduced me to the public and gave me a slight push with his elbow towards the small stage near the Holy Ark. Although my pockets were

filled with notes and the summary of my speech, I did not use them. I knew that the audience was under my control. It was entertaining seeing the embarrassed Rabbi who earlier had apologized to me for having to return home but who now stayed on, not moving.

***

Perhaps I was influenced by the spirit of Rabbi Israel Salanter because I talked for about three hours making good use of all the oratory techniques which I had adopted during my countless presentations. I had an attentive audience and spoiled them with spot-on sages sayings, jokes, tales, Bialik verses and Ahad HaAm's extracts.

The congregation grew larger and larger. Some of the listeners had possibly run home to fetch their neighbors and family members to hear the excited Zionist orator. As I ended the speech with the "Vision of the

Dry Bones" by Ezekiel, I was surrounded by jubilant listeners congratulating me and shaking my hand. I noticed one man among the exhilarated public who attempted to get closer to me but hesitated.

***

I was beginning to feel worn out by the strenuous speech and welcomed being taken care of by my hostess. She approached and said that a hot dinner was awaiting me. I was accompanied to my accommodations by several people who parted with compliments and handshakes.

The meal was superb. Having devoured it, I laid down to sleep. All of a sudden, I heard a slight knock on the door. When it opened, I recognized the man who had captured my attention in the synagogue. I smiled at him but he was standing stiffly. He was pale and breathed heavily."You are not well, are you?" I said. I offered him a chair and he sat down with an apologetic smile. "I was running in order to reach you before you went to bed, and then this asthma of mine!"

"You don't have to justify your visit. On the contrary, I am most delighted to have company for the evening since I have a couple of questions to ask you about your renowned town. But as I can see, you have a different matter to discuss, so go ahead."

For a minute it seemed as if he wanted to avoid the embarrassing subject but then he said, "Excuse me, sir, for my late visit. It is just that I was impressed by your speech like all of the others." He made an attempt to rise from the chair, but I felt that I had to make him talk about the mysterious subject since it apparently was extremely important to him.

We continued to chat about this and that because I wanted him to eliminate his shyness. When we began drinking tea, I said, "It is not nice for a person to talk about himself," I started, "but as the Sages say,

'When people do not know who you are, you are allowed to say that you are a wise student.' You probably do not know but my livelihood is not based on Zionist speeches. I am a lawyer and work as an assistant to an established solicitor in Kaunas who transfers complicated cases to me. I guess that you have some sort of sadness on your mind, so please feel free to tell me about it. If I am competent enough to give you advice, I will give it. If not, I know how to keep secrets because of my nature and the profession I chose."

The ice was broken! The man sat comfortably and thanked me for my gentle approach. "I have made a stupid mistake," he said, "and I now don't know how to get out of it." I asked, "But what is your mistake exactly?"

"I have come here to match you with my daughter," he pronounced finally. "She studies at the conservatory. You see, I was deeply impressed by your exalted speech at the synagogue. What spirit! What prominence! You were beaming with hope and confidence, so I thought such a beautiful soul like my daughter deserved a husband like you. She too is hoping to go to Palestine one day and to teach Jewish children to play the piano. I know you are about to leave tomorrow, but I feared that I would lose this rare opportunity which my daughter's destiny might depend on."

At that point, he stopped and was quiet. I understood him as he had been brought up in the atmosphere of constant worries about marriage which invariably was the center of the family agenda.

In virtually every town I reached, there were many transparent hints on the parents' part or the young lady herself offering a tour around the town's sites, forests and lakes. All of this was part of the general matchmaking effort of Jewish families. Nonetheless, there was something quite extraordinary going on now. The father's choice was based mainly on his strong belief in Zionism.

Actually, he came from a famous Zionist family. I realized that it was necessary to compensate him for his efforts and I could not give a straight-forward negative answer. I was glad to learn that there was a small bottle of wine which was kept for guests. I poured a bit for both of us to dilute the slightly tense atmosphere.

I then confessed that I had already been matched with a relative of mine when we were both in the cradle. It was not a lie. As a matter of fact, at the time, I was becoming interested in my cousin who years later perished in the Holocaust with all of her family.

The father spoke a great deal about his talented offspring who was invited to Leipzig by her relatives in Germany and currently studied at the conservatory there. Little by little, he acquired confidence. Even though nothing practical came out of his visit, we conversed about our families, life in general, and the opportunities for his daughter in Palestine. He modestly mentioned his brother who was a famous Jewish leader in Europe.

We discussed the crisis of the Zionist movement and the tensions between secular and religious Zionism which did not enjoy great support among religious Jewry. He was a clever person; our conversation was flowing smoothly, and the poor matchmaking attempt was forgotten.

Dawn was penetrating through the darkness when I saw my visitor down the narrow stairs leading from my room. I invited him to Kaunas and said that I would be happy to meet his daughter one day.

***

When I sank onto my cozy bed that night, I thought that only a longing for Zion could inspire a Jewish father to overcome his self-respect and shyness by believing that his beloved daughter could not expect more from her life than having an eloquent Zionist speaker as a spouse.

■■

The Five Torah Cities

Prologue:

It is necessary to include this story of the Five Torah Cities where I served as an official Hebrew teacher. In the course of my other stories, I obviously repeated my adventures but repetition is the way of the elderly so why should I be an exception to the rule? I hope the reader will forgive me. My impaired sight prevents me from reading my manuscripts.

It's important to remember that all those Jacob's communities have since then been massacred by the Nazi monsters and their Lithuanian assistants. The latter were extremely efficient in their work; not only did they murder thousands of innocent people but also saw to it that no remainder of the glorious Jewish tradition would be left in their country. Nothing remains: Neither graves nor monuments nor memorials.

It is therefore vital that we remember each Jewish name and institution which can add to our better understanding of the way of life that is gone forever. The decades that separate us from those events will surely add a special flavor to these stories.

***

These are the five towns:

Kupishok, my hometown where I worked as a teacher for two years in 1918 and 1919.

Neishtot-Sugint, near Tavrig, where I taught for three months during the summer holidays in 1920.

Kretingen, a border town near Klaipeda, where I worked for one academic year in 1924.

Wilkomir, a county center, where I taught for two years from 1925-1927.

Neishtot-Shirvint, near Shaki, where I both taught and managed a school from 1927-1930.

***

Each community has its story – in my community, the story is about a 'Melamed' – Meir Kodesh, my beloved father, may his memory be blessed, who loved his students and did everything to bring them closer to Torah and the Hebrew language – subjects about which he had profound knowledge. He possessed special methods to impart the love for Torah learning. He did not conceal his anger when it came to mischievous students but, all the same, he treated them with respect.

My father arranged a suitable learning environment – a separate wing of our house was dedicated purely to heder – the traditional Jewish school for boys between the ages of 7 and 13. My father accepted twenty-five students only and divided them into two groups studying in adjacent rooms.

In the first room sat thirteen pupils who studied Torah and Hebrew (reading and writing.) The other room housed those pupils who were already at the level of the prophets and Gemara learning, including Hebrew at a more advanced level. They learned to read the Bible with proper intonation as well as Hebrew books for children found in the heder's library. It was a great innovation to teach children fluent

Hebrew reading and they enjoyed such series as 'Perachim' (flowers), 'Nitzanim' (buds), and various tales.

***

The person who supplied the brochures and books was my elder brother, Shmuel (or Samuel.) He lived in Vilnius at the time, to dad's disappointment. He had left the modern Lida yeshiva of the Zionist Rabbi

Reinish and now tried to make ends meet in the capital. The material he sent was stored in a special bookcase at heder. On Shabbat eve, every student would receive a brochure for reading at home during the weekend.

This was the pedagogic ambience in which I grew up. Dad loved speaking Hebrew with his Ashkenazi pronunciation. Being the youngest member of the family, I was deeply attached to him during the fourteen years of my life at home. At least twice a week, he would take me for a walk in the fields between the afternoon and evening prayers. Those hours were devoted purely to Hebrew speech and my father vigorously preserved that tradition even at the time of the German occupation.

***

Kupishok was conquered by the Germans in a fierce battle one year after the war began. The occupation lasted for three years and ended with the defeat of Germany and its withdrawal from Lithuania. Later, in 1917, the enormous Russian empire was swept away in the whirlpool of the October Revolution. The Czar was overthrown and the country drowned in blood and red terror. Lithuania was later to become a Soviet republic – one of those formerly independent states which were enslaved by the Communist regime for many years thereafter.

Kupishok – Teacher and Friend

For the sake of historical truth, I must point out that my first teaching experience coincided with my first days of being an orphan. It happened after my father returned his soul to the Creator in April 1918. His death occurred some hours before a heavy curfew was imposed by the Germans so the burial ceremony had to be done in haste. The few people who made the procession walked up the steep road to the cemetery.

I, a 14-year-old, was brought there by a side-road since, according to an old Jewish custom, an orphan must be prevented from mingling with the funeral procession of his father.

Having walked a fair distance with Tuvia, the tanner, he suddenly turned to me and said, "Shlomo, your righteous father has died. The Lord will console you one day but what about us? Who will read the daily Gemara page with us between Mincha and Maariv? We are ignorant but thirsty to learn. It occurred to me that when you have finished the 'Shiva,' you could replace your father as our guide at the synagogue."

It so happened that Tuvia's words came true. And, indeed, at the age of fourteen, I was already quite knowledgeable in matters of faith since my father had taken good care of my education.

***

I did not have a particular fear of any audience nor did the daily Gemara page frighten me so I accepted the offer. What was much more surprising was the consoling visit of the German educational supervisor – 'schulbesirks inspektor' – who had respected my father tremendously. Having said some polite words about his virtues and his teaching talent, the inspector stunned me with an unusual request: To take over my father's post at the local Jewish school in Kupishok. He suggested to pay me the salary of my father (twenty marks a month – quite a sum of money at the time.)

For two years, I served in my father's shoes as a teacher of religion. At the time it aroused astonishment but not today – more than 75 years after the event. Sons should continue their parents beginnings and this was what I did. I was immersed in Judaism and Hebrew – virtually from birth – and knew the Holy Tongue both in writing and speech and could also recite the Bible almost by heart as well as read the Torah at the synagogue since my bar mitzvah days.

Every day I swallowed the Hebrew newspaper 'HaTzfira' (The Alarm) and the weekly 'World' which I read from cover to cover. The book of Talmudic folklore by Bialik and Ravinitzky had been my brother's present when it first appeared. The other creations of modern education were a bit dangerous to read in public, so I managed to obtain them secretly.

Needless to say, the various Rabbinic teachings, Rashi's commentaries and other types of religious literature were an indispensable part of my learning process. With hindsight, I must add that it wasn't a small bit of information, and I was indeed better acquainted with the sources than my classmates.

***

The issue of discipline did not exist. The German inspector officially introduced me to my students-friends and did not forget to mention that I was permitted to slap someone's face in case of discipline problems or laziness. Fortunately, I never used that privilege.

I loved the kids and they loved me. Sometimes I would tell them stories that I had read or even invented for the occasion. Not lacking imagination, I enjoyed story-telling and hope the listeners did too.

During the first year after my father's death, I served as a public envoy, leading prayers at the synagogue. There weren't many adults learned enough to fulfill the lofty task. Many fled the town during the mass flight, so the congregation contented itself with my childish voice but with my father's intonation. The respect everyone had for him combined with natural mercy for the poor orphan added to my prestige both among my pupils and their parents.

***

This success was probably the only happiness at my home which was in total depression after my father's death, the occupation regime and general austerity. The fact that my activities served as some consolation for mother filled my heart with satisfaction. The war was approaching its end and many families began to return to Kupishok. Liberation was in the air and I was asked by the parents in the town to renew the tradional heder of Meir Kodesh, of blessed memory, which I did.

***

The 'skameikes' (benches that were linked to the table following the school tradition of the time) were painted and two rooms were prepared for the mission. The voice of Torah and children's laughter were constantly heard in our yard. The only problem left was the study fees. The parents did not deprive me of my salary, God forbid, but the German mark deteriorated from day to day and had virtually no value.

A solution was found: The parents would pay through the medium of various goods that they themselves produced. My salary was expressed in such goods as wheat, barley, clothes, shoes, live birds and dairy products. Mother took these items from me and sold them in her little store so that we did not lack anything at home. I enjoyed the new, active lifestyle.

My mood was further improved by two pretty pupils of mine (both my age,) Pessia Cooper and Shifra Karpuch who, I could clearly see, were not indifferent towards me. I used to spend hours in front of the mirror carefully combing my hair. However, all of the sensitivity found its expression in intensive sessions of Biblical reading.

***

A bulky volume of Biblical stories and tales reached me at the time. It was called 'Bichurim' (written by Pinnes) and included endless articles which we absorbed with enthusiasm. It seemed as if our official morning lessons were not enough to satisfy the students thirst for knowledge.

My friends, members of Hirsh Ash's family – Leib-Reuven, Shimon, Azriel and Mordechai - influenced me to host these intellectual encounters at my place. They were joined by Michal Margalit, my Pinskoy counsins and my widowed aunt, Gittel Kadishevitz. Together with some others we read various texts in Hebrew and Yiddish.

***

During the evening prayers in our comfortable house, boys and girls of all ages participated. I was often the youngest and shortest of the company, but it didn't prevent me from being the undisputed leader in discussions.

The only sad moments for me began when they started to leave, the boys invariably accompanied the girls home whereas I was left with my lonely romantic thoughts. I was sometimes tempted to scribble some love verses on the margins of 'Leitzte Neis' (Latest News) – a Yiddish newspaper that reached us from Vilnius, bringing the hottest pieces of news from the bustling outer world.

***

The description of my pedagogic experiences in Kupishok would not be complete without mentioning the professional-personal battle which I led against an aggressive and stingy fellow-Jew. Here's the story:

I used to teach an extremely sweet girl at my heder. She was about seven or eight years old and succeeded in her studies. Every day she was accompanied by her mother, a gentle, good-looking woman who contrasted sharply with her husband. The latter, a wealthy merchant of agricultural products, had a bulky figure, treated his daughter's education with utter contempt and didn't even bother to negotiate study fees with me.

My agreement with the mother included an exchange payment in the form of two sacks, one of wheat and one of barley. It was clearly stated that one of the sacks was to be brought at the start of the semester, which lasted for six months, and the other after three months. The man, however, did not honor the agreement. He didn't deny the need to pay but evaded payment through all kinds of excuses and pretexts. He delayed payment for weeks, but I couldn't allow myself to exclude the girl from class because she and her mother were such likeable people.

It so happened that Lithuania was in that period liberated from the centuries-long Russian control and became an independent state. At first glance, it was good tidings for the people but there was a hitch: The peasants were constantly robbed during the occupation but managed to conceal a fair amount of their products such as fruit, vegetables, birds and wheat. They grew accustomed to the thriving black market and sold only tiny portions of goods at very high prices. As they heard about the impending redemption, it was clear to everyone that the exaggerated rate would eventually decrease. It looked as if there had been a secret agreement between all the peasants since one day they appeared with all their previously stored merchandise and sold it at extremely low prices.

A sack of wheat cost half or even a quarter as much as before. It was then that the deceitful father remembered he had a debt. One Sunday, he turned up at our house, threw down a sack of wheat which smelled of mold and muttered, "Here's your payment as agreed. Now you cannot say I deprived an orphan!" With those words he was off and I felt insulted and was boiling with anger.

The injustice of the treatment I received from the rude man could not allow my mind to rest. Mother tried to calm me down by saying, "He is just that sort of person, even his virtuous wife is not licking honey at his home and neither does anyone who comes into contact with him." But I was not to be pacified so easily and decided to act. Not everyone will do whatever comes into his head!

***

There was no permanent rabbi in the community. Both former ones (Hassidic and Mitnagdim) had fled the town. There was only one old Jew with a teaching permit but no formal duty as a rabbi. He was voluntarily consulted by people about matters of Kashrut. The person I searched for must be a recognized rabbi who could issue a formal verdict. I was certain that no Kupishok Jew would resist a rabbinic verdict.

***

Rabbi Tulov and his family lived not far from us. The Rabbi was a respectable man and the town residents felt honored by his presence. They were refugees from Vilnius and made a very positive impression. He seemed to have no particular ambitions in town, every day prayed at a different synagogue and did not claim a rabbinic salary from anyone. He and his family lived a modest lifestyle and only received some gifts from the local 'ba'alei-batim' (householders) who visited him on Saturdays to listen to his sermon.

He certainly was a sensible person and I decided to apply to him for a judgement. I asked the Rabbi to invite my opponent to a discussion and, indeed, a few days later I received a postcard notifying me that I should arrive at his house. This was one of my first experiences among many others that followed, when I fought vigorously and stubbornly for my beliefs.

The girl's father was one of the richest in the impoverished Kupishok community and was experienced to stand his ground. If I had been him, I would surely have known what to say, "We hadn't agreed on advance payment" and this was the weak point of my claim. I wasn't certain that the man would appear and, if he did, there was no certainty he would obey the verdict. Rabbi Tulov may not have been the town's official rabbi but he fulfilled all the obligations of that post.

These were the factors that I had to face in my desire to restore justice. Before I set out for the Rabbi's home, I had perused some sources including 'Shulchan Aruch', Mishna and Torah so that I arrived quite well-prepared on the day of the trial.

The Rabbi greeted me amicably and returned to the book he was reading. His wife offered me a seat and we waited for my opponent. He eventually came and apologized for being late. I saw a good sign in his apology and started my short speech, first with a slight hesitation. Gradually, my voice became stronger and stronger and I constantly felt the eyes of both listeners on me.

The Rabbi listened attentively, stopping me from time to time to inquire about details. I also noticed that my opponent's face changed as I was talking; he didn't deny my accusations, neither did he accept them. When I finished, I was amazed to see his expression; his normally sullen look had changed to a much softer and serious one. In a heavy tone, he asked the Rabbi to state his verdict and said he woud accept it. The rabbi could no longer hide his astonishment, invited us to sit near the big table in the middle of the room and left for a few minutes to ask his wife for a cup of tea for us.

In the meantime, I was stunned to notice the softened facial expression of the girl's father. "Zeit mir mochel," he said. (Please forgive me – Yiddish.) He stretched his stiff hand towards me. My eyes covered with tears. The Rabbi entered the room and was able to see for himself what had occurred during his short absence. The cups of tea were brought in, we sipped them slowly, and discussed worldly matters. At some stage, we felt it was time to thank the Rabbi for his efforts. My former opponent took out his wallet and placed a sum of money on the table. I, in turn, did the same.

The Rabbi tactfully turned his face away from the table at that moment.

"It's an honorable day," he said. "We all learned something, made peace with each other and now you are free to go. There is no need for an official verdict." He turned to me and added, "You won't be deprived of your payment."

Outside the house, before we separated, the girl's father handed me a banknote which compensated me for the sum I had just paid the Rabbi. "Tomorrow I'll be at your home with my daughter," he stated. On the next day, the man came carrying another sack of wheat and in addition a fat hen. We shook hands and he praised me extensively in front of my mother who beamed with joy.

***

Later someone spread this story around and we became a topic of the town's gossips.

Neishott-Sugint

The Chimney-Sweep's Son

The 1920-21 school year was my first encounter with the Hebrew 'Gymnasium' (high school) of Kaunas. I reached the capital of the then independent Lithuania alone without any material support or background in secular studies. During the period of the German occupation, I had studied at an elementary school where I had learned some spoken and written German. The only background I had in subjects like Russian, math and geography was from Ponevitz where I had spent some months before arriving in Kaunas.

At that time, the political and economic situation around the world was stormy and Lithuania was no exception. At the age of sixteen, I found myself in a whirlpool of difficulties being alone with my dreams and the master of my decisions.

In that restless state of mind, I commenced my studies in the 6th level of the Gymnasium and eventually managed to take an active part in all classes. It was then close to a miracle since the curriculum included four living languages: German, Russian, Hebrew and Lithuanian and one classical language – Latin. Geography, Jewish and general history, the Bible and Hebrew literature, art and sports were equally represented among the subjects studied.

I was accepted into this grade mainly because of my ability to read and explain a page of Gemara. The next day, however, it turned out that although my knowledge in Judaism was at a higher level than required, it didn't at all mean I would easily become integrated in other classes, especially exact sciences.

Luckily, my sister Peska (Pnina) worked in the Educational Department of the National Jewish Committee and arranged an exemption of school fees for me. In addition, I made a living by teaching Hebrew privately to the mutual satisfaction of my pupils and their parents. It was indeed a reasonable source of money but it distracted my attention from the great deal of homework we received at school. I must confess that I never excelled in subjects I didn't like, namely the exact sciences. Since I was a child, I invariably rebelled against the system and was not prepared to study what was compelled. In other words, I studied what I loved and tried my best to ignore the rest.

***

The Gymnasium did not succeed in altering my free-thinking personality.

I was not considered a brilliant student and in some subjects could hardly pass the exams. I even failed Russian completely! My friends did not contribute to my academic success; there were two idlers with a bit of money in their pockets who constantly offered me more enjoyable ways of spending the time rather than at school. And I didn't mind!

I was then about seventeen, good-looking but short, with a sharp tongue and a lively sense of humor.

One of my friends, Zevadia Levinson – the son of well-off parents – lived in a spacious, comfortable house in one of the suburbs of Kaunas on the picturesque bank of the Neiman River. That house became the center of our entertainment world when all school tasks were postponed until other times. Until today I cannot understand how I coped with the evil inclination to while away my time and remain an ordinary student. I was my own boss which meant a total lack of control or adult advice.

Nonetheless, I was quite popular among my classmates and some of the teachers even thought that I had the qualities of a leader. Whatever their opinion, I somehow overcame the obstacles at school. Not once did I punish myself for the endless wasted hours at various outings by preventing enjoyment for myself during the following days. I somehow plodded on through the first school year at the Gymnasium although it involved a great deal of mental effort and self-education.

***

My knowledge of Judaism, some fluency in German, which was still the language of teaching in a few subjects and my ability to express myself in the pursuit of justice secured me a pretty good position among my fellow-students.

The days of summer holidays were approaching. Where would I go? I asked myself.

The prospect of returning to Kupishok for two months did not particularly appeal to me. I already felt a bit remote from the provincial atmosphere of my hometown. My lust for adventure was pushing me towards new horizons.

And there came a surprise! One of the school's headmasters – Dr. Deutschlander, a colleague of the Gymnasium's founder Dr. Carlebach, was responsible for Jewish Education in the provinces in the Jewish National Committee. One day I bumped into him in the schoolyard and was invited into his office. He asked me about my plans for the holidays and eventually offered me to venture out to a town called Neishtot-Sugint and replace the local teacher of Hebrew and Bible.

The mission was supposed to take three months and the last month which would coincide with the school year didn't seem to bother him. Perhaps he thought one month was unimportant because of the many festivals or maybe he didn't care about my studies. He probably needed a teacher urgently and made his offer. My sister suggested not to turn it down because it could facilitate my economic situation in Kaunas.

I was supposed to get a salary in Neishtot. And so I set out to my uncertain future as a teacher who hadn't even finished his secondary education. My destination was Tavrig – the district center. Neishtot-Sugint was to be reached by no means of transportation, but by a horse cart, a common way of traveling in the then Lithuania.

***

A funny episode marked my arrival in that forsaken town. This Neishtot (in contrast to the larger Neishtot-Shaki) was situated right on the border with Prussia. So what should the town residents do if not smuggle goods across the border? Of course, dozens of shop owners and even simple citizens were buying and selling smuggled goods living in constant fear of the tax authorities. However, it was a very remote danger since the town was small and distant from the center. The local law officers were all bribed. Each and every policeman would receive various gifts and donations before festivals and sometimes for no special reason.

Everyone seemed to be happy with the arrangement but there remained the danger of the so-called 'aktzisnik,' a tax inspector sent from the district center or even the capital. Those were real pests! If an inspector like that appeared in town out of the blue, the local dealers could be in big trouble; there wasn't a single businessman who could not be accused of illegal trade. The local policemen, however helpful they wanted to be, could do nothing since the 'aktzisnik' was much higher than them in rank.

So how could the Jews protect themselves from the law? They watched out! The town was to be reached mainly by cart. Once in a lifetime, a car of some arrogant nobleman did get there and caused great astonishment among the adults – a cart without a horse! The kids would compete with it by running alongside. Fortunately, tax inspectors did not travel by cars and an unrecognized cart would be enough of a warning for the town's merchants.

When anyone saw an unknown vehicle approaching, a whisper was already spreading: Somebody alien at the gate. This was a sufficient hint to arouse action. In an hour's time - or less – the 'hametz' was cleared away: Cigarettes, drinks, textiles and other suspicious objects. The kosher goods occupied its temporary place on the counters until things got better.

Equipped with this short background, the reader will surely understand the anxiety caused by me, though short and skinny who was 'dressed to the nines.' I wore a black shirt with gold buttons shining in the sun and if that was not enough my cap had a glittering peak and a large silver insignia in the form of an eagle which made the outfit even more impressive.

A sharp-eyed Jew, who probably came with the same cart from Tavrig, caught sight of the individual in uniform with his official looking leather bag and was not slow to act. On arrival, he immediately forwarded the important information to those who needed it. The latter passed it on to others and the shopkeepers drew the conclusion and hurried to their stores while I got off the cart and noticed quite a few curious stares. They kept a fair distance and followed my every movement. Still, no one could imagine that the shining uniform and the cap were nothing more than the formal clothes of the Kaunas Hebrew Gymnasium.

I did not come with the mission of the authorities to detect those breaking the law. On the contrary, I was full of good intentions - to teach Hebrew and instill knowledge in the sons and daughters of Israel which was the new custom in schools under the aegis of the Joint.

In short, I stood and waited with all my baggage carried from Kaunas until the forgetful local National Committee activist remembered he had received a telegram from Kaunas informing him of my arrival. As the mishap was understood, the troubled shopkeepers vented their anger on the informer. "What a fool you are! How could you think that a short Jewish boy to be the all-mighty inspector? Have you ever seen a Jewish 'aktzisnik?'

The activist appeared at last, took me to the house where I would stay and then led me to the schol. This incident marked the beginning of a new teaching experience, very different from my late father's heder in our house.

***

Unknown to me then, I was at the start of a life-long career interrupted only by a three-year period as a lawyer in Kaunas before my aliya. In Neishtot-Sugint, for the first time I was an official teacher of the Jewish National Committee, the central institution of those times.

I was again totally independent without family or a home but with a certificate notifying that I had finished six levels of the Kaunas Hebrew Gymnasium and failed the exam in Russian literature which was to be retaken. (In fact, I never did!)

***

My general official appearance gave me some air of importance in the eyes of the town's residents and added to my self-confidence. However, surprising as it may sound, I remember the black-haired girl at my hostel much better than my pompous entrance in the school.

The small building housed two or three classrooms. Alongside me worked two old-fashioned 'Meladim' who taught Torah and Rashi. I was to teach Hebrew and grammar according to the new trend in Jewish education. Some of the students in the higher grades were not much younger than me.

Some days after my memorable arrival, I was transferred from my hostel to a private home where I enjoyed amenities: Accommodations, food and laundry service. All of these were my host's responsibility. He specialized in chiney-sweeping which was seasonal and offered a scarce living; in the summer, only a few people needed a 'sweep' for obvious reasons, so the man was happy to add a little to his meager resources. I was lodged in a spacious room and profited from three delicious meals a day.

The young family members studied at the school and were proud to have such a respectable guest in their home. The eldest son was in the top grade and displayed some interest in studies, but he still needed encouragement. There was also a daughter in the family, a good-looking seamstress who for some reason never missed the opportunity to linger in my room when serving food or making the bed.

***

My education assignment in Neishtot was short and relatively uneventlful. I didn't make friends among the local youth and the teaching hours were just about average. There were, nevertheless, two outstanding episodes: The tragedy of a German girl who taught me Russian and an adventure which I got myself into while trying to help a boy whose soul strived for enlightenment.

The 'Progymnasium' in Kretingen

I arrived in the city as a young teacher for an entire academic year. Kretingen was a border town situated near Kleipeda, which used to have a significant Jewish community. In 1923, I passed my final exams and received a matriculation certificate. My future remained unclear.

Being a penniless but ambitious orphan, I had to make my own decisions. Firstly, I decided to enter the University of Kaunas which meant an exemption from Lithuanian army duty which was a totally useless venture for those drafted. Secondly, I found a job as a teacher in one of the newly opened Hebrew secondary schools on the periphery of town.

There were dozens of such schools opening up throughout Lithuania. They all shared a common problem: The lack of teaching personnel. The Jewish community considered education of utmost importance especially since the Lithuanian government treated the Jewish population with great respect. As the republic did not particularly welcome the Russian influence, Hebrew was preferred as the language for teaching the Jewish citizens.

***

Those Hebrew speaking schools served as a perfect base for talented teaching personnel and created a number of outstanding educators and leaders. Many of the institutions were established during the years of Jewish cultural autonomy and had a high academic standard. Future generations must understand the dimensions of Jewish-Zionist education in what was then Lithuania. Subsequently, this entire cultural layer was massacred and destroyed by the Nazis.

***

Mr. Lippetz, head of the 'Tarbut' network in Kaunas, sent me to teach in a 'Progymnasium' in Kretingen, a city with which I was not familiar. I was employed as a teacher of Hebrew and literature as well as the Bible since these were the subjects I had already taught as a private tutor in Kaunas.

The only person I knew in town was Mr. Klommel, the schools' headmaster, originally from Rokishok, a town near Kupishok. I had previously talked with him about my work situation. On the agreed day, I arrived at the Kretingen Railway Station with my modest belongings.

***

Sheer luck! The moment I got off the train and stood on the platform with an embarrassed look, I saw a good-looking girl with an elegant, flowery umbrella in her hand. We smiled at each other and she asked whether I was looking for a comfortable room to rent. Amazing, I thought, for it was exactly what I needed at that moment.

It turned out that the girl, Golda Zolkov, had been sent by her aunt to find a tenant for the vacant room in their house, someone preferably single and intelligent. Needless to say, I was full of enthusiasm and followed her. She helped me to find a coach and led me to her house. We chatted pleasantly on the ride until we reached our destination. Clearly, Providence took care of me this time!

The landlady, a respectable woman who spoke Yiddish, showed me my room which was in the attic. I hadn't been spoiled by luxury before so the modest, though clean furniture suited me perfectly. In the meantime, I became acquainted with the family. The five Zolkov sisters spread some positive rumors about me in town.

I also had a conversation with Mr. Colombus, Chairman of the local parents' committee, who invited me for a Sabbath meal. The Headmaster, a tall, heavy-set man, a gifted mathematician and Hassid, introduced me to the students and teachers. I rapidly began to adapt to the school and community life of Kretingen.

***

This was my first job as a full-time teacher and I enthusiastically got down to work. Firstly, I tried to unite the students of my class and turn them into a learning society. We gathered in the evenings, chatting in Hebrew. My relationship with the pupils as well as with their parents was very friendly. The Headmaster wasn't too fond of these gatherings but he did not prevent my efforts.

***

I had some success with the local girls, especially after my lectures in front of the Hebrew-speaking audience of Kretingen. One day I made a presentation in the Zionist spirit which impressed the intelligentia of Klaipeda, the neighboring town.

Klaipeda formerly belonged to Prussia and was the regional center of Jewish culture. The Parents' Committee allowed me to organize extracurricular activities, including a youth club which proved to be an absolute success! We staged a Hebrew play with the participation of the students and their teachers, along with many other enjoyable functions.

***

My relationship with the other youth organizations in town was polite but not warm so I decided to leave town at the end of the school year. Also, my studies at the Faculty of Law at Kaunas University demanded greater attention than occasional trips from the provinces.

At Passover, I met Dr. Etzioni, the sponsor of the Jewish Gymnasium in Wilkomir which was a major center of Jewish life in Lithuania. With the assistance of Dov Lippetz, I signed a contract with the Wilkomir Jewish Gymnasium.

The following year I would teach Bible and Hebrew literature in this prestigious institution. It was a major step forward in my professional career.

***

With regret, I parted from my students and their families in Kretingen. The Headmaster unsuccessfully urged me to stay for another year. I left the town with a feeling of accomplishment.

For many years afterwards, I exchanged letters with my former students and we reminisced about our pleasant times together.

Teachers in Kretingen 1924

Wilkomir – Teacher, Educator and Youth Guide

Wilkomir was an important regional center, as it was a center of Jewish thought and a battleground for many ideological wars. The community was extremely diverse; there was the Zionist movement, the anti-Zionists and various religious streams. The anti-Zionists consisted of anti-religious leftist movements united in their common resistance to 'Zionist hegemony' in Jewish communities.

The Zionists suggested that the solution to the 'Jewish problem' was far away in Palestine; they were the ideological enemies of the left who considered Yiddish to be the language of the future and called Hebrew an obsolete tongue.

Regarding social issues, the leftist movement voiced opinions ranging from bourgeois to communist. Yudel Mark, a prominent educator, talented orator, and an intelligent person, chose Wilkomir as the center of the world of 'Yiddishism' in light of the cultural autonomy that Jews had received.

Already in the first years of Lithuanian independence, Mark had opened a Jewish school which taught in Yiddish. He attracted the best anti-Zionist teachers. The school soon began to fill with Wilkomir youth sharing the same political ideology. Some of the students came from small provinces. There were students who enrolled in the school because Yiddish was their primary language and the studies were now easier for them.

Political convictions were not foremost on the minds of the teachers but the students, particularly those in the higher grades, were captured by Communist ideas and struggled for the rights of the deprived. This was the only Yiddish high school in Wilkomir.

***

Diaspora supporters had a serious confrontation with members of the Zionist movement. The fact that they were only a minority in the Jewish community only strengthened their Marxist-Yiddish ideology.

A major religious stream in Wilkomir was the Orthodox community which consisted of a few hundred families. They sustained a yeshiva, studied Torah, and occasionally participated in the political debates, especially before the local Jewish central institutions held elections.

One of the most influential speakers of this community was Moshe Cohen, an educated and respectable man. He represented the political party 'Agudat Israel.' I had the privilege to befriend both him and his daughter, Hadassah, who was to eventually become my wife and with whom I spent fifty-seven happy and eventful years.

***

Dov Lippetz decided to establish an alternative to leftist education with a Zionist-Hebrew Gymnasium. He served as Headmaster for some time and then returned to Kaunas which was the center of Tarbut activities.

A suitable successor was found – Dr. Joseph Etzioni – who was a vigorous Zionist, energetic educator and a mysterious character. He had a colorful personality which deserves a separate biography. I was lucky to work with him daily for two years.

***

I arrived at the Wilkomir Gymnasium in August 1925 in a group of five young teachers, two women and three men. We had spent long hours traveling together on the dilapidated roads. Our shared experiences made us good friends by the time we arrived at our destination.

We spent our first night in a hotel owned by Raphael Grushkin, an educated Jew and the grandfather of Yair Stern, the future leader of Lehi. After a few hours of rest, we introduced ourselves to Dr. Etzioni who in turn introduced us to his deputy, an easy-going and energetic man named Pintzuk, as well as the other teachers.

***

It was time to take care of worldly matters and find permanent sleeping arrangements. My fellow teacher, a handsome individual named Israel London who was born in Mariampol, was kind enough to lead me to a hotel in the town center where we rented two rooms, one near the other.

***

My schedule was very diverse since the school lacked teaching personnel at the secondary level. I taught Hebrew, literature, the Bible and political economics for a total of thirty-six hours each week. In addition to that, I taught general and Jewish history to the lower grades. My formal training was very modest but I had read intensively and had learned from my father. I was slightly apprehensive before my first session with the higher grades.

As I entered the room, I saw dozens of young people, some of them around my age. Many were children of Jewish refugees who were beginning to return to their abandoned homes. Before the war, they populated the border towns between Russia and Germany but were expelled when the Czar decided that the Jews betrayed Russia during the First World War.

One of the most hilarious myths was that the Jews were hiding telephones in their beards in order to keep in touch with the enemy. Having suffered in Russia during their expulsion, the Jews were now returning to Lithuania.

***

When the War came to an end, thousands of Jewish families flooded their hometowns in Lithuania. Some of their children had grown up in Russia where they had studied and even graduated from universities. The Lithuanian authorities, however, did not acknowledge their certificates.

The young people were forced to go back to school and pass their exams again. The schools were inundated with students who entered the higher grades in order to pass the Lithuanian matriculation examinations.

About half of my students in the eighth grade were the ones who paid the price for this new policy. Not all schools were happy to accept these students for the final year but the Wilkomir Hebrew Gymnasium gave them the opportunity.

***

Before I entered the classroom, I had already envisaged the discipline problems that I would have to face. My previous teaching experiences did not prepare me for these new difficulties. I realized that teaching a 14-year-old was different than dealing with 17 and 18-year-old students. The latter could not be slapped; their parents might not be interested to come for a conference. Clearly, there was need for a different approach.

***

I had heard various stories from teachers who, trying to cope with discipline problems in their classes, couldn't fall asleep. I tossed and turned that night but swore I would not give up. I would try to find the right approach for the students and would not ask the headmaster for assistance as he had instructed, even in the case of the most serious discipline trouble.

My father had been a teacher highly respected in our community and my short stints in Neishtot and Kretingen had never involved conflicts with students. I thought that in the worst possible scenario, I could go back to Kaunas and return to the lower grades.

***

The bell rang and Dr. Etzioni appeared in the teachers' room and said, "You've got an 8th grade literature class." "I know, Mr. Headmaster," I answered energetically. "I'm on my way."

"I will go in with you to introduce you to the students," he kindly offered. But I politely refused and said that I preferred to appear alone.

When I entered the packed room, the students stood up. They were all taller than me! I asked them to sit down and felt forty pairs of eyes directed at me with great curiosity.

With my students in Wilkomir

From Right: Dr. Etzioni, in the center: The principal Dr. Lubowski (Libai);
The author is to his right.

C.Z. (?) youth in Wilkomir

Tales from My Father's Home

Telling you the story about Mendel-Leib Rabinowitz demands a confession on my part – I wasn't the most diligent student in town in the realm of Talmud. It does not mean to say that I was not knowledgeable or sharp enough, but my natural curiosity constantly diverted me from matters of faith towards more secular reading.

Having noticed that, my father decided to take urgent measures: First, he constructed a study room for me which was isolated from the rest of the house. But that effort proved to be totally unsuccessful since seclusion gave me even more freedom to plunge into popular Hebrew books and magazines.

Then father came up with the idea of a private tutor - he hired a shrewd Hassidic rabbi who would spend a certain number of hours with me. But those lessons also came to a halt despite the relatively high learning fees father paid for me. The poor man couldn't stand my mischievousness.

Utterly desperate, my pious father was looking for a solution and, at last, decided quite cleverly that I would study with a partner (in Havruta). He chose just the right individual for the task: Efraim Oshri (later a Brooklyn Rabbi and the author of the famous "Khurban Lita" or "Annihilatio of the Lithuanian Jews").

Miraculously enough, the new system did work and we proceeded from one Gemara page to another and in case of problems used to turn to my father, a Talmudic scholar himself, for guidance. The only day, however, when we couldn't consult him was Thursday - the Market Day - when father gave my mother a hand at her store on the Market Square. Indeed, that day was a bit of a celebration for all shopkeepers in town, since crowds of Lithuanian peasants were flowing into Kupishok from nearby villages.

So who did we go in case of Talmudic difficulty? Mendel-Leib Rabinowitz - one of the most renowned scholars in town. However, he was also busy at his gloomy shop of agricultural implements. I remember we once entered his packed store and watched him bargain with a peasant.

They seemed to be deeply absorbed but he asked: "And what do you boys want?" We shyly answered that we had a 'kashe' (a Talmudic question). Having heard that, he left in the middle of the argument, abandoning all his customers. He went into a dark back room and invited us to join him. There we presented our question and Mendel-Leib remained with us until the issue was resolved no matter how many customers were awaiting him.

***

This is just one example of those devoted souls for whom nothing is more important than sacred Jewish values and the study of Torah.

NOTE: Mendel-Leib Rabinowitz was born in 1866, the son of Baruch-Mordechai Rabinowitz and his wife Chana-Feiga and died December 30, 1931. He was the father of Basa-Dvora Rabinowitz, the wife of Beno-Laiser Meyerwitz.

His daughter and her family were murdered in 1941. He probably had a son whose wife came from Daugavpils, but no records have been found as yet about this family and what happened to them during the Holocaust.

We Tore Up the Devil

The Lord wished to bestow His favor on the people of Israel, so He granted them many festivals. These were the days on which we, the Jewish children of the Eastern European Diaspora, exempt from the burden of Torah study in the heder, were free to enjoy the many pleasures of the holidays.

Mother would wash my hair on the eve of the festival and I would dress in my holiday clothes. The house was filled with the delicious smells of the special food my mother and sisters were preparing for the evening meal. Every festival had its own characteristic aromas and tastes.

Despite their apparent similarity, the festivals are nevertheless very different from one another. Some are joyful and playful, whereas others are more sober, sometimes even sad. Take for example Passover, which we looked forward to for a month after the joyous Purim feast. We awaited the Passover Seder with its enjoyable and symbolic activities: The four cups of wine, the four questions, reading the Haggadah, the traditional songs, stealing the Afikoman, the game with nuts, and so on.

Or Shavuoth, a very short festival, only two days, but full of pleasurable surprises: The meal of cheese blintzes and other milk dishes, the synagogue redolent of greenery, and Tikun Shavuoth, the adventure of spending the entire night in the synagogue reading passages from the Torah and partaking of the cakes and coffee which one of the righteous women would bring from time to time to strengthen the hearts of the men who filled the synagogue until dawn.

What festival is more joyful than Sukkoth, beginning with the first nail we knocked into the sukkah at the end of Yom Kippur. I helped my father with the building of the sukkah by passing him the hammer and nails and arranging the thatch so that we would be sheltered from the sun during the day but see the sky and the twinkling stars through the narrow openings at night. What could be more pleasant than eating in the decorated, crowded sukkah which we had built with our own hands and fulfilling the commandment of sitting in the Tabaernacle.

Not to mention the lovely festivals of Purim and Simchat Torah in which we fulfilled the commandment to celebrate light-heartedly and with great enthusiasm. We can add to the 'happy' festivals Tu B'Shvat, the fifteenth of the month of Shvat.

Since this is not a religious festival, we were not given a holiday from heder until the afternoon when we were allowed a couple of hours of holiday merriment. We produced our packages of dried fruit, fruits which were rare in the cold climate of the Galut. The poorer children of the class, who were not able to bring these exotic fruits, did not suffer any deprivation for the teacher would place the fruit in one large dish and divide it equally among us. There were no more lessons that day. The teacher would leave us to our own devices and after much rowdy play we would go home in an excited holiday mood.

These are some of the joyous festivals which contrast with the festivals in which sadness and solemnity hold sway. Among these are the fast days like the Ninth of Av when there were no lessons in the heder because it was our day of mourning for the destruction of the Temple. From the cradle, we had heard stories about the atrocities perpetrated during the destruction and when we were older we studied passages from the 'Book of Lamentations.'

There was no contradiction between the ancient custom of little children throwing thorns on the mourners sitting in the darkened synagogue on low benches reciting lamentations with the thorns sometimes caught in the beard of a mourner raising either a smile or his ire. The heaviness of spirit we felt as this day approached as if the catastrophe had occurred in our own day and we ourselves had suffered all the hardships and bitterness of the Exile. Throwing the thorns was thus the fulfillment of a commandment for us and the sorrow flowed from the depths of our pure, young souls.

The feeling was the same on Yom Kippur, the Day of Atonement. Even though it is a holiday and the children studying the Gemara knew the legend about the dancing in the vineyard in the time of the Temple, there was no doubt about the nature of this day whose place was firmly fixed in the list of solemn festivals. Many of the prayers recited in the synagogue were punctuated by the sobs of the women. But most distressing to me was the sight of my father's tears.

Everything was clear to me concerning the happy and sad festivals except in the case of Rosh HaShanah, the New Year. I could not decide to which category

these two significant days belonged. Two contradictory feelings struggled within me. At the beginning of the month of Elul, I already became apprehensive. The blast of the Shofar after the morning prayer awakened in me serious anxiety about my fate in the coming year and my mind was filled with thoughts of repentance.

There isn't a human being in this world who has never sinned, all the more so this nine-year-old boy who, because of his many misdemeanors, was considered by everyone to be a mischievous scamp. I was not yet of an age to be held responsible for my sins, this responsibility being held by my father until I reached my Bar Mitzvah day when he would read the prayer absolving himself of the father's responsibility for the sins of his son. However, he wisely did not completely forego the punishment which I deserved, and I received my fair share of having my face slapped and even suffering the indignity of being put over his knee and soundly spanked.

I thus had no actual reason for apprehension about my fate for, as our Sages said, "Afflictions purify a man's sins." In a strange way, I was even somewhat grateful to my father for punishing me as I saw this as an absolvement from punishment from on High in the future. Nonetheless, I couldn't totally ignore my thoughts of repentance and behaved with great restraint from the first day of the month of Elul until the day after Yom Kippur reinforced by my mother's admonition every morning as I left the house, "In the month of Elul, even fish tremble in water."

At the same time, it was hard to ignore all the joys that Rosh HaShanah afforded a child like me, like the blasts of the Shofar which reached their peak before the Mussaf prayer. For an entire month, from the beginning of Elul, the Shofar would be heard every morning in the synagogue after 'Shacharit.' More than once we children succeeded in snatching the Shofar for a few moments and competed with one another in trying to blow it until we were caught by Shabtai, the Shammas, who retrieved the 'holy instrument,' roundly scolded us and threw us out of the synagogue.

In this way a month passed until at last we heard the sounds of the Shofar on the New Year. Seven times we would hear the blasts which slowly faded and then suddenly there would be absolute silence. Then the soft, spine-tingling voice of the Rabbi, his face almost completely hidden by his prayer shawl would say, "Tear Up the Devil!"

'Tashlich,' the curious custom practiced on the first day of Rosh HaShanah of symbolically casting ones sins into the water, was something I enjoyed witnessing, even though my father dubbed it women's foolishness. A procession of men followed by the women would proceed to the river where they would say,, "And I will cast all my sins into the depths of the sea," and they empty the contents of their pockets into the flowing water.

As I was well-informed about the known or rumored wrongdoings of many of the town's inhabitants, I would choose a victim and observe his sins as they were thrown into the river. I watched Meir Stein, the banker, who stole the savings of poor widows and orphans, and Benzi, the cheating moneylender, and Joelke, the rebel, who was reputed to eat unkosher food when he went on business to Gentile villages.

There was no hint of sadness on the eve of Rosh HaShanah as we sat down to the festive meal. The table was beautifully set, the candlesticks polished, the challah twisted in the shape of folded hands. On the table was a bunch of grapes, rare in the cold climate of Lithuania, ready for the blessing 'Sheheyanu,' the golden honey in a dish in which to dip a piece of bread when saying the blessing for a good and sweet year; the pile of New Year greeting cards with which my sister had decorated the table; and, most important of all, the large fish head, and next to it a smaller fish head on which father and mother would make the blessing "May we be as the head and not as the tail."

For me, the fish head was the greatest delicacy, one which I also enjoyed on Sabbath eve. On the eve of Rosh HaShanah, however, there was additional pleasure in the joyful obligation of saying a special blessing over the fish head. I felt a little guilty about enjoying the festive meal so frivolously on this solemn festival.

In this way Rosh HaShanah had been celebrated year after year until that fateful year of fear and apprehension. This was the year of the blood libel against Mendel Beilis in Russia, which threatened the large Jewish population with terrible pogroms if, God forbid, evil judges were to find

Beilis guilty. He had been accused of murdering a Christian boy for the purpose of using his blood for baking matzot for Passover.

This was an obscene libel which the enemies of our people had used for hundreds of years as a pretext to persecute us and spill our blood. The Beilis blood libel at the beginning of the twentieth century was the worst of them all for millions of Russians Jews depended on the outcome of his trial. The Czar's advisors planned the trial very shrewdly and thoroughly. We awaited the trial with great trepidation.

During that period, one day Nachum Leib, the postman, entered our house with a pile of letters in his hand. He extracted one from the pile and in his slightly husky voice read the beautiful curving letters in the Russian language forming words on the envelope: "To Mr. Meir Kodesh in Kupishok."

You may well ask why he read the address out loud when he was already in our house with the letter in his hand? He had come for the special purpose of delivering it and it was therefore incumbent upon him to read out the address. This obviously also gave him much pleasure and a chance to show off his reading ability.

My father was most surprised to receive this letter from such a distance as they did not arrive very often. As this was an unusual event, my father hinted to my mother that she should offer Nachum a glass of tea while he searched in his purse for the two kopeks to reward him for delivering the letter.

As soon as the postman left, my father hastened to examine the envelope. He too feasted his eyes on the long address written in Russian, turned over the envelope and read the name and address of the sender, wondering who Rabbi Abraham Dov Poppel from Heidotishok was (in the vicinity of Vilnius.)

After several moments, he suddenly remembered that this was a distant relative from his father's side, renowned from his youth for his worthiness and promise of greatness, handsome in both appearance and spirit, outstanding in the possession of both religious and secular knowledge, God-fearing and conscientious in his attention to the needs and well-being of his congregation.

Father placed the letter in his pocket and returned to his pupils who, in his absence, had begun to quarrel. When at last his pupils went home for dinner, he sat down at the table to read it. I will attempt to convey the contents as accurately as possible after some eighty years have passed since I read it. (I could not but notice that, annoyed as he was at my inquisitiveness in reading the letter, my father evinced a flicker of pride that his young son was able to read Hebrew so fluently.) The letter was written in beautiful Hebrew, sprinkled with sayings of the Sages. And here is a shortened version of what Rabbi Poppel wrote to my father.

The Month of Elul, 1912
Tuesday,
Heidotishok.

Dear Rabbi Meir:

I am appealing to you about the following matter. We are now going through hard times for the Jewish people in the light of the terrible blood libel which our enemies have imposed upon us. Mendel Beilis is in prison awaiting trial and only God can bring justice and free us from these shameful accusations.

At this difficult time, we must have recourse to repent. I believe that if the repentance of one individual can reach the seat of the Most

High, then the repentance of an entire congregation will certainly 'tear up the devil' and deliver us from sorrow, accusations, and wicked, harsh decrees.

I have therefore gathered together seven worthies of our town in order to discuss the matter of charity and repentance. As it is said by our Sages, "Charity begins at home." No doubt Rabbis and teachers in other Jewish communities will do the same in order to forestall the evil through repentance, prayer and charity and the Lord will hear our supplication, forgive our sins, and bring about a fair trial for Beilis and bring peace to our people.

Now the High Holidays are approaching; the Days of Judgement when on Rosh HaShanah we are all judged and on Yom Kippur, when the sentence is passed. We are in need of an experienced cantor to intercede for us with our Heavenly Father. There is nobody in our congregation with all the necessary qualities – experience, an impressive appearance and a pleasing voice.

In previous years, we contented ourselves with one of our own people, but this year is different, and we decided to search for a cantor outside the bounds of our community who will be better able to arouse the Lord's mercy. Since I know that you are graced with all the qualities of a very fine cantor, I am beseeching you to come to us for the High Holidays and to serve as our cantor.

If you are willing to accede to our request, we would appreciate a speedy reply. Be assured that your expenses will be covered generously, and that virtue is its own reward.

As I was an expert in the Holy Tongue, I avidly read the Hebrew magazine to which my father subscribed and was aware of the Beilis case and the danger which threated him and all the Jews of the land. I also understood the intention of the Rabbi who had invited my father to serve as cantor.

Although I did not know the Rabbi and his name was not familiar to me, I was nevertheless fully aware of my father's qualities and why they had approached him. Indeed, he was renowned for his skill in prayer reading and his melodic singing. Many prayer readers even tried to imitate him but with no success.

Despite his ability, father was very modest, unlike some other members of the congregation who would push their way to the reader's stand and entertain the congregation with their chanting. Instead, he would only go up when invited to do so and even then only after a great deal of persuasion. I was very proud when the Rabbi and the Gabbai would aproach him and quietly ask him to honor the congregation by reading the Mussaf. He would smile modestly and comply, taking his large prayer book and washing his hands before going up to the reader's stand, as though this was the first time he was serving as cantor on the Sabbath. On the High Holidays, he would volunteer to read the Mussaf (the prayer after Kol Nidrei.)

However, father never went to another town to serve as cantor, and it never entered his head or that of any member of his household to leave home for the High Holidays and to go to a strange congregation. I waited to see what would happen, asking myself if he would really accept the invitation. And what would my wise mother have to say about it? For it was very unlikely that he would do anything of this nature without first discussing it with her.

In my presence, everything continued in the usual way but from my parents' bedroom I heard whispering with my name repeated a number of times. I pretended that I knew nothing and just waited impatiently and with great curiosity to see what would happen.

And sure enough, one morning after the prayer service, about two weeks before Rosh HaShanah, father stopped me as I was about to leave for heder, lightly stroked my cheek and said, "Listen Zalmanke, I have news for you. Next week, God willing, we will go to visit grandfather as we do every year to wish him a happy New Year and from there we'll go on a long journey."

My grandfather, my father's father, served as the Rabbi in a small community which could be reached in thirty minutes by train. Twice a year, before Passover and the High Holidays, the entire Kodesh family would gather from all parts of Lithuania in order to wish him a happy holiday. We would spend about half a day in an uproarious mixture of words of wisdom, Hassidic melodies, the gathering of aunts, and children's games. At the end of the day, we recited the evening prayers and then departed to take the train to our different destinations.

I loved these family gatherings mostly because of the tumult and I had no fear of grandfather's questions about my studies. The fact that his grandson was acquainted with a page of Gemara did not impress him. According to him it was natural that young boys studied the Holy Scriptures to develop their intellect. What was more important in his opinion was good manners which, in my case, were presumably not perfect. My father was occasionally criticized by my grandfather for my naughtiness. The result of these conversations I felt on my body when we returned home.

As the day of the family gathering came to an end, the younger generation would receive grandfather's blessing. We would line up according to age and the seniority of our parents. He would place his hands on the head of each of us and whisper a blessing. We thanked him and so ended our visit.

This time, when father revealed to me the news about our projected journey, I couldn't restrain myself from admitting to having read the letter. He pretended to be surprised and even lectured me on the ban placed by Rabbi Gershom on reading other people's correspondence. However, he himself was so alarmed at the thought of the severity of the ban that he hastened to add that it apparently did not apply to a son who reads letters addressed to his father!

Although obviously not angry with me, he did forbid me to tell anyone else about the invitation. But our closely guarded secret soon became common knowledge and a topic of discussion among the members of our congregation. Well-wishers respected my father's decision, whereas other critcized him, asking how a respectable Jew like my father could think of abandoning his home during the High Holidays to chase after honor in a strange town.

My reticent mother acccepted the adventurous journey silently. Her eyes showed sadness but also an undertone of pride was evident in her voice when she related the contents of the letter to her sister, Tzippi, who nodded her head and said how fortunate my mother was that her husband's good reputation had spread so far. "What a pity," she said, "that you can't accompany him."

Mother could not even think of closing her store for ten days, the livelihood being so meager. Also, the cow and the chickens had to be attended to and the potatoes picked. So what could she do? She was a strong woman and knew how to endure difficult times.

When the hour of parting arrived and Mendel, the coachman, brought his wagon to a noisy halt at our door to take us to the railway station situated outside the town, mother did not cry, even though this was the first time she was to be separated from her husband and youngest child for the holidays. She parted from my father in the bedroom, out of modesty, and emerged slightly flustered and teary-eyed. She smiled at the coachman, hugged me tightly, and then gently pushed me away. "Hurry Zalmanke, get on the wagon and be careful. For goodness sake, don't put your head out of the window of the train! Behave nicely and listen to your father and be a good boy! Don't bring shame on our family!"

I was the one who cried! She wiped my tears with a corner of her apron. My father and I climbed onto the wagon and joined the other passengers. In a short while, we were sitting in the railway carriage on our way to grandfather's house.

***

Our visit this year was somewhat different from previous years, for everyone knew about father's undertaking and looked upon him with greater respect. He was secluded for a long time in a separate room where grandfather gave him instructions, warnings and good advice. Father came out of the room slightly more bent, as if an added burden had been placed on his shoulders, for grandfather was very particular about everything to do with worship. One can surmise that he left out nothing that is incumbent on a cantor. A proof of this was my father's tears when he received a blessing from his aged father.

I was also granted special attention from grandfather on this visit. He explained to me the special responsibility of a cantor throughout the year, but especially during the High Holidays and in troubled and fearful times such as these. He warned me not to jeopardize my father's mission by thoughtless behavior and gave me his blessing.

***

From grandfather's house we proceeded directly to our destination. I had never been on such a long journey in a train, and had never spent such a long time with my father in a closed compartment. To tell the truth, I felt a little uncomfortable being in the care of my father without the gentle intervention of my mother. It seemed to me that my father was also not at ease with the situation. As usual, he spent most of the journey reading, but every now and then he would attend to me, feeling my forehead to make sure I was not ill, and taking out the food which my mother had prepared in abundance to sustain us during the long journey. I looked out of the window and enjoyed the scenery.

From time to time the train would stop at a station, letting off passengers loaded down with their bundles, and taking in others. Our compartment remained almost empty. A Jew who entered and tried to engage my father in conversation soon gave up after father replied to his probing questions very tersely and went off to look for more congenial company.

As it grew dark, I sat beside my father and tried to imitate him by reading a passage from the Gemara which I had packed in my luggage so as not, God forbid, to be idle during the journey.

But soon enough I could not conceal my yawns. This did not go unnoticed by father, who put down his book and started to prepare a bed for me on the upper bunk. After reading the Shema, I climbed into my bunk and he covered me and dimmed the lights. I quickly fell into a deep sleep.

***

We reached our destination at dawn. Not many passengers got off at this station and the Rabbi's messenger had no trouble identifying us and leading us to the carriage which was to take us to the town a few miles away. The Rabbi and his household had gotten up early to welcome us to their home. In addition, a number of townsmen were also in the house of the Rabbi at this early hour preparing the morning prayer.

The men sat down at the table to drink a glass of tea before 'Shacharit,' unlike the Mitnagdim who refrained from drinking or eating before the morning prayer. While drinking their tea, they examined my father on his knowledge of Torah and appeared to be satisfied with his answers, for they very quickly loosened their tongues and spoke to him as though he was one of them.

During this conversation about local matters, we learned that this year, for a reason which I cannot recall, there was a problem in the fishing industry and that there was a danger that the fishermen would be unable to provide us with fish for the holiday. I didn't take much notice of this at the time, even though I was to be directly involved with the shortage of fish, as I will shortly describe.

My father quickly settled into his group and made preparations to accompany them to the synagogue. I seemed to have been forgotten, and it was only when he was putting on his coat that my father turned to me and said, "You, Zalmanke, will stay home, pray on your own, and the Rebbetzin will put you to bed to make up the hours of sleep that you missed. We have a lot of work before us, and need physical and spiritual strength during the High Holidays which are approaching to 'tear up the devil' in our prayers."

***

No sooner had the men left, when the Rabbi's wife and her eldest daughter began to attend to me. While inquiring about our family, they made up a comfortable bed for me, closed the shutters, and I soon sank into a refreshing sleep.

A gentle pat of my father's hand awakened me at noon. He had already managed to unpack our luggage which my mother had packed so efficiently:

Clothing in one pile, underwear in another, presents for our hosts, and even my

school books, as if I wouldn't find any books in the Rabbi's home!

I dressed and joined the family for lunch. After reciting the blessing following a meal and reading a page of Gemara with my father, I was given permission to go outside. I had never been in a strange town, except for my grandfather's town which was very small and where I knew every Jew. Now I was curious to confront the unknown.

Our arrival was already known to all the Jews of the vicinity. Inquisitive boys were loitering near the Rabbi's house and inspected the visiting youngster who had come with his father, the cantor, to stand at his side during the service. We soon became friends and they led me to the courtyard of the large synagogue.

My new friends told me about their 'melamed' (or teacher), about the tricks they played on him, congregation gossip, and their own private stories about their homes, their families and so forth. They were also well informed about the Beilis case, and even gave me the latest news which I hadn't heard yet because of our preoccupation with our journey. A number of them read the paper which reached their homes just as I did.

All the things we had in common brought us closer together and I returned to the Rabbi's house surrounded by many friends and very content despite the separation from my mother and the fear and trepidation concerning the great responsibility which I bore together with my father. I was grateful for this adventure, and already imagined the stories I would tell my friends when I returned home.

***

The festival began. It was strange to see a woman, not my mother, blessing the candles. Even the candlesticks were different from ours, and the way the Rebbetzin performed the blessing was different to the way my mother did. When I was little I used to cling to my mother when she blessed the candles, often feeling her burning tears as they fell on my face and I would cry together with her.

Suddenly I felt anger towards my father for separating me from my mother on the eve of this holy day, even though I lacked nothing and everyone in the house spoiled me and showered me with affection. The Rebbetzin even tried to persuade me to let her wash my hair before the festival but I refused, since having my hair washed was not something I enjoyed. No matter how tightly I closed my eyes, the soap suds would find their way in and burn them. Father rescued me from our well-intentioned hostess and took upon himself the responsibility for getting me ready for the holiday. I was quite pleased with myself when, cleaned and combed, I looked at myself in the mirror after putting on the new clothes which had been made especially for our journey.

***

In the synagogue, father was ready to begin the saying of Psalms for the New Year. The rest of the year the Book of Psalms was the province of the simple folk, whereas the more learned worshipped through the study of Torah. Not so on Rosh HaShanah. On this day everyone is equal before the Lord and His judgment, and the saying of Psalms is raised to the highest level. And so I sat down next to my father.

Clearing my throat, I began enthusiastically to recite, "Blessed is the man who walks not in the counsel of the wicked." But the enthusiasm began to wane as strange thoughts entered my mind and vied with my good intentions to direct my lips and heart to the praising of God. I started to wonder what my mother was doing at that moment, and what about my friends? These thoughts had been put into my head by the Devil and I, small and weak, did not know how to overcome his machinations.

My father was absorbed in his repentance, as was everyone else, and I felt neglected and alienated in these strange surroundings, with nobody to support me in my time of stress. I felt sorry for myself. My eyes filled with tears. Not the purifying tears of repentance which atone for one's sins, but tears of anger against my father who had abandoned me and who had separated me from my tender-hearted mother.

Also anger against myself that I was unable to overcome my evil inclination and that I was abusing the trust given to me by this holy congregation. The words stuck in my throat and I became silent and sank into a daydream. My father sensed my distraction and his nudge restored me to full consciousness and I continued to pray, but without inspiration and with a heavy heart.

At the end of the service, people began to approach my father, whom they regarded as an honored guest, to greet him and wish him a happy New Year. They also stroked my cheek and some even showed interest in me which helped to raise my spirits. The special honor conferred on us when the Rabbi himself came up to us to wish us a happy New Year also cheered me somewhat.

My father took my hand and accompanied by members of the congregation, we returned to the Rabbi's house. But no sooner had we entered, the set table appeared alien to me and my heart sank once more. With difficulty I refrained from bursting into tears. I felt hurt that my father did not notice my distress.

To add to my displeasure, there were no small challot for me to bless as was the custom at home where my mother would bake these little loaves especially for me. Even the dipping of the challah in honey, to symbolize a sweet year, was performed differently. At home, each one would receive a beautiful plate with a spoonful of amber-colored honey, whereas here there was but one communal bowl, and each one dipped his piece of challah in it and recited the blessing. I was too shy to do so; it was as though the custom had been changed deliberately just to annoy me.

The Rabbi and my father made the blessing over the wine in the rather sad melody used during Rosh HaShanah, the honey was tasted and then we came to the blessing of the fish head, which was to cause me much embarrassment and suffering. After the benediction, "Who has kept us alive and sustained us to reach this present time," we reached the main benediction, "May we be as the head and not as the tail." At this point, the Rebbetzin was to bring out the fish head, giving each one a portion and, saying the blessing, we would enjoy eating the stuffed fish, the gefilte fish, which from the beginning of time until the present day has been considered a Jewish delicacy.

Even though I wasn't in the best of moods, I looked forward to making the blessing and then enjoying the fish. I had completely forgotten about the very poor catch the fishermen had had that year. I was also not aware that a member of the congregation, who was concerned that his beloved Rabbi would not be able to bless the head, spent a great deal of money from his own pocket and somehow managed to obtain a small fish which he sent to the Rabbi.

So, unaware of all the facts, when I perceived that the Rebbetzin would serve the fish head only to the Rabbi, I was filled with wrath. I jumped up from my seat as if bitten by a snake and rushed out of the room to the dismay and consternation of all those seated at the table.

Father rushed out after me, followed by the Rabbi, the Rebbetzin and their children. They found me lying on my bed and sobbing. Father, as usual, started feeling my forehead to see if I had fever and begged me to tell him what was hurting me. To this day, I am unable to explain my strange behavior. I was an intelligent boy who was not regarded as spoiled or infantile. How then could I have been overcome with such childish and insolent anger that I answered father's concerned question with the absurd answer, "The fish head hurts me!"

He, however, guessed the meaning of this, for he shamefacedly turned to his astonished hosts and apologetically explained that it was a childish caprice, that I was accustomed to make the blessing over the fish head at home and was distressed that this year I was not being permitted to carry out this commandment.

Father's explanation added to the consternation of our hosts. For a moment there was complete silence in the room. Everyone stood around my bed as if I were seriously ill, not knowing how to relate to me.

It was the Rabbi himself who solved the problem with great charm and understanding. He placed his hand on my head and eagerly exclaimed, "You are quite right, Zalman. You deserve to make the blessing over the fish head. Get up, wash your hands, and come to the table because we're waiting for your blessing." This was an amazing and wonderful solution to the problem.

The Rabbi and the rest of the company returned to the table and waited for me to fulfill the Rabbi's request. He explained his action to my father and to his family, "Our dear young Zalman did us a favor. He is truly the messenger of Israel's advocate. Every year we stand on the Day of Judgement, poor and empty-handed, waiting God's mercy. This year, when we are in such great danger, we are more than ever in need of a virtuous emissary who is the purest of the pure to make the blessing. The benediction, 'We should be as the head' is one of the most important blessings on Rosh HaShanah. It means that we should be like the head and not, Heaven forbid, degraded and oppressed like the tail. An unexpected miracle has occurred! Dear Zalman, who is innocent of sin has undertaken to represent us on this Day of Judgement and to recite this important blessing which will, because of his innocence, surely reach the Most High."

As he was speaking, I entered the room, downcast and ashamed, and took my place at the table. The Rabbi, as though he didn't see me, continued to speak and, turning to my father, said, "You are fortunate Meir that thanks to your son's blessing and his innocent tears our prayers will be answered."

First noticing my presence, he presented the dish to me and said, "Zalman, would you please recite the benediction and be the first to taste the fish, after which we shall also make the blessing." I glanced at my embarrassed father who smiled reluctantly and gave me a sign of assent. I took the dish and in a clear voice recited, "May we be like the head and not like the tail." Everyone said, "Amen," and waited for me to taste the fish first and only then did the Rebbetzin divide the fish head into small slices so that everyone could have a taste.

Achieving my desire for the fish head did not bring me much joy but I was certain that my tears had been justified. Most assuredly, the fish head belonged and had always belonged to me alone. Nevertheless I felt that this time my demands had been exaggerated and that I had hurt my father.

The meal, as was usual with holiday eve meals, was very tasty but the atmosphere was subdued. At the conclusion, we said the traditional prayers and, as is customary on the eve of Rosh HaShanah, read Psalms.

I struggled to stay awake, wanting to remain with the men: The Rabbi, his son Aaron, who was older than me, and my father. The Rabbi again saved the day, suggesting to my father that we go to our room to rest. "You have much work before you, Rav Meir, and so does our Shlomo Zalman, your assistant. Go to bed. I shall also retire soon." My father answered jokingly, saying, "One must obey one's host as long as he doesn't tell you to leave." He closed the book in his hand and led me off to our room. He put me to bed without mentioning my capriciousness at the table. I began to recite the 'Shema' but my eyes closed in the middle of the prayer and I fell fast asleep.

My sleep was light. A little oil-lamp shining in the narrow passage cast a heavy shadow in our room. Father was asleep but he groaned from time to time and tossed and turned as though he were troubled. However, he continued to sleep. Not so I, for waking up and seing the strange room in the light of the oil-lamp, it was forcibly brought home to me that I wasn't in my own bed and my beloved mother wasn't with me. I was also apprehensive about what the future had in store for us.

One of the local boys, older than me, had told me some bad news. Just that morning he had read that the authorities had found a priest by the name of 'Paranaitas,' an anti-Semite, who claimed to know both Hebrew and Aramaic, and to be well-versed in the Talmud. He claimed that he had found the secret commandment in the Talmud to slaughter a Christian boy before the Passover and to use his blood in the baking of matzot.

The court in Kiev where Mendel Beilis was to be tried had approached this priest who had agreed to give testimony at the trial as an expert on Jewish law and tradition. There was great danger that the evil authorities of this oppressive state were preparing a show trial. Who could save us?

Suddenly I was beset by terror. How could one be sure that God would not abandon His people? There was damning evidence for our many sins. We also had the hand of the prosecutor, who was the devil, and the 'angel of death' against us.

The Day of Judgement was approaching, and the people of Israel would gather in synagogues around the world to pray for a good year, a year of forgiveness and atonement. Repentance, prayer and charity would avert a bad verdict. But for this, it is necessary that the counsels for the defense be powerful and completely righteous. I, myself, was one of the counsels for the defense! The Rabbi had said so and he knew what he was talking about. He had the countenance of an angel with a cheerful face, a pleasant manner, and an air of distinction.

Can he also divine our secrets? Does this righteous man also know that I, the defense counsel of Israel, who was brought to this town with my father to divert the heart of the Judge to give a good verdict, is not a paragon of virtue? Is there a man who has never sinned? Sometimes the evil inclination overcame me and I committed sins against God and Man.

All at once I felt the weight of the burden my father had placed on my shoulders. As if to annoy me, my sins and misdemeanors came to mind, even those I had committed in infancy!

I remembered all the forbidden food I had gobbled up. When I went down to the cellar to fetch onions, potatoes or pickled cucumbers for my mother, I took advantage of the errand to sip from the honey. But this was not the worst sin! There was also the forbidden taste that the evil inclination, may he be cursed, forced on me on that market day when our house was filled with villagers selling their wares.

When they left, they forgot a clay pot filled with that particular unclean meat. The evil inclination urged me on, "Taste it. Just a little taste!" I did so and my stomach turned! For days afterwards, I could not rid myself of the taste of the 'trayfe,' the un-kosher food. Remembering this caused me to wonder how I could possibly redeem myself on the Day of Judgement.

Then something happened which I shall remember until the end of days. I was filled with self-pity, pity for my iniquitous soul, and with pity for my poor father who had to bear the punishment for my sins. For four more years he would have to carry this burden. But above everything else, how would I be able to face the Most High tomorrow in the synagogue on such a solemn day, a day when all Jews would be judged and the devil was already sharpening his evil tongue to malign us.

I was filled with sorrow and even thought of waking my father. I burst into tears, covering my head with the blanket so that he would not hear me. And wonder of wonders, the tears gave me relief. A strange idea entered my head. What if I tried to speak to my evil inclination? After all, he was also a Jew and, as my father had explained, the other side of me. I prepared in my mind what to say to him, "Please, evil inclination, let me be spared during the High Holidays, here in a strange place. Why should innocent and honest people suffer because of my transgressions?"

In the midst of these thoughts, I recalled the incident of the fish head and realized that I had acted foolishly. I had behaved like a spoiled child and had brought shame on my father and on myself. Even though the kind-hearted Rabbi had turned bad into good, as though it was due to me that the blessing would be accepted, I did not flatter myself that this was so. I was aware that a religious duty achieved through a wrongful deed does not count.

Many years have passed since then, and I don't remember in exact detail the dialogue with my evil inclination. But one thing I do remember. The result was good. My tears dried, the heaviness in my heart began to dissolve and, at last, I fell into the sleep of the just.

When I awoke, I recited the morning prayers with great conviction as was fitting on such a solemn day. As was the custom among the Hassidim, we had a festive breakfast of cocoa and home-made pastries. I strode along with my father, the Rabbi, and his son to the synagogue. I felt that my evil inclination had listened to me and I was untroubled. We had made an agreement and he would not lead me astray.

The synagogue was almost filled, even though we had arrived early. The congregants were preparing themselves for many hours of worship. Soon the place was filled to capacity. The children surrounded me, but I tried to ignore them and to imitate my father and the Rabbi who were wrapping themselves in their prayer shawls which they wore over the white robes they had donned at home.

I immersed myself in the prayer book and from time to time would sigh deeply and direct my thoughts to Heaven. The cantor for the morning prayer was the Rabbi himself. This was a token of respect and the congregants felt more secure on the Day of Judgement when he conducted the Service.

Before the hour of the blowing of the Shofar arrived, the synagogue attendant announced a break. The 'shul' emptied out and we too went home. The Rebbetzin begged me to eat and drink something as the day was long and I would soon have to help my father who would be reading the Mussaf prayer. I was persuaded to drink some coffee with milk and eat a piece of delicious cake she had baked. I sat and ate quietly and after a while we returned to the synagogue.

On the 'bima,' the Shofar blower was preparing himself for the holy blasts and the special prayer, with tears pouring down his cheeks. I stood beside my father and the Rabbi ascended the bima, as was the custom, to read the passages for the blowing of the Shofar.

As the Rabbi began to recite, an hysteria seemed to overtake the congregants. Terrible cries and sobs filled the house of worship. They repeated the passage with tears of supplication seven times, accompanied by the wailing from the women's section. The voices gradually died down and there was silence.

The Rabbi once again rose to his full height and began to sing the moving traditional melody, 'Out of Distress I called the Lord.' The Rabbi read passage after passage, six passages in all, each one beginning with a letter of the words, 'Tear Up the Devil.' The congregation loudly repeated each passage after the Rabbi. At last the Shofar blower recited the blessing, preceding the Shofar blasts.

***

My heart was pounding in trepidation. Would the shofar blower succeed? Would the blasts be clear and lengthy, and not disrupted by the devil? But we could rely on the shofar blower, Reb Eliyahu, a simple Jew whom the Lord had blessed with this talent. There was nobody like him. His Shofar blowing was his pride, and his success was the hope of the congregation.

The Shofar blowing was over and the time for the Mussaf prayer drew near. All eyes rested on us. Once again there was a short break. Father took me outside and spoke to me as to an associate, giving me final professional instructions. I was to sing two whole sections of the prayers solo. My father and the Rabbi had discussed this innovation of giving the task of the cantor to a young child. The Rabbi had convinced my father that my prayer would reach the Most High for no one is purer than a child.

We re-entered the synagogue and returned to our places next to the eastern wall. My father, wrapped in his talit, holding his prayer book, was summoned by the Rabbi to the bima to read the Mussaf prayer. The eyes of the whole congregation were fixed on him. My father slowly approached the bima with me close behind, identifying with him completely and praying for his success. Father put his head in his hands and through his talit I could sense his tears as he whispered, "I am ready and willing."

Then his voice was heard, clearer than I ever heard it before, singing the traditional melody, "Here am I, poor of deeds..." It was now my turn to make my voice heard by giving the tone, in the language of cantors. Thank goodness, my voice also came out loud and clear. Even though my eyes were lowered I could feel the surprise and satisfaction of the congregation when they heard the cantor.

But suddenly my father's voice broke and he was strangled by tears. My father was famous as a tearful cantor who went from one mood to another according to the context of the prayer he was reciting. My own crisis of apprehension had passed, also my shyness. I even forgot my young age.

The whole community of Heidotishok had called my father and me to help it at this solemn time to overcome the accusers of Israel, to 'tear up the devil', and to arouse God's compassion for this congregation and for alle the people of Israel in this time of trouble. All my fears of the past couple of days of being unworthy for this task disappeared.

***

Father led the congregation, skillfully stopping at times so that I could join in. Looking up from my prayer book I saw that I had won the admiration of the congregation. Father also glanced contentedly at me. I was overjoyed, and sure that the Lord would accept our prayers. We had the second day of Rosh Ha-Shanah to look forward to, and I was certain that my father would continue to fulfill his task admirably, and that I would stand proudly by his side.

It was a good feeling. If only my mother were here!

The Family Story of the Pinskers

My Uncle Samuel from Kupishok

I had five uncles in Kupishok, my hometown in Lithuania. Two of them, Mendel and David, were my mother's brothers, descendants from my grandfather Meshulem Mordechai. His first wife died while still young and left three daughters: Sterna, Hannah, my mother, and Tzippi.

Then grandfather married for the second time. His wife's name was Dina. She bore him two sons and two daughters, Batiah and Rachel. All of them established families in Kupishok and were good neighbors to each other. My mother's brothers, Mendel and David Kadishevitz, passed away in their youth.

The girls got married. Aunt Sterna married a man named Ginzburg and moved to Dvinsk or Dinborg. He died before I had the chance to meet him. The rest of the families lived in Kupishok. Mother married my father Meir, the son of a rabbi in Donmonek. Aunt Tzippi married Samuel Pinskoy, Aunt Batia – Hillel Zilber.

Aunt Rachel finally married Abraham Glick. He was a soldier in the Russian army during the First World War. He was one of the last soldiers who retreated from the advancing Germans. He expressed his desire to stay with us. Uncle Samuel, being a caring person, agreed and accepted the unknown soldier. Soon we provided him with civilian clothes. We, as children, found a new partner for housework. Subsequently he married Rachel who was single and aging. That's how we got another uncle, thanks to kind Uncle Samuel.

***

Now I will start with the life story of Uncle Samuel, the father of Joe
Pinskoy's family, who live in Wallingford, Connecticut. This story in its
translation into English is dedicated to his children. These relatives
appeared out of the blue due to Joe and his wife, Eve, both warm and
hospitable people. The parents taught their children (daughters, Gladys
and Joyce and son, Clive) to be linked to their family. Not only did they
develop warm feelings towards their Israeli relatives whom they found in
the 50's, but they also transferred these feelings to their children who in
turn strengthened them.

Thus, in the last years of my life, I feel a spiritual need to build a
bridge between generations and to tell the sons and daughters growing
up under the sky of the free United States of America about their
ancestors in distant Lithuania.

Aunt Tzippi and Uncle Samuel's story would not be complete if we
didn't meet Grandpa Meshulem Mordechai (Motie) Kadishevitz – our
family's patriarch.

Grandfather Meshulem Mordechai

In Kupishok, everything started from Grandpa Meshulem Mordechai,
or Shulem-Motie, as he was called. I'm writing these lines while I'm
slightly confused and my eyes are darkened. For this reason, it's difficult
to recall the events with many details. They are all in a fog and mixed
with things I have seen or heard since then. The following is what I
remember about my grandfather.

He died when I was probably still in the cradle, while my memories
start from the age of two or three. It seems that his name emerged quite
frequently either in family conversations or perhaps as folklore. He used
to be a dominant figure in the community, everyone listened to him

carefully. He spoke in a pleasant manner and with a great sense of humor.

***

Shulem-Motie's style was straightforward and very colorful. A great many of his stories spread about the town as jokes. Let me tell you one of them. My grandpa was a tradesman who exported linen products to Russia in the nineteenth century. Dozens of poor tradesmen used to go to local villages and buy linen from the peasants. Afterwards they sold their merchandise to my grandfather. He was obviously respected by those for whom he was the source of their livelihood. Some used to flatter him a great deal and inquired about his well-being. He used to accept those expressions of respect properly although he reacted to them with his own humor which wasn't necessarily respectable from the language point of view.

They say that while walking back from the sauna, he was invariably met by merchants. The latter blessed him with 'tzur rephue' (a Yiddish blessing after taking a sauna.) According to the custom, the proper answer would be 'thank you' but it wasn't the case with him. In the cold and snowy winter days, he responded, "Kish me t...." (kiss my a..). Quite a sharp answer to a simple act of courtesy!

When people wondered about the reason for this rudeness, he explained, "A weak, ageing Jew comes out of a hot sauna into the freezing cold wrapped up in fur clothes and is hurrying home. Suddenly, these pests stop him with their stupid greetings. If he replies politely, they will naturally begin to ask him other questions. Was the water boiling or just hot? How was the steam? What news did they talk about in the sauna? and so forth. In the meantime, he is in danger of catching a cold or even pneumonia, God forbid, whereas after a response like mine, I get rid of the pests and go on!"

***

My grandfather bought quite an extensive piece of land in the market square that was later used for building a number of flats and shops. In his lifetime, he divided the possession between his sons and daughters. By this, he prevented a fight over their inheritance which can bring hatred, but it did result in jealousy. Almost all were shop owners with similar merchandise. The problem started when the peasants bought the stuff from one of the sister's shops instead of another sibling which was nearby.

His third daughter, Tzippi, he gave in marriage to a young man from a respectable Hassidic family. His name was Samuel Pinskoy (later changed to Pinsker.) He was a polite individual with a pleasant voice which he used in the local synagogue and talking at meetings. Samuel also was bright and had a wonderful sense of humor. As a dowry, he received two small shops in the town center and a plot for building a house not far from where we lived. The family grew but their financial condition worsened. A man with initiative and energy like his obviously did not want to live from hand to mouth without trying to improve the state of affairs.

In those days, penniless Russian Jews started thinking of making money in distant places. At the end of the nineteenth century, some developing countries attracted people with initiative and willingness to improve their financial situation. North America, New York especially, promised new opportunities to immigrants.

Another country was South Africa. After the war that freed South Africa from British rule, permanent and temporary immigration started. After they arrived in the new country, the immigrants began saving each penny, even on food, and many helped their families still in Europe when they themselves became more successful.

In the meantime, their family grew larger. Unfortunately, not all babies lived long. To the very end of her life, my aunt mourned the little angels, boys and girls who died right after their birth. Only five of them survived – three sons and two daughters. Joseph, the eldest, Beryl, and David, and the girls – Regina and Chaya.

Painfully, my uncle separated from his family and went to distant South Africa for a long time to try his luck. I was then very small, or maybe I wasn't even born yet. Nevertheless, I remember well the time when he came back. He looked quite different from the other Jews in town in his modern clothes. His beard was beautifully trimmed and his earlocks were shortened. Samuel's stories and jokes about the blacks and Dutch heroes who fought the British Empire made him very popular. He was always encircled by curious listeners striving to hear more about wild animals wandering in the forests and about gold mines. He never told his personal story about the way he had earned money even though I occasionally talked to him during my rare visits to Kupishok after I reached manhood.

In later years, his eldest son, Joseph, told me about those years his father had spent in South Africa earning money for his family and separated from his close relatives. But there was a happy ending! Samuel came back to Kupishok and immediately expanded his shop, adding more expensive goods. Now, anyone who wanted to cover his body from head to toe turned to Samuel Pinskoy's clothing store.

Some years passed and I left the Kupishok world with its small shops and entered the modern era. I would make short visits back twice a year to be with my mother and sister. During those rare visits, I invariably stopped by Uncle Samuel's store to listen to his calm words, full of wisdom and life experiences.

***

I do not remember Aunt Tzippi's house in the years of survival with five little ones and a husband far away. That life was very similar to her sister Hannah's, my mother. I can't help being amazed at the way those Jewish women, so tender and charming, could bear such harsh periods: The necessity of earning a living, bringing up their children, and struggling with terrible poverty. And at the same time, they preserved their self-esteem and were respected by other people.

It is difficult to comprehend how they could bury child after child, console themselves, and still hold themselves proudly despite all the disasters. What poet or writer would dare write Life Poems about our mothers and grandmothers, heroines of life and love.

The Pinskers

My memories about this side of my family started to flourish near the end of my life: They occasionally emerge from darkness, as if they demand to tell about their lives, perpetuate their stories. There is a great deal of truth in this claim since the number of survivors from that period is decreasing.

Age does its share and others were eliminated by the Nazis like mice or insects. Their homes have been destroyed. Nothing has remained! Should they be forgotten? Not only because they were our brothers and sisters, grandparents and parents, but they were kind people, good even in moments of hardship.

They were persecuted, humiliated and despised simply because they were Jews but their souls were lofty and noble. To their graves and gas chambers, they took their hope for the future!

May their memory be a blessing.

Aunt Tzippi

If you read Hebrew, you would be able to enjoy my poem called 'This Was the Kupishok That Was' in which I depict the life story of my parents, brother, sisters and friends. But since your Hebrew maybe is not yet up to standard of reading literary pieces, I will satisfy your curiosity by telling a family story in English.

Perhaps not one of the descendants will understand the story of Aunt Tzippi; it will simply seem unreal to them. Imagine a petite woman living on her own for several years, having to take care of her children and business (the family had a small shop) when her husband left in order to earn his living in remote South Africa.

But you might be wondering what she was doing at the time of her husband's journey. Not surprisingly, her life was tough beyond words! She was bringing up her children, at least two she buried because of malnutrition and disease. She arose every morning at sunrise and during the winter even earlier. The cow had to be fed, the garden (which provided the family with vegetables) had to be cared for, and food, prepared.

Tzippi would carry water from the local well on her back, watered the garden, and took the cow to the pasture. Then came time for the morning prayer and after that her working day started!

She then walked to her little store. That's the way she spent six days a week arriving home late and exhausted. As the Sabbath was approaching, my aunt baked some challot and cakes for her family. In addition, at Pesach, this hard-working woman had to prepare wine and perform another seventy-seven chores. She also had to write happy letters to her husband saying that everything was all right! Strange as it might seem today, her life was not so different from many other women in Lithuanian Jewish towns at that time.

When Uncle Samuel arrived back from South Africa, they built a house near ours and lived peacefully together. Aunt Tzippi continued to work with her husband in the shop thanking the Lord for all the good He had done for her and her family.

I do not know what she said or what she thought about when the cruel Lithuanians brought her to the Nazi murderers. I suppose, even at that fateful moment, she did not curse the Lord since she believed in His mercy.

***

The Children

The Pinskoy's had seven children, five of them lived but the other two were taken away still in their infancy. This was the unfortunate death quota that was never surpassed in Lithuanian Jewish families of that time. Taking the appalling sanitation conditions into account, it was a miracle that those five survived!

I will try to tell you a little about each of the children the way I still remember. It is obvious that David (Sidney in America), Chaya and Regina are ingrained in my memory as they lived near us in Kupishok until I left at the age of sixteen or seventeen.

***

My Cousin Joseph

Let me start with the sons. By the time I grew up, Joseph had already left home in Lithuania. He used to be extremely energetic and quickly escaped from the poverty of a small town. He earned his living through part-time jobs in Vilnius. As I remember, he joined a group of young people who fought against the Czarist rule which oppressed all the citizens, especially the Jews. The party he joined was the Jewish-Socialist party called 'The Bund.' Its members strove to put the ideas of Marxism into practice.

The Jews of Lithuania had good reason to wish a political change since they were constantly oppressed, prevented from getting good jobs and were forced to live in specific areas. Since Jews were not given the opportunity to work in agriculture, the public sector or the army, the only occupations that remained were commerce and peddling. Only a few Jews reached top positions in the field of medicine, law or finance. Joe was not among those few.

Therefore, he eventually headed for America. In the first years of his life there, he saved every penny and, as a result, rose to a fairly high social and economic level. He used to be a strong and persistent person. He was a man of principles so it was not easy to argue with him. At the same time, he was good-hearted and devoted to his family.

Being a relative living in a distant country, I received a great deal of attention and warmth from Joe. I recall how he located me in Jew York in the 1950's and we went to the graduation ceremony of his daughter Joyce in Boston. On my next visit to the states in the '60s, we met again and he simply made me crazy with his anti-Zionist political views. I also remember how he would bring us to Wallingford from time to time and did everything possible to make my wife and I feel welcome.

One Sabbath morning he had to bring his wife's mother to the synagogue. She probably did not ride on Shabbat, so he took her arm and led her there, despite his own reservations concerning Judaism. Joe was indeed special. Every time I visited him, his friends from Lithuania were in his home. He would generously help those who were not as successful.

***

The following generations would do well to follow in the footsteps of a giant of an individual like Joe Pinsker, a true 'mensch.'

***

···

My Cousin Beryl

My cousin Beryl was the next son. He was much older than me. I always liked him for his kindness. Exactly like his elder brother Joe, he left Kupishok at a young age and eventually ended up in Vilnius. There he learned the trade of watchmaking and started to work. Later, at the time of the German occupation, he returned to Kupishok for some years and opened a workshop in Uncle Samuel's house. After the death of my father in 1918, may his memory be blessed, I would go across to Uncle Samuel's house and watch the gentle and skillful work of Beryl.

At the end of the German occupation, I left Kupishok for Kaunas in order to study in a Jewish comprehensive school. The Pinsker family remained behind. Sometime later, destiny arranged an intimate and tragic meeting between Beryl and me in Kaunas.

Before I tell you the entire story, I want to give you an insight into the horrors of the Lithuanian army. The oppressive Czarist rule left its mark on the military system. Army service was considered extremely difficult, so everyone would do his best to avoid it. The recruited soldiers were literally turned into slaves by the atrocious discipline of the officers. The latter wasted the military budget on their own needs, walked around in perfect suits and lived in good apartments. At the same time, the soldiers suffered from malnutrition and horrific sanitation conditions. The drunken officers tortured their subordinates by beating them and forcing them to run many miles loaded with ammunition, hungry and freezing from the winter cold. This was the way the regular soldiers were treated;

the persecuted Jews suffered even more. Even a corporal could insult the bloody Jew who tried to soften his commander's temper by giving him presents.

During the rule of the Czar, Jews often fled the country as they got closer to army age. America was the ideal shelter. Another way of bypassing the dreadful military service was to buy the desired exemption certificate by giving bribes to the senior officers. The demand for the exemption was so great that there were special agents who made the arrangements. Any physical defect of a Jewish boy was considered a great blessing!

The poor teenagers tortured themselves for months in order to appear weak and ill in front of the medical committee. Everyone attempted to have a weak heart, flat feet, bad hearing and sight since these defects provided people with the much desired certificate.

Apart from the physical torments, there was also the problem of keeping kosher. Many Jews observed kashrut whereas in the army they had to eat from the communal bowl filled with rotten meat.

When the Lithuanians became independent, they turned out to be no better than the Russians. On paper, it was forbidden to discriminate against Jews, although in practice they suffered even more than before. Therefore, I still cannot fully understand why Uncle Samuel did not succeed to free his son Beryl from the paws of the Lithuanian military machine. Beryl was recruited and placed in a battalion near Kaunas.

At that time, in 1920, I was already studying in the capital before obtaining my matriculation certificate. I was an orphan - young and enthusiastic. My knowledge of Hebrew and Jewish tradition, which I had brought with me from my father's home, helped me to earn a bit of money giving private lessons. I gradually became accustomed to my independent life and even started to enjoy it. I had a room of my own and did anything I wanted. For the sake of historical truth, I didn't always do what I was supposed to do. Among my friends, there were guys from well-established families. We had a lot of fun together - but that is a separate story...

***

My cousin Beryl visited me in my school and continued to stop by fairly often. He sometimes stayed in my room for a couple of days and we spent many enjoyable hours together despite the age difference.

One day, unexpectedly, I learned that my cousin was ill and hospitalized. When I arrived, I found him lying on a cot with a severe stomach-ache.

He remained in the hospital for some two weeks and I visited him almost daily. Eventually he was on the way to recovery and on a Wednesday they said that he would be released the next morning.

I promised to come and take him from the hospital. On Thursday I gave up a school day and in the morning headed for the hospital in a carriage. On my arrival, I entered Beryl's room and found him dead on the couch. There was no one around. I was frightened and perplexed. When I summoned the nurse, she was a bit moved. When the doctor arrived, he was much less understanding and suggested that I take the body to the Jewish cemetery.

More than seventy years have passed but I can still vividly remember that horrible hour in a strange city, lonely and penniless. I somehow got over the feeling of anguish and sent a telegram to Uncle Samuel and Aunt Tzippi. They soon arived in Kaunas exhausted from mourning their son and from the long journey.

***

This is how Beryl's young life came to an abrupt end. Perhaps fate wanted me to be close to him in his last days. May his memory be blessed!

***

∎∎∎

My Cousin David

This is an altogether different story. During the first seventeen years of my life, David and I lived together. Our houses were adjacent to each other and we were good neighbors and good friends. At some stage, our relationship changed since David left for the United States. Many years later we met again during my first visit to the States in 1954.

I found him in a small town in Connecticut where he lived with his exceptional wife. He earned his living at a shop; his home did not have a happy atmosphere. It was hard for me to recognize the new David, closed and sad. He was very glad to see me though. I could not complain about his hospitality but I felt as if we did not have a common language anymore.

Even though my relationship with Sidney (which was his name in the States) was a bit cool, it wasn't like that during our childhood. He was then called 'Doydke Tzipes' which derived from his mother's name – Tzippi. Jewish women were often deprived of certain religious rights (the reminder of male dominance in Judaism) but it surely wasn't the case in my home. There, my mother enjoyed great respect and influence. Raising kids 'fer Got unt fer menschen' (for God and people) was her major responsibility.

David and I had studied in the same heder, played with the same kids and were both punished by our fathers. As a matter of fact, I was smacked more often, since Uncle Samuel was much more liberal than my strict father. He was slightly older than me but I sometimes proved to be better at religious subjects at school.

Starting at a very young age, we both actively helped our parents in their shops. On market day, we would stand on the look-out in order to prevent thefts when the store was packed with customers. At the end of market day, we used to help clean the street in front of the stores.

Before we reached maturity, the First World War broke out. Lithuania was precisely on the border between Russia and Prussian Germany. The war was fierce and there were many casualties. The civilian population of Lithuania was trapped between the two military forces and suffered from both armies. Everyone, and Jews in particular, went through terror, torture and persecution. With the temporary defeat of the Russian army, the government started to look for justification. Naturally, there was no better scapegoat than the Jews.

Not much time passed before the German soldiers conquered Kupishok after a fierce battle which resulted in thousands killed and injured. The small Jewish town turned into utter confusion full of Russian wounded soldiers, Jewish refugees and German conquerors. We, the Jewish children, suddenly became the interpreters because of our knowledge of Yiddish, which is very similar to German. The German soldiers constantly robbed our parents' shops which was similar to the vandalism of

the Russian army.

In this confusion, each person had to try to look out for his own welfare. David succeeded to do so and even taught me how to help the Germans in order to receive presents from them.

***

The occupation lasted for about three years. My father died and I had the freedom to do anything I fancied. David, my other cousins and I became the leaders of the young people in town. Our parents' stores were virtually empty, the economic situation was tough so we decided to assist our families in any way we could.

We somehow acquired the goods that the nearby peasants needed and even went to the villages with some salt, clothes, sugar, and soap. In return, we obtained milk, butter, flour and several dozens of eggs. As a matter of fact, David used to be quite eloquent when it came to commerce, just like his mother Tzippi. He would argue with the peasants in order to get a better deal. As I did not reveal great talent in the business field, he helped me.

Evenings passed in a different way altogether. The Germans often imposed a curfew on the town from sunset until sunrise. As a result, the teenagers gathered at somebody's house and we used the evenings for studying, reading and singing. In this field, David accepted my superiority and loyally followed my instructions.

When I left Kupishok for the capital, I heard about the Zionist dream. When afterwards I occasionally went back to visit, David was managing a large shop full of a variety of goods. His parents were his active assistants. He would complain to me about life in a small town and even expressed his desire to leave either for Palestine or America. He sometimes visited me in Kaunas where we spent wonderful evenings together with our other relatives.

After the tragic death of his brother Beryl, David presumably got fed up with Lithuania and left for the States to be near to his brother Joe. When he fled, he was not aware that his entire family would be cruelly murdered by the Nazis several years later.

***

As I said before, David established himself in America, got married but for some reason did not have children. It seems to me that his life was not very joyful. Still, he deserves being remembered by his relatives.

***

• •

The Daughters

I would like to finish this family story with several lines about the two daughters of the Pinsker's – Regina, the elder one, and Chaya. We were about the same age but had utterly different destinies. Fate was not merciful towards them. Regina (or Gena as we called her) succeeded in establishing a family which eventually broke up. Chaya, on the other hand, had to be satisfied with dreams.

Even though our families were neighbors, I did not see them as often as David. Their practical mother was extremely active in everything that concerned her family and the economy. Their yard was full of chickens, there were two cows and a turkey for Pesach.

The girls, Chaya especially, were very helpful and I remember watching her carry two buckets of water early in the morning. Gena was more spoiled; I never saw her working in the garden or carrying bags of groceries from the market.

When we grew up a bit, the two sisters and I became closer. The reason was the up-and-coming Jewish youth movements. We began to be involved in learning Hebrew as well as attending all kinds of events where I had the role of an organizer. Gena and Chaya invariably took part in our parties. Gena was famous for being able to speak perfect Yiddish. Chaya was often in the center of Jewish folk dancing and singing.

• •

***

After I had left Kupishok, Gena was married for a short time. She had one or two children. Several years later, my fiancé Hadassah and I arrived in Kupishok in order to meet my family. One evening Gena tried (unsuccessfully, though) to teach us to tango. I still recall the melody of that dance and it always reminds me of my cousin. That was the way we parted ... forever.

***

Conclusion

This is the end of the Pinsker story. Much to my regret, it has no happy ending, unless you consider death a happy end since it is a complete liberation from suffering and hardship. I do not know what my dear aunt, uncle and their children thought about when they were thrown into the hands of the ruthless Nazi murderers.

I want to believe that they were consoled by the miraculous survival of their two sons – David and Joseph. The last words of Tzippi and Samuel probably were blessings to the future of their children, and grandchildren who would be born in safety and freedom.

Naturally, they did not leave material wealth to future generations. The little they had was robbed by German and Lithuanian criminals. It says in the Bible, "I can hear the voice of your brother's blood from the Earth." (Genesis, free translation.) Instead they left the most valuable inheritance possible – the moral strength to cope with difficulties, to achieve what one needs with wisdom and love.

This is the heritage which will be passed on and is the most priceless possession one can ever have. Therefore, I hope and pray that the splendid legacy of Kupishok will live on in your and your children's hearts.

Nayshtot Shaki – I, the high school principal with the famous philanthropist
from the US Rosenblum and his daughter

Hadassah is introducing her intended Shlomo to her family in Vojlon
(Veliuona, Lithuania)

חוליה

אלו ההתחיים שלה חי קרב שלמה אבא אמא

ואר חנויות שלט קא חן של זה הדורית

מהגמיסיון הדברי זיוסיף עלרוית חולה לה

אל התנאים דלקן :

1) על הדורית זיוסיף השמים את חן קרב

שלמה כתוב ניה ניה הגמיסיון דמעברת על

ישראל לן שלאב. (200)

/ זה הדורית עשיות ראש שלגה קרב לגאלות את

שטרותי זה 800 אלה מלאת ליל כאבל

הניסי על הגמיסיון זרסה לה .

והדה : השערת /גריאת מאוית לאב

סראסיו / לחומשה שער התגל . את המפברת

מקבל /ני קרב זה שעיר אלא חבל שלה .

כן חי קרב שלגה מקרל שלון את הנהלת

הגמיסיון הדברי זיוסיף וכן את הוראת

המקברות הדברי שמאבות הגילויות.

וסני אות הדראה עשרית וטו אלה נשר.

3) ואן של חולה זה לוא נתקפו לשנית

הגלבות 1927-8 על הסכמה הדברית

אבא להאריך את החולה הזה גם להבא

4) ההולה הזא קא מקרל דלקן אאנרי אולון

ני ערכב תדברת שלאבר קולדה

זה ול הדורית יוסיף י.תגלון

שלגה בל

2/8 1927

Our trip to Shurjont (???) Germany

Municipal committee in Nayshtot Shaki (Kudirkos Naumiestis, Lithuania) during the 500 years celebration of Vytautas the Great; From right to left: Chief Catholic priest, head of the police, district physician (seated), Kodesh – principal of the Hebrew local high school, principal of the local Lithuanian high school

Freshmen at the high school in Neustadt

Neustadt Teachers in 1928

Hadassah and her brother Dr. Aharon Cohen

May G-d avenge his blood.

Shlomo Kodesh and his wife Hadassah

Dr. Aharon Cohen with his wife and daughter

My mother and my two sisters Pnina and Dina

Daughter Hannah Muller-Kodesh, her husband Zvi, her son Avi and her daughter Shir

Musia, my father's sister, her husband rabbi Friedman and the children

Epilogue:

There has been a myriad of books written about the Holocaust but this manuscript – these stories – tell of a prior period at the beginning of the last century... a period of our history which has all but been forgotten.

Many years have passed since these experiences – some seem just like yesterday – the highs and the lows which everyone must face in his life.

I arrived in Palestine in 1933 and immediately became immersed in developing the Ulpan movement, which has been the foundation of teaching new immigrants from all over the world the Holy Tongue.

Prior to the establishment of the State of Israel, I traveled to America and disseminated information about the concept of the Jewish state in the day schools and yeshivot there.

Subsequently, on behalf of the Government, my travels took me to London, Rome, Paris, Berlin, Caracas and other locations in the Jewish world.

Even now, after almost seventy years in my beloved Eretz Israel, I am still as optimistic about our future as I was when I first arrived.

In my retirement, I can only hope and pray that the words from my stories will remain in your mind and heart as they have within me over the decades.

Ashdod, 5760/2000

NAME INDEX